# CHICAGO'S BEST RESTAURANTS
## by SHERMAN KAPLAN

*Happy Calories!*

*Sherman Kaplan*

# CHICAGO'S BEST RESTAURANTS

## by SHERMAN KAPLAN

**SurreyBooks**

CHICAGO

*CHICAGO'S BEST RESTAURANTS* is published by Surrey Books, Inc., 230 E. Ohio St., Suite 120, Chicago, IL 60611.

Revised edition: 1 2 3 4 5

This book is manufactured in the United States of America.

Library of Congress Cataloging-in-Publication data:

Kaplan, Sherman, 1941-
    Chicago's best restaurants / by Sherman Kaplan. – 1st ed.
    308 p.  cm.
    Rev. ed. of: Best restaurants, Chicago & suburbs. 4th ed. c1986.
    Includes indexes
    ISBN 0-940625-61-X (pbk.): $8.95
    1. Restaurants – Illinois – Chicago – Guidebooks.  2. Restaurants Illinois – Chicago Metropolitan Area – Guidebooks.  I. Kaplan, Sherman, 1941-  Best restaurants, Chicago & suburbs.  II. Title.
TX907.3.I32C47   1993
647.95773'11 – dc20                  92-46085
                                         CIP

Editorial and production: *Bookcrafters, Inc., Chicago*
Art direction: *Hughes & Co., Chicago*
Cover illustration: *Michael Carroll*

For free catalog and prices on quantity purchases, contact Surrey Books at the address above.

This title is distributed to the trade by Publishers Group West.

# CONTENTS

# HOW TO USE THIS GUIDE

**C**hicago's *Best Restaurants* contains reviews of 225 restaurants that rank among the best of their kind in the city and suburbs – whether you're in the mood for a great hamburger or a gourmet seven-course dinner. It reflects the judgment of the author and no one else. I have not relied on committees, solicitations from restaurants or readers, or the work of other reviewers or critics to form my opinions; thus, the point of view expressed here is consistent. Chances are that if you visit and like the first few restaurants you read about here, you will like all the others, too. But, as the Romans put it, *"De gustibus non disputandum est"* – there is no arguing about taste.

We've organized the book to make it as easy as possible for you to find exactly the restaurant you're looking for. Restaurant reviews are arranged alphabetically in the body of the book. For each entry you can see at a glance how I rate the restaurant, the type of cuisine it offers, where it's located, about how much it costs, and other specifics. Three indexes provide you with an overview of all restaurants by *cuisine, location,* and *price range.* I've also included an index of my personal favorites, "Sherman's Dream List," for those rare occasions when money and diet are no object and you don't care how far you have to travel for a great meal.

## Rating System

Restaurants in this book are rated on a 20-point scale, a system I've been using for years. The overall "K/R" (Kaplan Rating) represents my opinion of a restaurant's worthiness, based on its decor (up to 4 points), service and hospitality (5 points), food (9 points), and overall value (2 points). The absolutely top restaurants in this book will have an overall rating (K/R) of 20/20. And because the idea of this book is to guide you to Chicagoland's best restaurants, no eatery has lower than a K/R of 15/20.

In the restaurant world, nothing is written in stone: hours, credit card arrangements, parking and party facilities, and menus change regularly. If you have any doubts or questions about a particular place, don't hesitate to call them with your inquiries. If you cannot get the information you want over the phone, chances are you won't want to visit. That leads me to a related point. Restaurants often change management and chefs. What has been a good experience for me might not be so for you. This (or any) guide can only be a starting point.

## Price Range

I hate restaurant guides that seem to invent their own alphabet of symbols, and you need a translator to understand a review. The only symbols used here are the "$" to indicate price range, as follows:

| | |
|---|---|
| $ | Dinner for two under $30, *plus* tax, tip, and drinks; |
| $$ | Dinner for two $30-$50, *plus* tax, tip, and drinks; |
| $$$ | The most expensive dining: over $50 for dinner for two, *plus* tax, tip, and drinks. |

Keep in mind that cost and quality are not necessarily related. If you want to know my sense of whether a place is worth what it charges, check its K/R for value.

## About This Edition

A quick glance through this new edition of *Chicago's Best Restaurants* reveals some significant changes. Due to the tremendous growth in the popularity of Italian food, more Italian restaurants are listed. Similarly, there has been a renewed appreciation of American cookery, whether it be on the cutting edge of contemporary culinary art or more like the food your grandmother might have prepared. Therefore, you'll find an entry for "American" in the index of restaurants by cuisine. Third, Chicago and its suburbs have seen an explosion in Thai restaurants in the last few years. While this book features a fairly small number of Thai restaurants, given the many the city has to offer, I consider them among the best of that unique Asian cuisine.

There is a keen interest in healthier dining today. Cholesterol and fat have become more important to many diners than the name of the latest trendy chef. *Chicago's Best Restaurants* reflects this concern: information on heart-healthy menus is given in the individual data section if the restaurant is responsive to this need. That does not mean that those are the only restaurants where healthy dining is possible, however. Most restaurants can accommodate a diner's special needs. All one need do, for example, is ask for dishes without the cream sauce, or request that sauteing be done in a minimal amount of vegetable oil instead of butter. (For a detailed account of healthy restaurant dining, see *Eat Out, Eat Right!* by Hope S. Warshaw, also published by Surrey Books.)

That brings me to another point. Previous editions of this guide to Chicago-area restaurants have been published by companies outside

Chicago. Now, for the first time under the aegis of a Chicago publishing house, *Chicago's Best Restaurants* will be more readily available and can be more easily updated. It is our goal to come out with new editions every two years or less.

My thanks go to WBBM Newsradio 78 in Chicago, where I have been a news anchor for some 24 years and the radio station's restaurant critic for almost as long. Thanks, too, to my new publisher for having faith in this work. As in past editions, thanks also go to friends and family who have accompanied me on my culinary journeys. And, as always, thanks and love go to Eileen, my wife, who shares not just my meals but my life.

*Sherman Kaplan*
*Spring, 1993*

# AEGEAN ISLES
KR 17.5/20
Decor 3/4   Hospitality 5/5   Food 7.5/9   Value 2/2

- **Greek**
- **Highland Park**
- **$$**

561 Roger Williams Ave.
Highland Park
(708) 433-5620; (708)
433-5621
**Troubleshooter:** Angelo
Papasteriadis (owner)

**Hours:** Tues-Sun 4:30-11 pm
**Cards:** MC, VISA
**Reservations:** Accepted
**Handicapped:** Accessible
**Bar:** Full selection of Greek
wines, beer, and cocktails
**Parking:** Street
**Party Facilities:** Available for
private parties on weeknights

A major facelift has been given to the small dining room, including some wonderfully evocative art by the owner's wife. But this is not so much a restaurant for romantic intimacy as it is a place to share with friends and family. Children are delighted by the shouts of "Oppa!" as another portion of brandy-flamed cheese is delivered to someone's table.

The menu is typical of Greek restaurants. Though dinners include a small salad, delicious sesame-studded fresh bread, and sides of rice or potatoes, there are some tempting appetizers. Among favorites are taramosalata and dolmades. The former is a creamy smooth spread of salmon roe, delicate pink in color, which is eaten with thick slices of bread. Dolmades are grape leaves marinated and wrapped around a filling of rice and seasonings. The flavors are light, meant to be complemented with a glass or two of the rosé Roditys that is so popular in Greek restaurants. By the way . . . though it is not on the menu, ask for the garlic spread. Like the taramosalata, it is delicious spread onto slices of the Grecian bread. If you enjoy the fullness of garlic, this will become one of your favorites.

Cold octopus in vinegar is another treat, a bit more exotic than what you might be accustomed to if you have never visited a Greek restaurant before. All traces of sponginess have been pounded out; the octopus is cooked to tenderness and served with the bite of a vinegar marinade.

Entrees are easy to select at Aegean Isles. A combination platter is a primer in Greek edibles. The platter is loaded with pastitsio (noodles bound with béchamel sauce and spices), moussaka (like an eggplant lasagna), gyros (slices of meat from a rôtisserie), dolmades, plus rice, peas, and roasted potatoes. There's so much here, you probably will ask that leftovers be wrapped for some at-home snacking the next day.

Roast leg of lamb, shish kebab, and baked chicken seasoned with oregano are among other entrees, but Aegean Isles really shines with its whole fish. Usually red snapper or sea bass (sometimes both) comes freshly steamed with just a touch of lemon juice to highlight the nautical flavor of the fish. Various fashions of shrimp help round out the seafood menu. Desserts include one of my favorites, bougatsa, a sweetened custard-filled pastry flamed with Greek brandy and served hot. It's enough to have you shouting "Oppa!" all over again.

# ALOUETTE

KR 19.5/20
Decor 4/4   Hospitality 5/5   Food 8.5/9   Value 2/2

| | |
|---|---|
| • **French** | **Hours:** Daily 5 pm-midnight |
| • **Highwood** | **Cards:** All majors |
| • **$$** | **Reservations:** Suggested |
| | **Handicapped:** Accessible |
| 440 N. Green Bay Rd. | **Bar:** Full, excellent list of wines |
| Highwood | and after-dinner cordials, |
| (708) 433-5600 | brandies |
| **Troubleshooters:** Christian | **Parking:** Free lot |
| Zeiger (owner), Alex Abraham | **Dress:** Jackets and ties |
| (maitre d') | **Party Facilities:** Space for |
| | 30-100 |
| | **Heart-Healthy Menu:** |
| | Choices and diet needs met |

Alouette, which opened in 1977, is as handsome as ever with its country inn motif. And it is one of the most improved dining venues in the last few years. The restaurant has a large and loyal following, attracted not only by the uncommonly well-prepared cuisine, but also by the service, which is always attentive and genuinely warm.

Chef Reinhard Barthel, Jr., knowledgeable beyond his youth, prepares sensual dishes, often in exquisite detail. The visual artistry almost exceeds the taste.

Among appetizers, foie gras is presented in flaky brioche pastry, glazed with a demi-glacé, and garnished with crisp and bitter radicchio. In another presentation, plump snails are baked with garlic butter, parsley, Spanish onion, and a drizzle of lemon juice, all of which is covered with a pastry dome to hold in the complexity of aromas.

Diners can generally find a favorite classic or two on the often-changing menu. Veal Oscar comes with sweet snow-white crabmeat and tender asparagus spears beneath a béarnaise sauce blanket. Twin tournedos of beef are also served with a warm béarnaise, while an ambitious trio of filet mignon, veal medallions, and baby lamb chops comes with a trio of sauces.

The Alouette menu is not without inventiveness, as an order of salmon sauteed with a reduction of pimiento and cilantro accent reveals. Fresh fish is flown in daily, its presentation at the whim of the chef, though individual requests are met whenever possible.

In addition to its à la carte dining choices, Alouette features a nightly prix fixe menu, which should not be ignored by budget diners who might think fine French cooking is out of reach.

# AMBRIA
KR 20/20
Decor 4/4   Hospitality 5/5   Food 9/9   Value 2/2

---

- **French**
- **Chicago/Mid-North**
- **$$$**

2300 N. Lincoln Park West
Chicago
(312) 472-0076
**Troubleshooter:** Chef Gabino Sotelino (chef/owner)

**Hours:** Mon-Thurs 6-9:30 pm, Fri-Sat until 10:30 pm
**Cards:** All majors
**Reservations:** Required
**Handicapped:** Accessible
**Bar:** Full bar and wine service
**Parking:** Valet
**Dress:** Jackets and ties
**Party Facilities:** For up to 24
**Heart-Healthy Menu:** Selections

---

**A**mbria is firmly among the Big Four of local eateries (Carlos', Le Français, and the Everest Room are the others). Diners are not pampered so much as respected. Waiters know their foods and wines and will offer more than superficial knowledge when asked for a suggestion. There is a stylish sense of wit about the service that keeps things from becoming pretentious.

The menu changes periodically. The best way to get a feel for what Chef Gabino Sotelino has to offer is to choose Le Grand Menu

Dégustation. For a prix fixe, diners enjoy seven smaller courses, two appetizers, two entrees, salad, and assorted desserts. The dégustation is served only to entire parties and requires a 24-hour notice. Le Petit Menu Dégustation offers four appetizers and a light dessert, is less expensive, and does not require advance notice.

Among recent selections were ravioli filled with foie gras, cèpe mushrooms, and fresh thyme, bathed in a broth of duck glacé. Among other selections might be a wild mushroom terrine.

À la carte entrees have recently included several imaginative seafood presentations, such as John Dory in a pale butter sauce, or sea bass char-grilled on a tomato coulis, framed by thin-sliced sauteed new potatoes. Sweetbreads might come out sauteed all buttery rich and almost creamy in their silken texture, contrasted with a bedding of crisp celery and leek spears. As do many other entrees, they come with a collection of hand-carved baby vegetables, which add color and texture finesse to the platter.

Desserts are magnificent, ranging from the signature white chocolate mousse bathed in dark chocolate fudge sauce to creamy smooth crème brûlée, coconut glacé, fruit tarts, and full-flavored chocolate torte stuffed with whole pitted cherries and served with a caramel sauce.

# Amourette
KR 18.5/20
Decor 3/4   Hospitality 5/5   Food 8.5/9   Value 2/2

- **French**
- **Palatine**
- **$$**

2275 Rand Rd.
Palatine
(708) 359-6220
**Troubleshooter:** Christian
Zeiger (owner)

**Hours:** Lunch Mon-Fri 11:30
am-2:30 pm, dinner nightly
5-10 pm
**Cards:** All majors
**Reservations:** Suggested
**Bar:** Service bar, good wine list
**Parking:** Adjacent lot
**Heart-Healthy Menu:**
Selections include entrees that
contain 450 or fewer calories,
prepared without sauce, served
with fresh steamed vegetables
(individual dietary considerations
can usually be met)

Amourette is a cozy place, convivial, casual, with a sense of style. Cooking follows the best direction of modern French cuisine. But, in keeping with the bistro ambiance, you do not have to cash in the family jewels to dine here.

Among hors d'oeuvres is cold tuna with a salad of seaweed, reminiscent of Japanese-style presentation. A bit more rich might be traditional baked snails with garlic butter or a wild mushroom terrine. One of the more original ideas on the menu is pissaladière, a French-style onion pizza.

Dinner choices include roast rack of lamb or quail with breast of duck in a mushroom and onion sauce. Dover sole is prepared in two classic styles: almandine and meunière. Or consider a dazzling ragout made with red snapper filets, tipped with slightly spiced boursin cheese wrapped in phyllo dough, then bedded on spinach.

Other entrees to choose from include veal and lobster medallions in white wine sauce, a large veal chop with morel mushroom cream sauce, beefsteak with shiitake mushrooms and bordelaise sauce, roast duck with raspberry saucing, and rabbit in a zinfandel wine reduction with thyme for a woodsy, herbal accent.

Desserts are as exciting as previous courses. Crème brûlée is silken. Chocolate regularly receives its proper due, and fruit tarts are exquisite.

# ANN'S BAVARIA HAUS
KR 19/20
Decor 3/4   Hospitality 5/5   Food 9/9   Value 2/2

- **German**
- **Libertyville**
- **$**

114 W. Peterson Rd. (Illinois Rte. 137) at Milwaukee Ave. (Illinois Rte. 21)
Libertyville
(708) 367-5933
**Troubleshooters:** George and Bess Winters (owners)

**Hours:** Mon-Thurs 6 am-9 pm, Fri-Sat 5:30 am-10 pm, Sun 7 am-8 pm
**Cards:** AE, MC, VISA
**Reservations:** No
**Handicapped:** Accessible
**Bar:** Full, good beer selection
**Parking:** Free lot
**Party Facilities:** Only in summer, with outdoor beer garden for 70-80

The front of the restaurant is actually a German delicatessen with cooler cases stuffed with sausages and cheeses. Imported canned goods line shelves, while at least one large table is loaded with delicious-looking, thick and chewy pumpernickel and other Middle European breads. One part of the restaurant shares space with the deli, while another room is a bit more isolated. The atmosphere borders on Wisconsin rec-room; the menu is deliciously German.

Nightly specials are posted on the walls to supplement the regular menu. The list of German specialties includes such tried and true classics as kassler rippchen (smoked pork loin with kraut or cabbage), wiener schnitzel, sauerbraten, zwiebel fleisch (roast beef with noodles, onions, cheese, and gravy), and beef rouladen, just to name a few. The sauces are rich and flavorful, the portions ample, the meats tender. The schnitzel is tender, handsomely breaded and fried.

In addition to the sizable dinner portions, diners can enjoy a wide choice of sausages, ranging from mild veal brats to more spicy knackwurst or smoked Thuringer, to name just a few. The sausages are served with your choice of boiled potato or German potato salad, plus kraut or cabbage. The menu goes on to list a dozen or more other entrees and attractions.

You could begin with a couple of reasonably priced appetizers and soup. Delicious fried onion rings come with a horseradish dipping sauce. German fries are akin to American hash browns, but with the added bite of shredded onion.

Desserts include homemade strudel, Eli's cheesecake, Black Forest cake, and other goodies.

# ANN SATHER

KR 20/20

Decor 4/4   Hospitality 5/5   Food 9/9   Value 2/2

- **Swedish/American**
- **Chicago/Mid-North**
- **$**

929 W. Belmont Ave.
Chicago
(312) 348-2378
**Troubleshooter:** Tom
Tunney (owner)

**Hours:** Daily 7 am-11 pm
**Cards:** AE, MC, VISA
**Reservations:** Taken except
Saturday and Sunday mornings
**Handicapped:** Accessible
**Bar:** Full
**Parking:** Free lot
**Party Facilities:** For 20-220

## Other Locations

5207 N. Clark St.
Chicago
(312) 271-6677; Daily 7 am-
   10 pm
1328 E. 57th St.
Chicago
(312) 947-9323; Daily 7 am-
   10 pm

You would be hard pressed to find a more homey kind of restaurant than Ann Sather. The original Ann Sather remains at its famous Belmont Street location, while two newer locations offer virtually the same service and value.

No matter what time of day or night, every meal begins with a bowl of cinnamon buns and a variety of breads. The cinnamon rolls alone might be reason enough to come here.

Breakfast is served all day, highlighted by Swedish pancakes. Sausages and egg dishes, including a variety of three-egg omelettes, are always featured.

Getting into the dinner menu, choices run the gamut from salads and sandwiches to full-course meals. One good introduction to Swedish-style cooking is to order the Swedish sampler. The platter includes delicious roasted duck with a traditional lingonberry glaze, Swedish meatballs in gravy, potato sausage (which blends veal, pork, and potatoes), dumplings, sauerkraut, and brown baked beans.

Other selections regularly include pan-fried pork chops or chicken livers, veal steak, and old-fashioned chicken croquettes served with candied sweet potatoes and creamed peas. Seafood choices are equally ample, whether a platter of fried perch, catfish, or broiled trout. All dinners include two side vegetables, soup or juice, and dessert.

# ARBELA

KR 19/20

Decor 3.5/4   Hospitality 4.5/5   Food 9/9   Value 2/2

- **Middle East/Assyrian**
- **Chicago/Far North**
- **$**

6243 N. Western Ave.
Chicago
(312) 338-7200
**Troubleshooter:** Hanny Baba (owner)

**Hours:** Mon-Thurs 11:30 am-midnight, Fri-Sat until 3 am
**Cards:** All majors
**Reservations:** Accepted
**Handicapped:** Accessible
**Bar:** Full, good wine list. Entertainment Fri, Sat
**Parking:** On street or at city lot one-half block south
**Party Facilities:** For up to 120

**A**rbela is simply one of the best Middle Eastern restaurants in and around Chicago. Its heritage is Assyrian, and the dining room is touched with influences of Mesopotamia. The service is friendly, informed, and unrushed. The food is often heavily seasoned, complexly flavored, and aromatic.

Dinners include rice or potatoes and Middle Eastern pita bread, plus a green salad. Start with a platter of appetizers, which can be ordered à la carte or as a combination. The platter comes with skewered grilled chicken and beef shish kebabs; stuffed grape leaves; meat, spinach, and cheese pastry pies; feta cheese with salty black olives; a trio of spreads, including chickpea (called hummus), eggplant (called baba ghanoush), and seasoned yogurt; a style of pizza on a thin, crêpe-like dough; deep-fried ground chickpea balls (called felafel), plus assorted marinated vegetables. It's almost a meal in itself, or, as meant to be, an especially good way to become acquainted with a traditional array of appetizers, or mazza.

Especially outstanding is the baba ghanoush, in which the eggplant is roasted over a flame, its pulp taking on a dark smoked flavor that is haunting in its intensity. The meat, cheese, and spinach pies are the Middle Eastern version of filled dumplings; in this case, the pastry wraps are deep fried to a golden crispiness. Entrees include beef, lamb, or chicken shish kebabs, several styles of lamb, some roasted chicken, and some fish.

A highlight is sauteed lamb, which is not on the printed menu but might be featured as a nightly special. The lamb chunks are sauteed in oil, picking up the redolent flavors of sweet red and green peppers, plus onions and a bouquet of spices. Another special, simply named Middle Eastern chicken, features grilled chunks ringing a platter of steamed rice. The chicken has obviously been marinated and treated to a mix of seasonings whose spiciness underscores the meat.

Diners with smaller appetites can order any of several sandwiches. Shawrima, the Arabian version of Greek gyros, comes shredded with lettuce, tomatoes, and onions on a large French roll. Its flavors are well married and satisfying. The sandwich works especially well with a side order of tabbouli, a cracked wheat, parsley, and mint salad in a mild vinegar dressing.

# ARCO DE CUCHILLEROS
KR 16.5/20
Decor 3/4   Hospitality 4/5   Food 7.5/9   Value 2/2

| | |
|---|---|
| • **Spanish** | **Hours:** Tues-Fri 4 pm-11, Sat noon-midnight, Sun noon-10 pm (Sun. tapas buffet noon-3 pm) |
| • **Chicago/Mid-North** | |
| • **$$** | |
| 3445 N. Halsted | **Cards:** AE, MC, VISA |
| Chicago | **Reservations:** Parties of six or more |
| (312) 296-6046 | |
| **Troubleshooters:** Miguel and Francisco Sanchez (owners) | **Handicapped:** Accessible |
| | **Bar:** Full, small but excellent list of Spanish wines and sherries, homemade sangria |
| | **Parking:** Street |
| | **Party Facilities:** On Mondays, or before regular restaurant hours other days |

Only a handful of small tables fills this tiny restaurant, where an open kitchen lets diners watch many of their orders being prepared. Bare brick walls and tile floors, as well as Spanish motif graphics, help set the decor and mood. The restaurant is modeled on a Spanish tapas bar.

Tapas are nothing more than appetizers, meant to be consumed several at a time, or "grazed." At Arco de Cuchilleros, there are more than three dozen choices on the menu, plus two or three daily specials. While not especially elegant in preparation or presentation, they are tasty and in fairly generous portion.

Start with a selection of cold choices, perhaps a bowl of gazpacho soup with its fresh vegetal flavors. This gazpacho is unusual in that it has a cream base. Nonetheless, the flavors are there, and it is a delicious, though somewhat too rich, version of gazpacho.

Order a pitcher of sangria for those at your table, and then begin to do some serious tapas selecting. If you have a taste for garlic, be sure to get potatas ala-oli, in a decidedly full-flavored mayonnaise. Add a lentil bean salad, sharpened with oil and vinegar. And do not miss marinated olives, juicy and delicious. Among other selections from the cold tapas menu is tuna, which is similar to ceviche in its marinade of lemon juice. But soy sauce has been added to the blend, lending a decidedly unusual flavor and color. In fact, the dark color of the tuna may be alarming. Overcome any hesitation, however, and dig right in. One other seafood selection brings a mix of shrimp, clams, and mussels laid out in a circle on a bed of lettuce and julienne vegetables, to which is added vinaigrette flavored with the fresh pulp and juice of oranges. This may be a highlight at the table.

From among the hot tapas, try an individual portion of paella, a casserole of rice, sausage, chicken, and seafood, traditionally and uniquely Spanish. Garlic is used in abundance on shrimp in a butter-and-white-wine sauce.

A quick scan of the menu will lead diners to any of several other selections. Desserts include Spanish flan custard. Service is friendly, though your server may need some occasional prompting.

# ARNIE'S

KR 17.5/20

Decor 4/4   Hospitality 4/5   Food 8/9   Value 1.5/2

- **American**
- **Chicago/Near North**
- **$$$**

1030 N. State St.
  (Newberry Plaza)
Chicago
(312) 266-4800
**Troubleshooter:** Arnold J. Morton (owner)

**Hours:** Lunch Tues-Fri 11:30 am-2:30 pm, dinner Sun-Thurs 5:30-10 pm, Fri-Sat until 11:30 pm, brunch Sun 10:30 am-2:30 pm.
**Cards:** All majors
**Reservations:** Required for Sunday brunch and weekday lunch, suggested at other times
**Bar:** Full
**Parking:** Validated discount parking in Newberry Plaza garage or valet/lot parking
**Party Facilities:** Rooms for up to 30-80 sit-down, 125 reception; entire restaurant for up to 300 sit-down, 400 reception

Though Chicago restaurateur Arnold Morton has a reputation for innovation, he is also wise enough to stay with the tried and true. His namesake restaurant, Arnie's, is an outstanding example.

The restaurant is nearly two decades old, and while it may not be on the cutting edge, its style and decor remain unique. That decor, art nouveau eclectic, brings together an illuminated stained-glass ceiling with pressed-tin borders, tropical wall murals, swagged curtains, deco fixtures, and seating that manages to look current. Considering that many of today's restaurants call bare brick and open ductwork decor, Arnie's can still be almost shocking in its extravagance.

This is a restaurant that smacks of Power Lunching; at dinner, patrons may be less competitive, but the tone of expectation, albeit more romantic, is still there.

The dinner menu is not particularly extensive; a cursory glance might disappoint adventurous diners. But there are some real finds. Arnie's was among the first Chicago restaurants to prepare fresh pasta primavera, and it is still being done, the correct way, at tableside. This is more than showmanship; immediacy is the key to the dish so that vegetables do not become wilted or overcooked. Nor should the noodles be allowed to congeal in a cream-based sauce that could thicken even during the short trip from kitchen to table.

There exists at Arnie's a sense of fullness about many of the entrees. Nothing is bland in a cuisine that can on occasion match the boldness of the restaurant's decor. A seafood trio of salmon, shrimp, and lobster comes crosshatched off the grill, dressed with a complementary trio of sauces and an edging of wild rice. An interesting threesome of veal brings real Marsala, Florentine, and Piccata together on a single platter accompanied by spinach fettucine. House specialties include real two-fisted, man-sized steaks whose dimensions would give pause to all but the most ambitious diners. Arnie's classic rack of lamb brings six to eight chops with a bouquet of mixed fresh vegetables. Another staple of the restaurant is a Sicilian veal chop, coated with an egg-and-cornmeal batter and sizzled to a pink doneness.

# AVANZARE
KR 19.5/20
Decor 3.5/4   Hospitality 5/5   Food 9/9   Value 2/2

- **Italian/Northern**
- **Chicago/Near North**
- **$$$**

161 E. Huron
Chicago
(312) 337-8056
**Troubleshooter:** Manager on duty

**Hours:** Lunch Mon-Fri 11:30 am-2 pm, dinner Mon-Thurs 5:30-10 pm, Fri-Sat 5-11 pm, Sun 5-9 pm
**Cards:** All majors
**Handicapped:** Accessible
**Bar:** Full, wine list includes over 100 bottlings, most Italian
**Parking:** Nearby lots
**Party Facilities:** For up to 80
**Heart-Healthy Menu:** Selections

Avanzare was among the first Northern Italian restaurants to hit it big with the expense-account crowd as well as mere seekers of good food. Its handsome dining room allows for plenty of space between tables, which makes it ideal for Power Lunching or romantic dining. One glance at the menu reveals that this is not your basic "red tomato sauce" kind of restaurant. When Avanzare does a red sauce, it is something special. Among appetizers, fresh sea scallops come baked with angel-hair pasta, bathed in a light natural broth that hints of saffron. Carpaccio is lightly oiled, dusted with grated Parmesan; this is worlds away from steak tartare. Among pasta courses, you won't find marinara and Bolognese, which are the limits at less ambitious restaurants. Instead, bow tie noodles, called farfalle, come with grilled chicken, a wealth of garlic, and broccoli in a clear lemon pepper broth. In another choice, wide lasagna-style noodles are lavished with expensive prosciutto di Parma and big porcini mushrooms sauteed in butter, all topped with grated Parmesan cheese.

Among entrees, the restaurant has served grilled beef filets with seasonal mushrooms, fresh leaves of spinach, and a butter sauce embellished with white truffles. Seafood specials can change daily. Grilled tuna could come marinated in the unusual combination of soy sauce and the Italian apéritif Cinzano. The platter is garnished with gnocchi and tiny stemmed enoki mushrooms. Sea bass might appear grilled and served with a delicious pesto Hollandaise. From a choice of lighter meats, veal scallopini may be sauteed and served with Italian ham and sage, coupled with polenta in Marsala wine.

# BANDO
KR 16/20
Decor 3/4   Hospitality 4/5   Food 7/9   Value 2/2

- **Korean**
- **Chicago/Northwest**
- **$$**

2200 W. Lawrence Ave.
Chicago
(312) 728-7400
**Troubleshooter:** Manager on duty

**Hours:** Daily 11 am-11 pm
**Cards:** AE, MC, VISA
**Reservations:** Taken
**Handicapped:** Accessible
**Bar:** Full, good selection of Oriental beers
**Parking:** Street
**Party Facilities:** Yes

**B**ando is unlike any other Korean restaurant I have ever visited. Bando certainly looks like no other Korean restaurant in Chicago. The decor includes an indoor waterfall and crystal chandeliers. As at some other Korean restaurants, diners are seated at large tables, each of which has a central gas-fired grill for dinners that require some tableside presentation.

The restaurant seems well supported by Chicago's Korean-American population – this is always a good sign of authenticity. The menu lists many Korean dishes found in other restaurants. There are some genuine high spots. For an appetizer, you should not miss what the menu describes simply as "pan fried mixed vegetables." Actually, this is a platter-filling pancake about the size of a 12-inch pizza. Various cooked vegetables are arranged attractively, somewhat like spokes around a center hub. The batter is studded with pieces of clam, which lends a slight, but not unpleasant, fishy undertaste. This can be easily disguised with a little sesame soy and ginger sauce, liberally studded with garlic and pepper.

Among other appetizer choices, pan-fried dumplings, known in most oriental restaurants as pot stickers, are tasty little morsels akin to fried ravioli. Other appetizers run the gamut from sashimi to fried fish and oysters and a couple of styles of tempura.

Traditional Korean dining should include some kind of substantial soup. Yellow corvina, a Pacific Ocean fish cut up into chunks, is served in a hot pepper fish stock with nuggets of other seafood, including a large oyster. This dish is a good example of the traditional approach, although it might not appeal to American tastes.

Elsewhere on the menu, the Bando version of dak bokuhm, which the restaurant calls dak-yah-chae-bolkum, is quite different from the fried chicken in a spicy sweet-hot glaze served in other Korean restaurants. Bando's dish seems more like steamed chicken and vegetables in a clear sauce that is without much flavor or character. Even bee-bim-bop – a casserole of rice, assorted vegetables, and a fried egg all tossed together – is somehow different, perhaps largely because of what I suspect is a sweet bean-based sauce used to bind the ingredients.

An attempt is made at friendly service, though language can be a barrier. Bando Korean Restaurant is not for the diner unfamiliar with Korean foods; it is a different approach to Korean cuisine.

# BÊTISE
KR 18.5/20
Decor 3.5/4  Hospitality 5/5  Food 8.5/9  Value 1.5/2

- **French**
- **Wilmette**
- **$$$**

1515 Sheridan Rd. (Plaza del Lago Shopping Center)
Wilmette
(708) 853-1711
**Troubleshooter:** Nancy Barocci (owner)

**Hours:** Lunch Mon-Sat 11:30 am-2:30 pm, dinner Sun-Thurs 5:30-9:00 pm, Fri-Sat until 10:00 pm, Sun (brunch) 11 am-2 pm.
**Cards:** CB, DINERS, DISCOVER, MC, VISA
**Reservations:** Suggested
**Handicapped:** Accessible
**Parking:** Free lot
**Party Facilities:** Semi-private for up to 45

The concept of bistro dining is taken somewhat upscale at Bêtise. The name means "whimsical" or "playful" in French, though the cooking really seems somewhat more serious than that.

This is not to suggest that Bêtise is stuffy or remote in any sense. The dining area is large and noisy when crowded, as befits a bistro. The à la carte menu is supplemented by daily specials, which only makes the choices all that more difficult.

Everything is tempting, from a soup du jour, which might be American-style corn chowder, to luscious desserts including crème brûlée and chocolate raspberry terrine, to a taste of prune-and-armagnac-flavored ice cream.

Dining at Bêtise offers a fairly wide array of imaginative choices. One could begin with a classical approach to onion soup. Salmon fumé is given originality, served in small coronet-shaped rollups on a crisp potato chip, with a whipped cream cheese filling. In another selection, mussels are placed in a circle on a small platter, each filled with a mirepoix of diced vegetables and enough garlic to make its presence apparent. Even tastier are snails with slivers of fennel amid a smattering of lobster meat, all bound together by chèvre cheese.

This prelude is equaled by the dinner selections. Though roast chicken with shoestring fries is not among the most memorable choices, a stylized chicken stew under a flaked pastry dome is more challenging, as vegetables crowd for equal attention.

Even better is rabbit with a plating of risotto flavored by brandy and apples. The loin is stuffed with spinach and roasted to release its mild flavors. Other dinner selections include several styles of fresh fish, such as seared salmon with roasted bell pepper coulis or marlin steak, grilled and served with a corn relish accompaniment.

One recent special may be typical of how the kitchen treats lamb. In this case, cuts of loin are grilled to a pink fullness, sliced into wedges, and laid out on a platter with deliciously roasted carrots, steamed leafy greens, and a light red wine reduction of the lamb's natural juices. This sort of dining is close to perfection.

# BICE
KR 18/20
Decor 4/4   Hospitality 5/5   Food 7.5/9   Value 1.5/2

| | |
|---|---|
| • **Italian/Northern** | **Hours:** Lunch Mon-Sat 11:30 am-2:30 pm, dinner Sun-Thurs 5:30-10:30 pm, Fri-Sat until 11:30 pm |
| • **Chicago/Near North** | |
| • **$$$** | |
| 158 E. Ontario St. | **Cards:** AE, MC, VISA |
| Chicago | **Reservations:** Recommended |
| (312) 664-1474 | **Handicapped:** Accessible |
| **Troubleshooter:** Robert Ruggeri (owner) | **Bar:** Full, good wine list, specialty drinks |
| | **Parking:** Valet |
| | **Party Facilities:** Yes |

**B**ice is the kind of place where one is likely to see movers and shakers in the fields of advertising, PR, entertainment, even food. It is stylish, it is first class, it is expensive. The large dining room seats about 150 in a decor that suggests a contemporary European design. Service people carry out this suggestion, thanks not only to their well-tailored dress, but also to their sophistication in soliciting orders and making suggestions.

The menu stresses Northern Italian dining. Though offerings change nightly, many items will appear often enough to give the restaurant a sense of culinary continuity. Among recent selections from the antipasti listing, vitello tonnato – sliced cold roasted veal with a purée of tuna and caper sauce – was about as classic as this recipe can be. Lamb carpaccio – thin, nearly translucent slices – came with nuggets of hearts of palm and slices of Parmesan cheese.

The more commonly seen beef carpaccio is served with mustard dressing and Parmesan. Another variation, sliced cured beef with a quartet of artichokes, comes in a lightly lemoned olive oil. Cured beef remains cured beef no matter how it is prepared.

Pastas can be ordered as entrees, though I think pasta is more enjoyable as a separate course, perhaps shared with companions. The fettucine and porcini mushrooms is so intensely flavored as to leave a bite at the back of the throat, which is as this dish should be. Other pastas, from a list of several, might include linguine with pesto or shells with broccoli, anchovies, and sun-dried tomatoes. The kitchen also prepares freshly made risotto, enjoyable right down to the last chewy grain.

Entrees include several Northern Italian classics, as well as some selections not often seen in Chicago. An order of stuffed quails features a matched pair of the plump little birds, along with a wedge of polenta and a garnish of sun-dried tomatoes. Though good, the stuffing is a bit too breaded. Grilled swordfish is more direct, simply embellished with olives, capers, tomatoes for color, and fresh basil leaves for light flavor. Black sea bass has been served recently with mushrooms and cabbage, varied enough to be interesting, but not so intense as to interfere with the fish.

Among meats and poultry, the menu includes roasted rack of veal with plum tomatoes, sliced breast of duck with sauteed mushrooms, lamb chops with a spiced peppery relish, and a traditional veal saltimbocca. Desserts can be as simple as freshly made gelati or as elaborate as cheesecake with pine nuts and raisins.

# BINYON'S

KR 16/20

Decor 3.5/4   Hospitality 3.5/5   Food 7/9   Value 2/2

- **American**
- **Chicago/Loop**
- **$$**

327 S. Plymouth Ct.
Chicago
(312) 341-1155
**Troubleshooter:** Don Wallace (owner)

**Hours:** Mon-Fri 11:30 am-9 pm, Sat 4:30-9 pm
**Cards:** All majors
**Reservations:** Suggested
**Bar:** Service bar
**Parking:** In lot next door, valet service after 4:30 pm
**Party Facilities:** For 8 to 120

**B**inyon's goes back to the days of Prohibition when Chicago was a wide open town of Black Maria's, violin cases that were anything but musical, and bootleg hooch. Since those years, the city has tried to tame a reputation more honored in fiction, perhaps, than in reality. But that Binyon's is a permanent fixture in the Chicago dining firmament is no fiction.

The restaurant has the warmth of a private club or taproom, although the hustle and bustle is a far cry from the hushed halls of a private gathering place. But that's why people throng here. More than 1,000 people can be served at lunch from a menu as basic as fish, chops, and steaks. Even the salads have a larger-than-life quality.

Entrees such as sauteed veal kidney or sweetbreads are no longer on the menu. It's not that Binyon's is keeping up with the times, but tastes do change. Thus, diners will find more pasta and seafood. But steaks, chops, and ample portions remain the staple at this old line dining emporium. All dinners, by the way, include soup or salad plus a fresh vegetable and a choice of potatoes or rice. Turtle soup, once only an occasional selection, is now a fixture on the menu and should not be missed.

Not far from the Federal Building complex or Chicago's financial heart at Jackson and La Salle, Binyon's has always been a favorite with the pin-striped suit set, as well as with local gadabouts. And, while regulars number in the hundreds, there's always room to welcome someone new.

# BISTRO 110
KR 19/20
Decor 4/4   Hospitality 5/5   Food 8/9   Value 2/2

- **French**
- **Chicago/Near North**
- **$$**

110 E. Pearson
Chicago
(312) 266-3110
**Troubleshooter:** Doug Roth
(co-owner)

**Hours:** Mon-Thurs 11:30 am-10:30 pm, Fri-Sat until midnight, Sun until 11:30 pm
**Cards:** All majors
**Reservations:** Suggested for parties of 5 or more only
**Handicapped:** Accessible
**Bar:** Full, extensive wine list, many by the glass
**Party Facilities:** None

There's something to love about a restaurant that puts a whole head of roasted garlic on your table along with the bread and butter. It's a signature of Bistro 110, as much a part of the restaurant as its noisy, bustling atmosphere.

The restaurant's wood-burning oven turns out orders of chicken, fish, and side vegetables, as well as the heads of garlic. Other house specialties include several kinds of pastas, sandwiches, and desserts. Our waiter claimed the wood-burning oven generated heat as high as 900 degrees. Maybe so, but I just wanted dinner, not my car painted and baked.

Entrees include some classic bistro food including, but not limited to, traditional steak and fries, cassoulet loaded with chunks of duck and lamb and slices of fatty sausage, and, of course, the white beans that are at the heart of the recipe. More than a whiff of fennel and garlic add to the complexity of seasonings, all of which is enriched with some crème fraiche.

Appetizers range from roasted mushrooms and French onion soup baked in a crock to oven-roasted calamari with the flavor of basil-infused olive oil, plus roasted potatoes and tomatoes. The delicious basket of fries is large enough to keep the whole table nibbling away.

The restaurant features an enclosed sidewalk café setting, which gives those lucky enough to get a table there in the winter some wonderful views outside.

# BLACKHAWK LODGE

KR 19/20

Decor 4/4   Hospitality 5/5   Food 8.5/9   Value 1.5/2

- **American**
- **Chicago/Near North**
- **$$**

41 E. Superior St.
Chicago
(312) 280-4080
**Troubleshooter:** Manager on duty

**Hours:** Mon-Thurs 11:30 am-10:30 pm, Fri-Sat until 11:30 pm, Sun 5-10 pm
**Cards:** All majors
**Reservations:** Suggested
**Handicapped:** Accessible
**Bar:** Full, excellent wine list, good selection of beers
**Parking:** Valet after 5 pm
**Party Facilities:** Available
**Heart-Healthy Menu:** Selections

Blackhawk Lodge is as American as the apple pie on its dessert menu. The restaurant's appearance is rustic, but not primitive, with bleached wood flooring, light colored paneling, and heavy fieldstone fireplaces.

The food is balanced between traditional American and more imaginative, contemporary cookery, though it isn't cutting edge. A welcoming basket of buttermilk biscuits and corn muffins sets the tone.

Filet of tuna comes with a liberal crust of black peppercorns on a bed of sweet, caramelized onions, with roasted red potatoes on the side and sour cream-based dill dressing. The tuna is flawless, perfectly grilled, still moist, even meaty. Other seafood choices include grilled salmon, sea scallops seared in a skillet, grilled whole fish of the day in a marinade of herbs, mustard, and lemon, and barbecued shrimp cooked New Orleans style.

Following contemporary tastes for creative poultry, Blackhawk Lodge offers some real delights. Roasted garlic chicken has a delicious smoked flavor permeating every bite. Whole cloves of garlic add their own savory influence. The menu also lists barbecued, smoked, and fried chicken choices, the latter served with mashed potatoes and gravy for a real down-home taste.

Appetizers are truly delicious. Roasted eggplant is served with a top of pureed sun-dried tomatoes and sweet onions. Angel-hair pasta, in either appetizer or entree portion, comes with a mix of smoked mushrooms, fresh-cooked spinach, and a little chopped tomato that appears more for color than flavor. Only barley soup, which the menu points out is made with five kinds of beans, was a tad disappointing, not because it was incorrectly made, but because it just may have been overwhelmed by everything else.

# BLIND FAITH CAFE
KR 17.5/20
Decor 3.5/4  Hospitality 4.5/5  Food 7.5/9  Value 2/2

- **Vegetarian**
- **Evanston**
- **$**

525 Dempster St.
Evanston
(708) 328-6875
**Troubleshooter:** David Lipschutz

**Hours:** Mon-Thurs 10 am-9 pm, Fri until 10 pm, Sat 8 am-10 pm, Sun 8 am-9 pm
**Cards:** AE, MC, VISA
**Reservations:** None Fridays through Sundays, otherwise for 7 or more only
**Handicapped:** Accessible
**Bar:** None
**Parking:** On street or lot one-half block south
**Heart-Healthy Menu:** Yes

**D**o you remember when you were little how your mother urged you to eat all your vegetables? Mom doesn't exactly prowl the tables at the Blind Faith Cafe, but certainly she's there in spirit at this most famous of all area vegetarian restaurants. You don't have to be a vegetarian to enjoy the Blind Faith Cafe. Just go for the good food, lots of it, and most at extremely reasonable prices.

Begin with one of the appetizers, such as tempeh fingers. These may remind you of fried mozzarella sticks, except that they are made from tempeh, fermented split soybeans. The taste is pleasant, the texture cheese-like. The hummus and tabbouli have the authenticity you will find in better Middle Eastern restaurants and make great pre-dinner snacking.

Soups include miso, a Japanese soy soup; vegetarian chili; or the soup of the day. Mushroom barley soup, a recent special, comes in a clear stock, with lots of chewy slices of the fungus and delicious kernels of grain.

Foods like tofu or tempeh, because they are so neutral, can show up in any number of ways. You might want to try sauteed tempeh. What comes to the table looks like stir-fried chicken and has a slightly oriental flavor, no doubt from a soy sauce seasoning. The flavors are delicate, not heavy; the tempeh is shaped into firm little nuggets with a sauté of broccoli, onions, and mushrooms atop a bed of brown rice. There is even a vegetarian jambalaya, awash with everything you would expect in such a dish, except the meat. This one proves "vegetarian" does not mean "bland."

There are some meat imitations at Blind Faith Cafe. Try pecan scallopini. This is not a bowl of nuts! A patty of texturized vegetable protein (tvp) is grilled, laden with a brown sauce and melted mozzarella, and served on a bed of linguine.

When the recipe is not imitative, things can be even better. Pasta pesto is redolent with fresh basil and garlic. Instead of pignoli nuts, this recipe uses cashews, which may not be the way it's done in Genoa, but it's still quite good.

As you might expect, Blind Faith Cafe can accommodate special diets. It's really an interesting change from standard dining. And, who knows . . . you might just want to jog a few kilometers after dinner!

# BLUE MESA
KR 18.5/20
Decor 4/4   Hospitality 4.5/5   Food 8/9   Value 2/2

- **American/Southwest**
- **Chicago/Mid-North**
- **$$**

1729 N. Halsted St.
Chicago
(312) 944-5990
**Troubleshooter:** Phil
Marienthal (owner)

**Hours:** Lunch Mon-Fri, Sun (brunch) 11:30 am-2:30 pm, dinner Mon-Thurs 5-11 pm, Fri to 12 pm, Sat 11:30 am-12 pm, Sun 4-10 pm
**Cards:** AE, DINERS, DISCOVER, MC, VISA
**Reservations:** Recommended
**Handicapped:** Accessible
**Bar:** Full, specialty margaritas, Mexican beers
**Parking:** Valet
**Party Facilities:** For up to 45

**B**lue Mesa could be considered an adobe outpost with a warm touch of Santa Fe brought to the streets of Chicago. The restaurant is a picture of New Mexican design, with its pueblo-style interiors, whitewashed walls, low-key art, cacti, and blooming desert greens. For warm-weather dining, there is also the patio.

With the appointment of a new chef comes an almost entirely new menu, which has evolved from basic New Mexican fare to a diverse representation of Southwestern Nouvelle. Anglo, Mexican, and Spanish contributions are represented by traditional recipes, which are even touched with some Asian influences.

For starters there is a variety of hearty soups, stews, and bountiful salads. Southwestern crab cakes may seem a contradiction in terms – and cuisines – but try it with the spice of green chili chutney. A version of pizza brings together artichoke hearts, sun-dried tomatoes, mushrooms, and roasted garlic under a layer of Chihuahua cheese.

As for entrees, consider specialties that include pasta zozobra – grilled smoked chicken and artichokes sauteed with tri-color peppers, then simmered in sun-dried tomato, basil and cream sauce, all served over penne, a tubular Italian pasta. Vegetarians will enjoy something like the meatless burrito, which is filled with corn, broccoli, leeks, and peppers, all bound together in a black bean sauce. Other selections include a variety of fajitas and grilled or blackened seafood.

If you are looking for the unusual in desserts, try chocolate fritters with vanilla and almond ice cream, topped with a peppered chocolate sauce, combining the intensity of hot with sweet for a unique flavor. For something a bit more laid back, there is always a slice of Key lime pie topped with burnt meringue.

# BOB CHINN'S CRAB HOUSE
KR 18/20
Decor 3.5/4   Hospitality 4.5/5   Food 8/9   Value 2/2

- **Seafood/American**
- **Wheeling**
- **$$**

393 S. Milwaukee Ave.
Wheeling
(708) 520-3633
**Troubleshooters:** Bob Chinn
and Marilyn Chinn Le Tourneau
(owners)

**Hours:** Lunch Mon-Fri 11:00
am-2:30 pm, dinner Mon-Thurs
4:30-10:30 pm, Fri until 11:30
pm, Sat 12-11:30 pm, Sun 3-10
pm
**Cards:** All majors, house
accounts
**Reservations:** Accepted for 5
or more (will cut wait in half)
**Handicapped:** Accessible
**Bar:** Service bar plus handsome
lounge with antique long bar
**Parking:** Free lot
**Party Facilities:** Semi-private
facilities on porch
**Heart-Healthy Menu:**
Selections

**B**ob Chinn's Crab House is a landmark in the American restaurant industry. Excluding fast-food chains, no other restaurant in the United States serves so many people each day. Twenty-five hundred dinners could be dished up on a typical day. With that kind of volume it would seem that some diners might have an inordinate wait for a table. That used to be the case. But a renovation in the mid-1980s, including a major expansion, sped things up remarkably. People may still feel as if they are moved in and out like so many widgets on a conveyor belt, but once you're in the hands of a waitress, things become much more cordial.

Soups are delicious. The seafood gumbo is the kind that sneaks up on you. Your first spoonful fills the mouth with comets of flavor. Then, when you think things are about to subside, a rush of pepper seasoning takes hold. This one is a real winner.

Entrees change frequently, as do prices, depending upon market conditions. Bob Chinn's Crab House really knows how to serve traditional lobster. After outfitting you with a bib to catch all the juices, your waitress will bring out a large wooden platter with the lobster butterflied, and most of the shell cracking done. The rest is up to you. Savor each delicious bite; saving the best for last, crack into the claws and remove the meat from the shell for the kind of dining that makes lobster the supreme treat it can be.

For fish lovers, Pacific onaga is often on the menu, fished from Hawaiian waters. Tuna is always a good choice. The large cut of tuna steak comes fresh from the grill, with hashmarks. The fish might be topped with a cracker-crumb seasoning mix that leaves just a bit of saltiness, and perhaps the flavor of Worcestershire on the tongue. Florida swordfish, Alaskan halibut, soft-shell crabs, as well as almost any other variety of crabs you might want, are featured in season. Since this restaurant does such a huge volume, turnover virtually ensures freshness.

Desserts include several chocolate goodies, cheesecake, ice cream, and Key lime pie, which is too sweet.

# BONES
KR 17/20
Decor 3.5/4   Hospitality 3/5   Food 8/9   Value 2/2

- **American**
- **Lincolnwood**
- **$$**

7110 N. Lincoln Ave.
Lincolnwood
(708) 677-3350
**Troubleshooter:** Paul Leff
(managing partner)

**Hours:** Mon-Thurs 11:30 am-11 pm, Fri-Sat until midnight, Sun brunch 11-3 pm, dinner 3-9 pm
**Cards:** All majors
**Reservations:** Suggested
**Handicapped:** Accessible
**Bar:** Full
**Parking:** Free lot
**Party Facilities:** For 35-90, receptions up to 110
**Heart-Healthy Menu:** Selections

You know all the warnings about cholesterol and fats, but who could go to Bones and still eat like a monk? Bones is the epitome of sensual dining. Go there to delight in gnawing, gnashing, and "gnoshing" on hickory-smoked ribs or tender barbecued chicken drowned in a sauce as thick and sweet as syrup.

Bones is almost always busy, which means you really should phone ahead for reservations. Otherwise, prepare for a stackup that makes Friday afternoons at O'Hare look restful. To the restaurant's credit, the handsome sports bar is as good a place as any to wait.

Once you're seated, amidst a mix of dark woods and cartoon drawings of celebrity figures hand-painted on the walls, a waitress will stop by soon to take a drink order and offer menus. The menu is fairly short, highlighted by the basics: barbecued baby back ribs, beef ribs, and chicken either barbecued or broiled.

Despite all its emphasis on meats, Bones does have some Heart Healthy recipes, which follow the American Heart Association's dining guidelines. True, it's hard to stick with broiled whitefish or chicken and pasta when a slab of baby back ribs slathered in sauce is yours for the taking. These baby backs are to ribs what the Hope diamond is to costume jewelry.

At Bones, there are two kinds of sauces: spicy, which is really kind of sweet, and mild, which is . . . well, mild. As for the teriyaki sauce, stick to Japanese restaurants for this stuff.

If all of this is not enough, someone with a pin identifying her as the Hospitality Schmoozer comes around with a large bowl of fried chicken for the asking.

Desserts are lavish and excessive, including something called skoog pie, which is layers of ice cream, caramel, pecans, and chocolate. Or you could try something simpler, like strawberry ice cream pie, with a puree of strawberry sauce and a crunchy graham cracker crust.

# BOSSA NOVA
KR 17.5/20
Decor 3.5/4  Hospitality 4.5/5  Food 7.5/9  Value 2/2

| | |
|---|---|
| • **American/Eclectic** | **Hours:** Daily 4 pm-2 am |
| • **Chicago/Mid-North** | **Cards:** All majors |
| • **$$** | **Reservations:** Suggested, especially weekends |
| 1960 N. Clybourn Ave. | **Handicapped:** Accessible |
| Chicago | **Bar:** Full |
| (312) 248-4800 | **Parking:** Valet and street |
| **Troubleshooter:** Victor | **Party Facilities:** For up to |
| Kasemir (owner) | 100 |

At Bossa Nova, the Spanish tapa is internationalized. The menu offers over 60 selections of interesting nibbles. But, as you might suspect with such a large array of choices, not everything hits a home run. Though Bossa Nova may not offer the very best tapas in town, there is enough variety to interest most anyone.

The menu is laid out into various categories beginning with a trio of soups, moving on through hot and cold tapas, skewered meats and fish, entrees, pastas, and pizza. Those items that are deemed particularly spicy by the chef are designated with from one to three jalapeño icons. Our tasting of several "three jalapeño" tapas leads to the conclusion that the chef is extremely sensitive. Designations such as Pasta from Hell or Suicide Chicken Wings sound more intimidating than they really are. But Dragon Noodles deliver all the heat that the name implies.

So if you really want something hot, be sure to make that clear to your waitress. Otherwise, there is some real imagination, and several eruptions of talent on the Bossa Nova menu. Perhaps the most exceptional, and certainly the most imaginative of several tapas tasted at our table, was a stacked combination that sandwiches grilled tomatoes and goat cheese between slices of eggplant in what the menu designates as a "Big Mak" (spelled with a "k"). The cheese insinuates itself among the other components for delicious flavor and satisfying texture. On the other hand, the house version of baba ghanoush, the Middle Eastern eggplant purée, is short on roasted flavor. But skewered swordfish comes alive with an accompaniment of mango relish, while crab cakes with red pepper rouille are so tasty you might wish this came in an entree-sized portion. Similarly tasty is seafood chili. A creamy broth holds shrimp and calamari with white beans; despite its appearance, the flavors are anything but monochromatic or bland.

There is no one dominant influence on the menu, with contributions from Asia, Europe, and the American Southwest most evident. Simple sweet potato fries make great snacking, especially with an icy cold imported beer; Mamba from the Ivory Coast is the equal of many a European lager.

Dining at Bossa Nova can be as varied and complex as you may choose, thanks to the extensive menu. Desserts can be rather creative, though chocolate fettucine is not as full flavored as one might want. However, a chocolate egg roll is delcious on all counts.

# BOULEVARD

KR 19/20

Decor 4/4   Hospitality 5/5   Food 8/9   Value 2/2

- **American**
- **Chicago/Near North**
- **$$$**

Inter-Continental Hotel, 505
   N. Michigan Ave.
Chicago
(312) 321-8888
**Troubleshooter:** Heinze
Gliege (maitre d')

**Hours:** Lunch Mon-Sat 11:30
am-2:30 pm, dinner daily 6-10
pm
**Cards:** All majors
**Reservations:** Suggested
**Handicapped:** Accessible
**Bar:** Service bar
**Parking:** Valet and lot
**Party Facilities:** For up to
600

**D**espite the trend toward more casual dining that is sweeping the
restaurant industry, the need remains for the special-occasion restau-
rant. Whether it be for business entertainment or a personal celebra-
tion, there is hardly anything better than a fine hotel restaurant. And
when the hotel is as elegant as the Inter-Continental and the restau-
rant as beautifully appointed as the Boulevard, there may be no
need to look any further.

Inter-Continental spent a fortune to spruce up and restore one of
Chicago's older, more elegant hotels. Every bit of the beautiful terra
cotta, bas relief, and metal work has been refurbished. Furnishings
are luxurious but still comfortable.

The Boulevard is up a graceful flight of stairs, and it sweeps
around a level overlooking the Inter-Continental's Michigan Avenue
entrance. This is the restaurant's biggest problem; whenever a crowd
has gathered below, the noise it generates floods the restaurant. Oth-
erwise, dining is dignified and unhurried.

The menu is à la carte, leaning toward American influences. A
careful eye and hand are given to plating; this is a restaurant that
does not take appearances lightly. Twin filets of grouper are
wrapped in potatoes, thin as parchment, resting in a pool of beurre
blanc mushroom sauce redolent with herbs. On the same platter sits
a basket woven from julienne zucchini sticks; inside the basket are
faux garden peas, actually zucchini. In another selection, poached
scallops and lobster, the seafood is topped by a yellow sabayon
Champagne sauce. Framing the platter are snips of varied colored
vegetables. Grilled lamb chops come three to the order, fresh fla-
vored, served on a platter whose center is a timbale mold of cous-

cous. An additional selection of grilled entrees ranges from a platter of vegetables with any of several sauces to venison eye of the round.

Accompanying courses are of similar distinction. Appetizers include a wonderfully flavorful mix of smoked eel and scallops in a light tomato sauce. A layered mushroom crêpe is tinged with thyme butter; fennel consommé is served from a large tureen over a small shrimp aspic, which dissolves in the warmth of the broth. Desserts, like other courses, are bountiful.

# BRUNA'S
KR 17.5/20
Decor 2.5/4   Hospitality 5/5   Food 8/9   Value 2/2

- **Italian**
- **Chicago/South**
- **$$**

2424 S. Oakley Blvd.
Chicago
(312) 254-5550
**Troubleshooter:** Luciano
Silvestri (owner)

**Hours:** Mon-Thurs 11 am-10 pm, Fri-Sat 11am-11 pm, Sun 1:30-10:00 pm
**Cards:** All majors, house accounts
**Bar:** Extensive Italian wine list
**Parking:** Street

T he dining room here is often heady with the aroma of garlic, oregano, and other seasonings. No one is likely to be overwhelmed by the decor, which, aside from a couple of perfunctory murals, is rather simple. But for good Italian food at reasonable cost, Bruna's offers a simpler approach at a time when Italian dining has become more or less "yuppiefied."

Many dinners are served with a vegetable and soup or salad. An à la carte pasta will add to your check, but none will cost more than $10, and pasta can be split among your party as a separate pasta course. Instead of a noodle pasta, you might want to be a bit more adventurous and try gnocchi. These are like little dumplings, though heavier. Gnocchi are especially delicious when served with the hearty meat sauce characteristic of Bruna's home-style cooking.

Linguine in clam sauce is another example of the simple, direct approach here. Among entree choices, lasagne is layered four-deep with broad noodles, meat, and cheese. Boned breast of chicken Parmigiana is covered with the standard house red sauce and, of course, ample melted cheese. The veal Parmigiana gets similar treatment. Veal, all of it tender, pale Provimi, makes up a large portion of the menu.

Bruna's is not too many years away from its fiftieth anniversary, and though under a different ownership for the past several years, it remains the home-style restaurant that marked its beginnings.

# BUB CITY
KR 18/20
Decor 4/4   Hospitality 5/5   Food 7/9   Value 2/2

- **American/Southern**
- **Chicago/Mid-North**
- **$$**

901 Weed St.
Chicago
(312) 266-1200
**Troubleshooter:** Bob Vick
(managing partner)

**Hours:** Mon-Thurs 11:30 am-11 pm, Fri until midnight, Sat 5 pm-midnight (bar closes 2 am), Sun 4-10 pm
**Cards:** All majors
**Reservations:** Suggested
**Handicapped:** Accessible
**Bar:** Full
**Parking:** Valet and street
**Dress:** Jeans and cowboy boots encouraged
**Party Facilities:** Ten rooms with total capacity for groups as large as 2,000
**Heart-Healthy Menu:** Selections

From the land of Moon Pies, Lone Star Beer, and sweet potato pies comes Bub City. You'll find more longnecks, as in beer bottles, than rednecks, as in Southerners, at Bub City, but this still is a restaurant where food is ample and fun. The Down South feeling is carefully researched and re-created, right down to the ramshackle exterior and "Truckers Welcome" sign. Inside, the collection of tables and chairs is rummage sale chic; the barroom is immense and appropriately noisy.

The menu emphasizes crab, ranging from blue crabs served on a large bed of ice, to crab fritters with a New Orleans rémoulade, to dungeness and other styles that require diners to get right in using crab cracker, mallet, and, of course, hands. Large plastic bibs help to protect your shirt front.

It is this hands-on approach to dining, beginning with an oily and heavily garlic-lathered bread, that characterizes the tactile fun of Bub City. Sure, for a couple of bucks additional, they will shell your shrimp, but if you don't like getting a little bit messy, Bub City is not for you.

Start with the appetizers that come in large enough portions to satisfy a table of four. Chicken wings are spiced, but not nasty; crab fritters are fried nuggets whose flavor is easily lost in the rémoulade. Fried jalapeños with cheese might not exactly be authentic Southern truck-stop grub, but they are nonetheless delicious. The peppers are deprived of their seeds (whence comes the heat), stuffed with a good, meltable cheese, coated in light batter, and plunged into the fry cooker.

Among dinners are several combination platters that give you wide taste ranges, including barbecued ribs and chicken, Texas-style beef brisket, and a crab feast.

Bub City also offers a selection of linguine dinners, all served in deep bowls. Among the choices is one with shrimp, scallops and crab, kind of a mild spiced Southern version of zuppa de pesce. The house version of shrimp Creole is, like everything else, in generous portion, its spiciness muted but not obliterated. Dinners come with sides of boiled potatoes and corn on the cob, best left uneaten. Desserts are terrific and include such classics as bread pudding with bourbon sauce, a variation on bananas Foster, or super sweet, sweet potato pecan pie. And, if you come in late summer, you might even catch the restaurant's annual Watermelon Thump and Sweet Corn Fest!

# BUKHARA
KR 17/20
Decor 4/4   Hospitality 3/5   Food 8.5/9   Value 1.5/2

- **Indian**
- **Chicago/Near North**
- **$$**

2 E. Ontario St.
Chicago
(312) 943-0188
**Troubleshooter:** Mr. Revi
(manager)

**Hours:** Lunch Mon-Fri 11:30 am-2:30 pm, Sat-Sun 12-3 pm, dinner Sun-Thurs 5:30-10 pm, Fri-Sat until 11 pm
**Cards:** All majors
**Reservations:** Suggested
**Handicapped:** Accessible
**Bar:** Full
**Parking:** Half-price in nearby lots or garage
**Party Facilities:** For up to 200 (Sun-Thurs)

**B**ukhara is unique among Chicago's Indian restaurants. For one thing, it breaks away from the storefront mold that marks most of them. For another, its menu, though not as large as other Indian restaurants', offers a distinctive cuisine.

Bukhara serves what its owners call Northwest Frontier cuisine from India. Unlike other Indian restaurants, Bukhara will freely serve beef, though a section of the menu also caters to vegetarian tastes. Diners sit at wood tables in large, almost oversized chairs. The white-washed walls and planked floors are decorated with Bukhara carpets, their intricate designs endlessly repeated. Virtually everything served, even a tossed salad, comes from the tandoors, those large clay urns heated with charcoal coals that are clearly visible in the glass-enclosed kitchen.

Any of the vegetarian offerings are fine for appetizers. Try dal Bukhara, a dish of lentils in subtle seasonings that leave just a hint of sweetness on the palate. Contrast the dal with aloo bharvan, an Indian version of stuffed baked potatoes. They are filled with a mix of cashew nuts, mild green chili peppers, raisins, cumin, and a traditional blend of dried ground spices called garum masala, used in Indian cooking much the way a French chef would use a bouquet garni.

In addition to your opening course, order a basket of mixed breads. The breads are important because diners are expected to eat with their hands, using the bread as scoops. You can have utensils on request but, since Bukhara gives each diner a large bib to protect clothing, using your hands is no trouble at all.

The several tandoor-roasted entrees at Bukhara have flavors un-like those of other Indian restaurants, even though entree names may be similar. For example, barah kebab has no resemblance to traditional kebab cooking, except that meat is in individual chunks. In this case, the meat is lamb, coated with a thick paste of seasonings and spices, and roasted to perfection in the tandoor. This is the kind of meat you want to nibble on right down to the very bones. Or try murgh malai kebab, which uses boned chicken that has been mari-nated in ginger and coriander, with a liberal addition of garlic. The flavors marry deliciously. A chicken entree, the house specialty named tandoori murgh Bukhara, has an entirely different, simple flavor that emphasizes the natural goodness of the chicken itself.

Though service can be a bit disorganized, if not haphazard, Bukhara is a unique restaurant for some unusual and delicious dining.

# BUONA FORTUNA
KR 18.5/20
Decor 4/4   Hospitality 5/5   Food 7.5/9   Value 2/2

| | |
|---|---|
| • **Italian** | **Hours:** Mon-Thurs 5-11 pm, Fri-Sat until midnight |
| • **Chicago/Northwest** | **Cards:** All majors |
| • **$$** | **Reservations:** Accepted |
| 1540 N. Milwaukee Ave. | **Handicapped:** Accessible |
| Chicago | **Bar:** Full, only Italian wines |
| (312) 278-7797 | **Parking:** Free lot across street |
| **Troubleshooter:** Mario | **Party Facilities:** For 50 + , |
| Szpyrka (owner) | Sundays only |

**B**uona Fortuna is an unpretentious neighborhood restaurant worth leaving your neighborhood to visit. The restaurant is fronted by highly polished woodwork with brass accents and classical col-umns flanking the front door. The interior is all wood-planked floor-ing, bare brick, and faux bronze panels. White paper over cloth tops each table, as does a fresh flower for color and warmth.

The food is imaginative, without contrivance. Something as basic as carpaccio, paper-thin slices of filet mignon, is served traditionally with a drizzle of olive oil, a coarse grating of Parmesan cheese, plus lemons, mushrooms, and capers. Bruschetta, at three slices to the order, is a bit overpriced but tasty enough with its topping of crushed tomato, basil, and oil.

The menu at Buona Fortuna says the restaurant serves green New Zealand mussels. In fact, the ones we got were the more common black shelled, but fresh and aromatic nonetheless in a rich garlic and tomato liquor. Traditional polenta with a side of sauteed mushrooms, fried or grilled calamari in balsamic vinegar, and asparagus and eggs with lemons and olive oil round out the first course selections.

One could take an à la carte salad at this point before moving on to pastas or entrees. Pasta courses are substantial enough to enjoy as an entree. The restaurant was willing to accommodate some of our special requests without difficulty.

One of the tastiest dishes at Buona Fortuna may be pasta with anchovy sauce. In this recipe, the anchovies are evidently cut into small pieces and cooked down in olive oil until they are all but disintegrated. Fresh breadcrumbs are added to the mix. The result is a delicious and well textured sauce that clings to each strand of noodle, a sauce not nearly so salty as anchovies might suggest.

More substantive for a main course would be pasta with seafood. Though the menu says shrimp and broccoli are served in a cream sauce, we asked for something without cream. Marinara was substituted and worked beautifully. Among the pastas offered, gnocchi is plated with porcini mushrooms, asparagus, and peas in a cream-and-tomato sauce. Angel-hair pasta comes with herbs, grated Parmesan cheese, and a light tomato sauce while mostaccioli is matched with sauteed peppers and oil.

Several meat, poultry, and seafood selections round out a menu that, though fairly short when compared to some Italian restaurants, offers diversity without resorting to dining clichés.

# THE BUTCHER SHOP
KR 18/20

Decor 4/4   Hospitality 5/5   Food 7/9   Value 2/2

- **American**
- **Chicago/Near North**
- **$$**

358 W. Ontario St.
Chicago
(312) 440-4900
**Troubleshooter:** Al Watkins
(manager)

**Hours:** Sun-Thurs 5-10 pm,
Fri-Sat until 11 pm
**Cards:** AE, DINERS, MC,
VISA
**Reservations:** Accepted
**Handicapped:** Accessible
**Bar:** Full
**Parking:** Valet
**Party Facilities:** For 30-100
and up

For the ultimate in do-it-yourself dining, spend an evening at The Butcher Shop, where you probably will be doing the grilling yourself. Diners can go up to the large cooler cabinets and pick out individual cuts. The steaks are choice grade and vary in cost depending on their size. You'll pay $2 more if the restaurant's chefs do the cooking for you.

But going to the grill is half the fun of The Butcher Shop. Working at a hickory charcoal pit, you'll have a full array of spices and seasonings to put on your steak, and of course, the utensils needed to do the grilling. Chances are you'll strike up a conversation with other people who have the same thing on their minds as do you . . . namely, how good that steak is going to taste after 20 minutes or so over the coals. If you should have a problem, either your waiter or one of the grill men will be there to help. All dinners come with a handsome salad and baked or au gratin potato.

There are a couple of other dinner choices on the menu besides the steak. Marinated chicken features boneless breasts grilled over charcoal and offered at market price. Lamb chops are a recent addition, while fresh fish, which can vary from day to day depending upon availability, is also priced at market. Roast prime rib is a fairly recent menu addition, in either 16-ounce or 32-ounce cuts. Desserts are typically all-American and include apple pie hot from the oven or tangy cheesecake.

# CADILLAC RANCH
KR 17.5/20
Decor 3.5/4   Hospitality 5/5   Food 7/9   Value 2/2

- **American**
- **Bartlett**
- **$$**

1175 W. Lake St. (two blocks west of Illinois Rte. 59)
Bartlett
(708) 830-7200
**Troubleshooter:** Tom Curran (general manager)

**Hours:** Mon-Thurs 11 am-10 pm, Fri-Sat until midnight, Sun until 10 pm (country breakfast buffet 9 am-2 pm)
**Cards:** All majors, house accounts
**Reservations:** Every night except Saturday
**Handicapped:** Accessible
**Bar:** Full
**Parking:** Free lot
**Dress:** Western gear invited
**Party Facilities:** For 25-800

There is no hitching post in the parking lot for tying up Old Paint, but Cadillac Ranch seems to have most everything else needed to replicate a Texas barbecue restaurant and saloon dance hall. The restaurant is quite large, with seats for about 220 inside, plus several more tables on the outdoor wraparound deck. In addition, there is a pool hall, a bar, and a dance hall for trying the Texas two-step and line dancing.

People go at it with gusto at a restaurant where the emphasis is on quantity and fun more than true culinary excellence. It's a place the kids will certainly enjoy, as will the adults who have to pick up the tab.

The menu is enormous and fairly predictable for this type of place. There are smatterings of Tex-Mex snacks, including nachos, tacos, and stuffed jalapeño peppers called Texas torpedoes. A combination platter for the table, or in smaller portion for one or two people, features a decent assortment, including chicken wings, some grilled skewered shrimp, and other nibbles.

The combination approach at Cadillac Ranch can also be taken with a dinner entree. The "Boomtown Bar B Que Feast" is truly that, though quantity seems to be more the goal than quality. For instance, it is almost impossible to get the shells off the fairly small grilled shrimp. And what the menu claims is beef brisket really seems like less flavorful thin-sliced roast beef with a barbecue sauce that does not really make up the difference. On the other hand, the large portion of chicken is delicious, while the slab of ribs is meaty, the kind that falls from the bones. Corn on the cob, roasted potatoes, and tubs of cabbage slaw and baked beans with bacon are brought to the table. The feast is served family style for four people or more, brought out on an upside-down garbage can lid.

Best bets for smaller appetites are hamburgers or cheeseburgers, the kind that have the heft of a real burger, not some wimpy fast-food version. Seafood includes catfish and crab legs; there are also several steaks. Cadillac Ranch chili is rather mild, though it is made with chunked steak rather than ground meat and, in authentic Texas fashion, served without beans. Desserts include fruit cobbler and fried ice cream, even frozen yogurt, though considering you have come this far, what difference do a few more hundred calories make?

# CAFE BA-BA-REEBA!
KR 20/20
Decor 4/4   Hospitality 5/5   Food 9/9   Value 2/2

- **Spanish/Tapas**
- **Chicago/Mid-North**
- **$$**

2024 N. Halsted St.
Chicago
(312) 935-5000
**Troubleshooter:** Gabino Sotelino (managing partner)

**Hours:** Lunch Tues-Fri 11:30 am-2:30 pm, Sat until 3:00 pm, dinner Mon-Thurs 5:30-11 pm, Fri until midnight, Sat 5 pm-midnight, Sun brunch 10:30-2:30, dinner 2:30-9:30 pm
**Cards:** All majors
**Reservations:** Accepted for lunch, limited for dinner
**Handicapped:** Accessible
**Bar:** Full, with emphasis on Spanish wines
**Parking:** Valet
**Party Facilities:** For 3-300
**Heart-Healthy Menu:** Limited selections

Tapas are Spanish appetizers, but there is hardly a way to describe their variety until you taste them. Created from meats, seafood, cheeses, and vegetables, many tapas can be sampled to create a complete meal. The idea is to build as you go along, following individual tastes and appetite.

Although tapas dining involves small tastes of many different foods, you nonetheless might want to try an entree. The clincher is paella, a classic Spanish casserole that combines chicken, Spanish sausage, mussels, and shrimp with saffron and baked rice. It's a splendid treat! In addition, several of the tapas may be ordered in larger, entree-size portions.

Desserts range from homemade ice creams to chocolate hazelnut cake to baked bananas in a thick caramel sauce.

# CAFE BORGIA
KR 16.5/20
Decor 3.5/4  Hospitality 3.5/5  Food 7.5/9  Value 2/2

- **Italian**
- **Lansing**
- **$**

17923 Torrence Ave.
Lansing
(708) 474-5515
**Troubleshooters:** Mike and Karen Jesso (owners)

**Hours:** Sun-Thurs 11 am-11 pm, Fri-Sat until midnight (closed 3-4:30 pm Sat)
**Cards:** AE, MC, VISA
**Reservations:** None
**Bar:** No alcohol, diners may bring their own
**Parking:** Free lot
**Party Facilities:** Ask for details

Cafe Borgia gives far south suburban diners an opportunity to enjoy some exceptional Italian cooking; it may not be a Renaissance experience, but it still manages to satisfy. Each evening specials for each course of dining are noted on a hand-written poster. Of course, patron may also select from the printed menu.

Among entrees, vitello porcini combines tender scallops of veal with a rich mushroom sauce enhanced by smoked mozzarella cheese, to which red wine is added along with a touch of sage. Beef braciole receives a similar treatment, made even richer by a side of risotto, the creamy Milanese rice. Breast of Chicken is given a versatile touch with a stuffing of cheeses. The chicken also comes with a side of risotto.

Cafe Borgia serves an interesting version of chicken Vesuvio, a creative departure from the conventional approach. In this version, a good helping of fresh rosemary is heaped onto the chicken, which is then baked with garlic and potatoes. Rosemary is not so delicate that it cannot stand up to the garlic seasoning that characterizes a good chicken Vesuvio.

The Cafe Borgia version of pizza with four cheeses brings a thin, crisp crust coated with its melted toppings hot from the baking oven. It's a far cry from the kind of pizza delivered to your door in 30 minutes or less!

The menu features nine pasta dishes. Most are in a rich cream-based sauce, though tomato sauce is also available.

# CAFE PHOENICIA
KR 18.5/20
Decor 4/4   Hospitality 5/5   Food 7.5/9   Value 2/2

- **Middle Eastern**
- **Chicago/Mid-North**
- **$$**

2814 N. Halsted St.
Chicago
(312) 549-7088
**Troubleshooter:** Tony Azo (owner)

**Hours:** Mon-Thurs 4:30-10:30 pm, Fri-Sat until 11:30 pm, Sun 4-9:30 pm
**Cards:** AE, DISCOVER, MC, VISA
**Reservations:** Suggested
**Handicapped:** Accessible
**Bar:** Service bar
**Parking:** On street, Fri-Sun free in lot at 830 W. Diversey Ave.
**Party Facilities:** Entire restaurant available for up to 80

To sample Cafe Phoenicia's approach to Middle Eastern Mediterranean means succumbing to a sense of lavishness, all the while knowing that your indulgences will not leave you uncomfortably overfed.

This is one of the more handsomely decorated Middle Eastern restaurants in Chicago. There is a wonderfully talented twosome of musicians whose repertoire of great American popular standards may seem out of place in this ancient Phoenician ambiance, but whose talents are otherwise most welcome and enjoyable.

The Cafe Phoenicia menu is easy to understand and sample. You might want à la carte appetizers, but the mazza, a bounty of small portions set out for diners to pick and choose from, is a better way to begin. Take warm pieces of pita and dip into the wonderfully aromatic smoked eggplant purée called baba ganoush. Savor the fresh flavors of fava beans in a tomato, garlic, and lemon sauce, or fresh-cooked spinach served cold with light garlic, lemon juice, oil, and shallots. Stuffed grape leaves are marvelously tasty finger foods, the leaves wrapped around a filling of either lightly seasoned ground meat or rice.

Strangely, Cafe Phoenicia's hummus, a chickpea spread that is a staple in Middle Eastern restaurants, is somewhat dry. Similarly, lahmajoun, slices of pita topped with ground lamb, akin to pizza, is without much flavor or texture.

All entrees come with a satisfying lentil soup. Entrees range from steaks to veal chops given a slight regional accent to more traditional choices such as cracked wheat balls deep fried and stuffed with meat and spices called kibbee. Seafood gets good attention in the form of trout stuffed with a spinach mixture or given similar treatment with scallions, cilantro, and dill, then charcoal grilled.

Couscous is found in several varieties on the Cafe Phoenicia menu, including vegetarian, grilled lamb, or chicken. The chicken couscous is wonderfully balanced so that no one flavor or seasoning tends to dominate. That kind of restraint is a characteristic of better cookery.

From among desserts, a milky pudding called mahallabeya is a refreshing dinner conclusion, while atayf, a folded crêpe filled with sweet cream and cheese, garnished with pineapple, nuts, and orange liqueur, is not to be missed.

# CAFÉ PROVENÇAL
KR 18.5/20
Decor 3/4   Hospitality 5/5   Food 9/9   Value 1.5/2

- **French**
- **Evanston**
- **$$$**

1625 Hinman Ave.
Evanston
(708) 475-2233
**Troubleshooters:** Andy Reis
(owner), Dan Tarver (maitre d')

**Hours:** Tues-Thurs 6-9 pm,
Fri-Sat until 10 pm, Sun 5-8 pm
**Cards:** CB, DINERS,
DISCOVER, MC, VISA
**Reservations:** Mandatory
**Handicapped:** Limited
accessibility
**Bar:** Full, award-winning wine
list
**Parking:** Valet
**Dress:** Jackets required
**Party Facilities:** For up to 30
weekdays, larger groups
accommodated Mon-Thurs

After the death of its founder, Leslie Reis, devoted patrons wondered what would become of Café Provençal. Now, in the capable hands of Leslie's husband, Andy, the restaurant remains true to its tradition of impeccably prepared food and great service.

From the moment one makes a reservation, the voice on the line suggests a degree of formality lost in most contemporary dining. The decor at Café Provençal makes it evident that the gracious dining of the past is secure.

Executive Chef Kevin Schrimmer does not ignore the more contemporary trends in French cookery. His recipes reveal a seasoned architecture based upon traditional foundations. But as is virtually demanded in dining today, a particular lightness characterizes most of what comes from the Café Provençal kitchen.

An asparagus flan appetizer is a case in point. This is really an ethereal mousse with an airy character that contradicts the intense flavor. Adding some complexity is a wild mushroom reduction that serves as sauce, aspirated with fresh thyme, chive, and chervil. Or consider grilled shrimp napped in a mango and ginger coulis for a rather bold divergence of flavors. More true to the roots of traditional French dining is a trio of pâtés, each slice resting against the others in a pyramid presentation.

Guests are greeted with an *amuse-gueule* as they are seated. A light but tart sorbet is presented between salad and entree as a palate cleanser.

Though there are relatively few entree selections on the printed and recited menu, that concentration seems to allow for extended care in preparation. Certainly, this is true for delicious salmon, presented in a surprising wrap of cabbage leaves, more apparent in texture than flavor. Beside the fish is a small sandwich made of whipped potatoes pressed between two woven potato chips. Also among seafood offerings is monkfish, poached, rolled upon itself, and plated with couscous, tabbouli, and a Peruvian Indian grain called quinoa, noted for its high protein content.

Among other selections is Chinese-inspired duck breast, sliced thin, cooked so that just a trace of pink is apparent. The duck is served with a light plum sauce, small meat-filled potato wontons, and, like other entrees, a garnish of fresh vegetables.

Though service is impeccable, some patrons may resent the automatic imposition of an 18 percent service charge.

# CAFE PYRÉNÉES
KR 18/20
Decor 3.5/4   Hospitality 5/5   Food 7.5/9   Value 2/2

- **French/Bistro**
- **Vernon Hills**
- **$$**

Illinois Rte. 60 & Milwaukee Ave. (Rivertree Court Shopping Center)
Vernon Hills
(708) 918-8850
**Troubleshooters:** Chef Jean-Marc and Marie Loustaunau (owners)

**Hours:** Lunch Tues-Fri 11:30 am-2:30 pm, dinner Mon-Fri 5:30-10 pm, Sat until 10:30 pm
**Cards:** AE, CB, DINERS, MC, VISA
**Reservations:** Accepted
**Handicapped:** Accessible
**Bar:** Service bar
**Parking:** Free lot
**Party Facilities:** For up to 85

Cafe Pyrénées' name suggests provincial, hearty food, not the refined and sometimes oversauced recipes associated with more urban French restaurants. That promise is by and large delivered. And, while Cafe Pyrénées might not be perched at the lofty pinnacles of French dining, the journeyman work of Chef/Owner Jean-Marc Loustaunau satisfies at reasonable cost.

If I have any criticism, it is only that there seem to be no signature dishes, no special flair in preparation that would distinguish this café from other good bistros.

From among appetizers, mushroom terrine with red bell peppers utilizes the peppers more for color than flavor. Somewhat more exciting is a grilled merguez sausage plated on couscous, in keeping with its North African origins, and served with a lightly peppered demi-glacé.

Recent entrees have included a trio of fish served with wild rice and chablis butter sauce. The portions are generous, the fish selection varied enough to be interesting. From other entrees, choices can be a substantial leg and breast of duck in traditional liver-enriched Rouennaise sauce; as classically uncomplex as rack of lamb with fresh herbs; or as inventive as chicken breast enlivened with a filling of Brie cheese and a Madeira wine sauce. Another half dozen or so choices round out the entrees on a given evening.

Desserts include pastries, tasty tarts, and crème brûlée, as well as a cheese selection. Service is virtually faultless.

# CAFE SPIAGGIA
KR 19.5/20
Decor 3.5/4   Hospitality 5/5   Food 9/9   Value 2/2

- **Italian/Northern**
- **Chicago/Near North**
- **$$**

One Magnificent Mile (second level), 980 N. Michigan Ave., Chicago
(312) 280-2764
**Troubleshooter:** Manager on duty

**Hours:** Mon-Thurs 11:30 am-10 pm, Fri-Sat until 11 pm, Sun noon-9 pm (brunch noon-4 pm)
**Cards:** All majors
**Reservations:** No
**Handicapped:** Accessible
**Bar:** Service bar, extensive wine list
**Parking:** Public garage in building
**Party Facilities:** For 15-500 at Spiaggia Private Dining and Conference Center one floor above Cafe Spiaggia

Located right next to its more posh and expensive sibling, Spiaggia, the Cafe shares the same kitchen and some of the same menu items at substantially less cost. This is a casual, romantic European café set up like a galleria along and overlooking the Michigan Avenue side of One Magnificent Mile. The emphasis is on Northern Italian foods, although other provincial Italian cooking is not ignored. Signature items include elaborate antipasti, gourmet pizzas from a wood-burning oven, and rotating specials that complement the printed menu. Not as pricey or formal as its namesake, this is a captivating alternative when you are not on an expense account.

# CAFFÉ FETTUCCINI
KR 17/20
Decor 3/4   Hospitality 4.5/5   Food 7.5/9   Value 2/2

| | |
|---|---|
| • **Italian** | **Hours:** Mon-Fri 11 am-11 pm, Sat 4 pm-midnight, Sun until 10 pm |
| • **Norridge** | |
| • **$$** | **Cards:** All majors |
| 4701 N. Cumberland Ave. | **Reservations:** For three or more |
| Norridge | **Handicapped:** Accessible |
| (708) 452-6400 | **Bar:** Full |
| **Troubleshooter:** Ed Maggerise (owner) | **Parking:** Free lot |

Even though Caffé Fettuccini is tucked away in a shopping mall, people search it out because it is well worth the effort. What makes Caffé Fettuccini so special is the quality of the cooking, which is consistently a cut above so many neighborhood Italian restaurants'. Zuppa di mare is fabulous. Not only is it abundant with enough food to feed three or four people without difficulty, but the quality of the ingredients is without fault. The large platter is ringed with fresh steamed mussels around a center of shrimp, tiny calamari, clams, scallops, octopus, and crab legs, all resting on a bed of linguine in a mildly seasoned tomato-based sauce. More to the point, no single flavor in the zuppa di mare interferes with anything else, so that the crab tastes like crab, the shrimp like shrimp, and so on.

Among other entrees, veal Milanese is a straightforward, large slice of meat with ample, but not mushy, breading. Veal Marsala is rich with mushrooms in its flavorful wine sauce. Although all dinners include a house salad or soup, a side of pasta, and complimentary fresh fruit for dessert, the à la carte menu holds some interesting choices. Scungilli, or conch, is outstanding, simmered lightly in a tomato sauce, and, as with other seafood we tasted, unobscured by any heavy seasonings. The baked clams are sweet and tender; the fried zucchini can bring an ordinary garden vegetable up to its outer limits. Service is convivial, though the restaurant can get crowded. If you are looking for a place to have a small, romantic tête-à-tête, you might look elsewhere. But if you have a taste for really good Italian cooking, you'll find it at Caffé Fettuccini.

# CAFFÉ LUCCI
KR 16.5/20
Decor 3/4   Hospitality 4/5   Food 7.5/9   Value 2/2

- **Italian**
- **Glenview**
- **$$**

609 Milwaukee Ave.
Glenview
(708) 729-2268
**Troubleshooters:** Joe Greco and Chick Stella (owners)

**Hours:** Mon-Fri 11 am-2 am, Sat 4 pm-3 am, Sun 4 pm-1 am
**Cards:** AE, house accounts
**Reservations:** Suggested
**Bar:** Full
**Parking:** Valet and free lot
**Party Facilities:** For 10-100

Its name suggests a café, but Caffé Lucci is much more than that. It is the kind of restaurant for people who really like to eat, without too much concern for calories. That, of course, gives the chef enormous latitude, and he makes full use of it with rich ingredients and seasonings.

Lucci's Special, as the menu calls it, brings scallops cooked in garlic butter, then topped with sauteed mushrooms. This may not be trendy dining, but if your cardiac surgeon gives the OK, it can be some kind of treat. Fried calamari come in an herbed batter and are delicious nibbles. Or try melanzane marinate, chilled eggplant salad with a liberal dose of garlic. The entree listings lean to a host of fresh pastas, plus fish, veal, poultry, and beef. Linguine del lago is a house special. A mix of large scampi and snails is sauteed in butter and served on fresh linguine that has been seasoned with tomatoes, basil, and garlic. Or try lasagna, touted by another restaurant critic as number one in Chicago. I don't know that I would go that far, but this is a meaty lasagna with a good balance of flavors.

Among seafood, orange roughy is baked and served in a mild lemon butter. Shrimp, broccoli, and fettucine brings its ingredients together in a garlic butter and cheese sauce. Baby salmon, sometimes offered as a daily special, is about as good as salmon can get.

Caffé Lucci makes no attempt to be trendy or on the cutting edge of food fashion. I cannot remember the last time I saw tournedos Rossini on a restaurant's menu, but Caffé Lucci has it. Service is accommodating, if not especially accomplished.

# CALIFORNIA PIZZA KITCHEN
KR 18/20
Decor 3/4   Hospitality 5/5   Food 8/9   Value 2/2

- **American/Pizza**
- **Chicago/Near North**
- **$**

414 N. Orleans St.
Chicago
(312) 222-9030
**Troubleshooter:** Rick Demarco (director)

## Other Locations

Water Tower Place (seventh level), 835 N. Michigan Ave.
Chicago
(312) 787-7300; Mon-Thurs 11 am-10 pm, Fri-Sat until 11 pm, Sun noon-10 pm; No reservations
551 Oak Brook Center
Oak Brook
(708) 571-7800; Mon-Thurs 11:30 am-10 pm, Fri until 11 pm, Sat 11 am-11 pm, Sun noon-10 pm; No reservations

**Hours:** Mon-Thurs 11:30 am-10 pm, Fri-Sat until 11 pm, Sun 1-10 pm
**Cards:** All majors
**Reservations:** Evening only
**Handicapped:** Accessible
**Bar:** Service bar
**Parking:** Street or public lots
**Heart-Healthy Menu:** Selections, vegetarian, cheeseless

Chicago is not only the city of big shoulders. It is also city of deep-dish pizza. Our fame is exported worldwide on the strength of thick crusts, pungent tomato sauce, layers of cheese, sausage, and pepperoni. Who would dare tamper with such a creation?

People from California, that's who! Talk about bringing coal to Newcastle: the owners of California Pizza Kitchen have done just that, except for one major difference – California-style pizza just isn't Chicago-style. It's like comparing Bridgeport to Bel Air. California pizza is wimpy!

Or so it would seem at first glance. For one thing, these are thin-crust pizzas that often ignore such basics as a good garlic-endowed tomato sauce. There's hardly a trace of sausage among toppings, unless it's duck sausage. In fact, one of the pizzas is made with Peking duck, another features grilled lime chicken, while yet another is made with (gasp) shrimp pesto.

Generally speaking, however, the idea works. There are many roads to Rome or, in this case, Malibu. What we have at California Pizza Kitchen is a sense of inventiveness that showed up first on the West Coast at trendy restaurants like Spago, then was picked up as an adjunct to some of the racier Chicago-area restaurant menus.

The menu does include a dozen or so pasta entrees that can be eaten as pizza companions or meals in themselves. Thai chicken linguine is made with Italian pasta instead of the traditional oriental-style noodles. The flavors seem more individually assertive in the bindings of a peanut-and-ginger sauce. The pasta comes topped with bean sprouts. What can I say . . . it's California-style, remember?

As for the pizzas, if you like this sort of thing, you'll be happy. Hawaiian-style combines Canadian bacon, tomato sauce, and chunks of fresh pineapple. Hey, who am I to argue? Some people in Chicago would never think of eating pizza without some dead fish on top called anchovies. To each his own, I always say.

There's no end to this restaurant's seeming inventiveness. Even a simple bacon, lettuce, and tomato sandwich is made in a pizza version, with lettuce and mayonnaise as a topping.

Service is friendly and fairly quick. The place is comfortably casual, with a great view of freshly exercised stock traders, lawyers, and other yuppies marching past from the nearby East Bank Club. Healthy foods, healthy views . . . awesome! Ciao, dude!

# CAPE COD ROOM
KR 19/20
Decor 4/4   Hospitality 5/5   Food 8/9   Value 2/2

- **Seafood/American**
- **Chicago/Near North**
- **$$$**

140 E. Walton Pl. (Drake Hotel)
Chicago
(312) 787-2200
**Troubleshooter:** Patrick
Bredin (maitre d')

**Hours:** Daily noon-11 pm
**Cards:** All majors, house accounts
**Reservations:** Mandatory
**Handicapped:** Accessible
**Bar:** Full
**Parking:** Valet
**Dress:** Jackets required
**Party Facilities:** For up to 10

Since the Cape Cod Room opened in 1933, it has been one of Chicago's best known destination restaurants. Its name is synonymous with the finest in seafood.

The red-checked tablecloths, mounted sailfish, weather vanes, exposed wood beams, and other nautical decor set the stage. Though space is at a premium at the tiny nine-seat oyster bar, the restaurant becomes more expansive as you move into the dining areas.

This is a restaurant that rests heavily on tradition. Much of the menu remains as it has for decades (of course, with high prices). Who could go to the Cape Cod Room and not order the Bookbinder soup? It is one of the few seafood specialty houses still serving lobster Newberg or thermidor. But its bouillabaisse is as contemporary as any, the Cajun swordfish will attract contemporary diners, and the Dover sole is among the finest. In fact, while the Cape Cod Room may look and even feel like part of the past, its seafood is as fresh as the morning.

# CAPRICCIOS
KR 18.5/20
Decor 3.5/4  Hospitality 4.5/5  Food 8.5/9  Value 2/2

| | |
|---|---|
| • **Italian** | **Hours:** Lunch Mon-Fri 11:30 |
| • **Northfield** | am-2:30 pm, dinner Mon-Thurs |
| • **$$** | 5:30-9:30 pm, Fri-Sat until |
| | 11:30 pm, Sun 5-10 pm |
| 300 Happ Rd. | **Cards:** All majors |
| Northfield | **Reservations:** Suggested |
| (708) 501-4556 | **Handicapped:** Accessible |
| **Troubleshooter:** Carlos | **Bar:** Full |
| Montiel (owner) | **Parking:** Free lot |
| | **Party Facilities:** For up to 45 |

Capriccios is in a new and stylish strip mall, but inside, its atmosphere is much more attuned to fine dining than one might expect. This is not to suggest stuffiness, but merely good food in handsome surroundings.

There is a bit of pretense in the service; all the hovering over beef or salmon carpaccio seems more than is really needed. But don't let all the waiters distract you from the attractive presentation. Whatever dish you select, the plating is so handsome, you might want to linger for just a moment to enjoy the beauty of what you are about to consume.

A calamari salad is a study in composition, the ringlets of squid arranged amidst a colorful vegetable julienne in a light vinaigrette. Chilled shrimp and broiled chilled scallops are served with a small round of goat's cheese; the dressing is lightly minted. Other selections range from oysters Rockefeller to simple steamed clams, made somewhat more complex by a dressing of garlic, chives, and wine.

One flaw with most American Italian restaurants, and Capriccios is no exception, is the way pasta is ignored as a separate course. More often than not it is treated as a substitute entree. The pity is that pastas at Capriccios are so good, they should be offered in smaller portions as a second course between appetizer and entree. Consider tantalizing angel-hair pasta, lightly dressed with toasted pine nuts and fresh garlic in virgin olive oil. Another selection might be spaghetti with pieces of lobster in a wine sauce.

As for entrees, veal Florentine comes in a tangy green peppercorn sauce with bits of tomato for color. The veal is stuffed with spinach, its flavor without the bitterness that can sometimes afflict this green leafy vegetable.

Other entrees include sauteed filet mignon medallions in porcini mushroom sauce, a traditional grilled veal chop with an herbed butter sauce, as well as other chops, seafood, and poultry. All entrees come with delicious soup or beautifully composed house salad. Desserts can be selected from a nightly tray.

# CARLOS
KR 20/20
Decor 4/4   Hospitality 5/5   Food 9/9   Value 2/2

| | |
|---|---|
| • **French** | **Hours:** Mon, Wed, Thurs, Sun seatings 5:30-6:30 pm and 8-8:30 pm, Fri-Sat 5:30-6:30 pm and 9-9:30 pm, upstairs seatings 7:30-8:15 |
| • **Highland Park** | |
| • **$$$** | |
| 429 Temple Ave. | |
| Highland Park | **Cards:** All majors, house accounts |
| (708) 432-0770 | |
| **Troubleshooters:** Carlos and Debbie Nieto (owners) | **Reservations:** Mandatory |
| | **Bar:** Service bar |
| | **Parking:** Valet |
| | **Dress:** Jackets required |
| | **Party Facilities:** For 25-60 |
| | **Heart-Healthy Menu:** Special consultations |

With a sophisticated new decor that utilizes dark wood, enamels, and dim sconce lighting, Carlos underscores its position as one of the very best restaurants in the area, if not the entire nation. Chef Don Yamauchi has created menus that are nothing short of dazzling.

I can think of nothing as impressive in recent years as Hawaiian ono, a Pacific Ocean fish that flakes like crabmeat and has a taste near that of lobster. The chef creates a stacking of the fish with lump crabmeat, pairing this with crisp potato slices and an infused oil that brings together the essence of rare saffron and reduced fresh orange juice. The beauty of the plating is surpassed only by the incredibly intense flavorings and wonderful textures.

Similarly imaginative is a presentation of sea bass, cut into broad triangular wedges and charred. Each piece is plated in alternate fashion with scallion pancakes, wonderfully intense smoked mushrooms resting on a bed of wilted spinach, then napped with a fruity red wine reduction.

Carlos has recently been offering some wild-game selections. Antelope from New Zealand is served with Swiss chard and a reduction of black olives for its sauce. One appetizer brought rounds of venison sausage with small cubes of New York foie gras. In another presentation, ravioli came stuffed with a game forcemeat, each piece topped with a slice of grilled squab, all of which was served on slices of whole garlic in its own sauce.

Among other selections that might be available, fresh lobster is roasted and presented in fennel broth with dumplings akin to Italian gnocchi that have been stuffed with mild goat's cheese. Shreds of fennel garnish the shallow bowl in which the lobster is served.

Even something as seemingly ordinary as the house salad that accompanies each entree presents a special surprise. Hidden among the tender green lettuce leaves is a leaf of red lettuce for color accent. It is this kind of planning, this attention to detail, that keeps Carlos in the very front rank of fine dining.

Desserts are no less exciting, with artistic creations of pastry, chocolate, creams, fresh fruit, and the like. The restaurant's wine list fills a library-sized volume. Service is without flaw.

# CARSON'S

KR 18/20

Decor 4/4   Hospitality 4/5   Food 8/9   Value 2/2

- **American/Ribs/Steaks**
- **Chicago/Near North**
- **$$**

612 N. Wells St.
Chicago
(312) 280-9200
**Troubleshooter:** Manager on duty

## Other Locations

5970 N. Ridge Blvd.
Chicago
(312) 271-4000
200 N. Waukegan Rd.
Deerfield
(708) 374-8500
5050 N. Harlem Ave.
Harwood Heights (near O'Hare
   Airport)
(708) 867-4200
400 E. Roosevelt Rd.
Lombard
(708) 627-3200
8617 Niles Center Rd.
Skokie (carry out)
(708) 675-6800

**Hours:** Mon-Thurs 11 am-midnight, Fri until 1 am, Sat noon-1 am, Sun noon-11 pm
**Cards:** AE, CB, DINERS, MC, VISA
**Handicapped:** Accessible
**Bar:** Full
**Parking:** Valet

Say "ribs" in Chicago, and the automatic response from most people is Carson's. Though not everyone would agree that these are the city's best ribs (a subject open to endless debate), those at Carson's are certainly the best known.

The reason these ribs win such accolades is the sauce – a pungent, spicy-sweet brew with a smoky aftertaste that rib lovers savor. The sauce's two-stage preparation is part of the secret. In step one, a popular commercial base is doctored with as many as eight spices and seasonings, plus a liberal helping of brown sugar. This is then slathered on the ribs, which are slow-baked in specially designed electric ovens. The ribs are finished beneath the open flames of a gas broiler. Again, they are washed with sauce, this time without the brown sugar to avoid burning.

In addition to ribs, Carson's serves some of the best steaks around. They range from a 22-ounce New York sirloin to smaller cuts for lesser appetites. Dinners come with salad or slaw, your choice of potatoes, and rolls with butter, making this one of the better bargains.

If you crave barbecue flavor but your taste does not run to ribs, order the whole roast barbecued chicken. Seafood is limited to orange roughy, which is broiled.

# CATCH 35
KR 20/20
Decor 4/4    Hospitality 5/5    Food 9/9    Value 2/2

- **Seafood**
- **Chicago/Loop**
- **$$**

35 W. Wacker Dr.
Chicago
(312) 346-3500
**Troubleshooters:** Paul Tumburger, Edgar Blair

**Hours:** Lunch Mon-Fri 11:30 am-2 pm, dinner Sun-Thurs 5:15-9 pm, Fri-Sat to 11 pm
**Cards:** All majors
**Reservations:** Accepted
**Handicapped:** Accessible
**Bar:** Full, excellent wine list. Live entertainment Tues-Sat 5:30-8:30 pm
**Parking:** Valet after 5
**Party Facilities:** Private rooms for up to 80
**Heart-Healthy Menu:** Orders can be tailored

Some restaurants reveal themselves to be special almost from the moment you walk through the door. Catch 35 is such a restaurant. Its 1940's art deco decor, with large murals of stylized ocean depths, the overhead lighting and high ceilings, the glass refrigerator cases that reveal an abundance of fresh seafood ready for preparation, all set the stage.

Anticipation of fine dining to come continues with the approach of a server, not just someone between jobs but a professional who knows how and when to anticipate and that the best recommendation on the wine list is not necessarily the most expensive bottle.

The panache that marks Catch 35 continues with its menu selections. Something as basic as Bahamian fish chowder has the taste of reality, chunks of fish to dig into within the tomato-based broth, with its myriad seasonings, all focused on good taste and balance. Oysters can be had from the raw bar or baked and will range in variety depending upon freshness and seasonal availability.

The Catch 35 version of crab cakes is baked, not fried, but it loses nothing from the transition to more healthful preparation. There is a light spice to the crab, but not enough to detract from the basic, underlying nautical flavor. Equally delicious is Szechwan scallops, one of several selections with a decidedly oriental accent. In this case, the broiled scallops are perfectly cooked, still tender in a dark, syrupy sauce whose natural sweetness is contrasted with the cheeky bite of peppers.

Other appetizers from the fairly short selection include chicken satay Thai style, with peanut sauce and cucumber relish, deep-fried calamari with tofu, and beer-battered shrimp.

Entrees range from several stir-fried choices often involving shrimp or, in the case of a dinner-sized Niçoise salad, pieces of yellow fin tuna. In another recipe, crab claws are combined with scallops and shrimp in tomato sauce, while shrimp, scallops, and rice noodles comprise yet another dish.

House specialties at Catch 35 include whole fish from the grill. Norwegian salmon is given a complex sweet/hot glaze while grouper can be prepared simply with garlic, olive oil, and fresh basil. Pompano might be coated in crumbled New Zealand water crackers and presented with a crabmeat filling and mustard mayonnaise.

All dinners include a side of fresh vegetables and rice or new potatoes as well as warm sourdough bread. Desserts are truly lavish, ranging from traditional American-style apple or Key lime pie to elaborate trifle cake soaked with Chambord.

# CELEBRITY CAFE
KR 17.5/20
Decor 4/4   Hospitality 3.5/5   Food 8/9   Value 2/2

- **American**
- **Chicago/Near North**
- **$$**

320 N. Dearborn St.
Chicago
(312) 836-5499
**Troubleshooter:** Mohammed
Gazi (manager)

**Hours:** Brunch Sun 9:30 am-2:30 pm, lunch Mon-Sat 11:30 am-2 pm, dinner Sun-Thurs 6:30-10:30 pm, Fri-Sat until 11 pm
**Cards:** All majors, house accounts
**Reservations:** Suggested
**Handicapped:** Accessible
**Bar:** Full
**Parking:** Discounted valet parking
**Party Facilities:** Entire restaurant for up to 100

I confess to some surprise at the discovery of how very good Celebrity Cafe is at Hotel Nikko. The menu emphasizes a contemporary American flair, and even with its à la carte pricing, dining costs are reasonable. Factor in the wine list, and there are some downright bargains.

One good way to begin is with pizza, easily enough to share as an opening course for a table of four. Inspired by Wolfgang Puck, these California-style pizzas have become almost too standard on restaurant menus. At Celebrity Cafe, only one kind is offered – a crust topped with spinach leaves and goat's cheese. The combinations work remarkably well, bound by a mild tomato sauce and a sprinkle of freshly herbaceous seasonings.

From that starting point an appetizer of mussels and clams is a good followup. They are served with cooked white beans, more for texture than taste, all of which is bathed in a garlic, oregano, and fresh basil broth that may have been simmered with a bit of white wine. A companion appetizer, maybe even a bit tastier, is grilled shrimp served with cut-up avocado and a corn salsa. It's an intriguing combination and, like virtually everything else at Celebrity Cafe, is served with an eye for handsome, artistic plating.

Also noteworthy are potato-and-turnip cakes with wild mushrooms. The sparse menu outline hardly does justice to the delicious blend of flavors, so light that they practically are like a kiss, yet substantial enough that one knows these are root vegetables and forest mushrooms in a natural combination.

From several entrees, sauteed venison is served with slices of venison sausage, tiny turnips, and spaghetti squash as side vegetables. Unfortunately, as with other meat selections tasted during our visit, things tended more toward the well done than to the medium rare (as we had requested). That was the case with a rack of lamb and veal rib eye, both of which were otherwise flavorful enough. The lamb came with deliciously roasted garlic cloves, while the veal rib-eye steak was stuffed with a mix of spinach, tomato, and grated Parmesan cheese.

A selection of seafood brings some intriguing combinations in line with what is definitely an adventurous approach to cooking. Most interesting might be sea bass wrapped in a thin tomato covering along with mushrooms and tomatoes in lemon butter sauce. Less complex is grilled salmon with a honey mustard glaze or swordfish braised with vegetables and potatoes.

Desserts from the cart include the kind of chocolate confections that refuse to take "no" for an answer.

# CENTRO
KR 18.5/20
Decor 4/4   Hospitality 5/5   Food 7.5/9   Value 2/2

- **Italian**
- **Chicago/Near North**
- **$$**

710 N. Wells St.
Chicago
(312) 988-7775
**Troubleshooters:** Alex Dana
(owner), Giovanni (manager)

**Hours:** Lunch Mon-Fri 11
am-3 pm, dinner Mon-Thurs 5-
10:30 pm, Fri-Sat to 11:30 pm
**Cards:** All majors, house
accounts
**Reservations:** Only 5-6:30
pm, waits can be substantial
**Handicapped:** Accessible
**Bar:** Full
**Parking:** Valet
**Party Facilities:** None
**Heart-Healthy Menu:**
Specials pointed out by waiters
when asked

Crowded, noisy, and congenial are words that most quickly come to mind about Centro. The cooking style leans firmly toward Southern Italian, with an emphasis on pasta and seafood. Portions are lavish and handsomely served. The Umbrian bread salad comes out looking more like a sandwich containing fresh, bright-red tomatoes, red onion, basil, olives, slices of cheese and salami, plus olive oil, garlic, and oregano. It easily could be a light supper for one or two.

Something heartier would be the sausage and peppers in similar gigantic portion. In fact, your waiter may very well issue a caution about portion size, adding that leftovers could easily be packed to take home. Start with a focaccia, the thick Sicilian round bread, topped like a pizza with tomato sauce and cheese, and accompany it with delicious stuffed eggplant. The sliced eggplant is dipped in a lavish egg batter, deep fried to a golden color, then stuffed with a filling of ricotta cheese; the ever-present red sauce adds bite and color.

Speaking of sauces, the house special is rectangular sheets of flat papparadelle noodles in a chunky red sauce that is just a little too harsh. There's nothing like good cavatelli, the finger-shaped noodle dumplings that have a special homemade quality. At Centro, cavatelli with broccoli is served in oil and garlic or baked with a blanket of mozzarella over lighter ricotta and red sauce. It is a wonderful flavor and texture combination. Several other standards include linguine in various sauces with shrimp, clams, mussels, or calamari. For something with bite, try fusilli a la arrabiata, corkscrew noodles in a peppery sauce that seems to leave the flavor of pimiento on the tongue, in addition to the chili peppers that give the heat.

One could do fine without ordering an entree, but several are listed, including chicken or veal Vesuvio, the indigenous Chicago contribution to the Italian-American larder. Veal Vesuvio consists of thin scallops sauteed in olive oil and garlic. Though not as robust as chicken Vesuvio, it is delicious in its own way.

For dessert, Centro brings out the usual suspects: tortoni, cannoli, several styles of cheesecake, zuppa inglese, and a creamy tiramisu, which needs a bit more unsweetened cocoa and coffee presence.

# CHARLIE TROTTER'S
KR 20/20
Decor 4/4   Hospitality 5/5   Food 9/9   Value 2/2

- **French/Nouvelle**
- **Chicago/Mid-North**
- **$$$**

816 W. Armitage Ave.
Chicago
(312) 248-6228
**Troubleshooters:** Charlie Trotter (chef/owner), Marilyn Schneider (dining room manager)

**Hours:** Tues-Thurs 5:30-9:30 pm, Fri-Sat to 10:30 pm
**Cards:** AE, CB, DINERS, JCB, MC, VISA
**Reservations:** Mandatory
**Bar:** Full, superb wine list with guidance from sommelier Larry Stone
**Parking:** Valet
**Dress:** Jackets and ties
**Party Facilities:** Luncheons for 20 or more, private space for dinner available, including personalized printing of menus (and menus without prices) on request

A description of Charlie Trotter's can hardly do justice to what is easily one of the finest restaurants in the United States. One does not merely have dinner; one has an experience to be savored and reflected upon.

Trotter is a young and personable chef who has knocked the culinary world on its collective ear since he opened in a renovated townhouse about five years ago. His style could be called nouvelle, but that word hardly describes his talents. He is meticulous, a stickler for perfection, with the eye of an artist.

Diners may choose from a five-course vegetable dégustation for $55 or a seven-course dinner, with meat and fish, for $75. The truly ambitious will be tempted by the twelve-course dinner for $100, whose various courses are selected by Trotter.

The menu at Charlie Trotter's changes often. The vegetable dégustation might begin with a terrine in which paper-thin sliced zucchini wraps a filling of eggplant moistened with saffron oil and the juice of a red bell pepper; the platter could be garnished with crisp wafers of celery root. Next could come a warm broth of sweet corn and beans in which is centered a packet made of artichoke, filled with a coarse mash of bell peppers. There is no way to describe the complexity of flavors that such ingredients can create.

Another course could bring a trio of ravioli, one filled with parsnip, another with carmelized onion, and the third with shreds of cabbage. Trotter appreciates the delicate essence of Japanese cuisine and is influenced by its ephemeral combination of taste and textures. Nothing is overstated; all is in proportion and balance.

In the larger seven-course dinner, a medallion of veal with lightly seasoned veal sausage could be the cornerstone. There is an architecture to Trotter's design; read from the menu, his ideas may suggest the Gothic, but in the execution they are more akin to the clean lines of contemporary art. For example, he will soften the impact of his game meat with a delicate reduction flavored with thyme and shallot.

For dessert, Trotter may create a quenelle of quinoa with pistachios and dried currants. Even better is a warm apple soup with a small apple dumpling in the middle; a small scoop or two of apple sorbet will add its essence. Desserts climax with chocolate. Bittersweet chocolate cake comes with a warm center from which oozes a dark, flavored sauce. To the side are scoops of honey and molasses ice creams.

# CHEZ PAUL
KR 17.5/20
Decor 4/4  Hospitality 4.5/5  Food 7.5/9  Value 1.5/2

- **French**
- **Chicago/Near North**
- **$$$**

660 N. Rush St.
Chicago
(312) 944-6680
**Troubleshooters:** Bill Contos
(owner), Chris Iassello
(maitre d')

**Hours:** Lunch Mon-Fri 11:30
am-3 pm, dinner every day
5:30-10:30 pm, closed holidays
**Cards:** All majors
**Reservations:** Suggested
**Bar:** Full, with French vintages
back to 1929
**Parking:** Valet
**Party Facilities:** For up to 70

For decades, Chez Paul has represented haute cuisine dining in Chicago. Though no longer on the cutting edge of culinary trends, the restaurant has nonetheless stepped back from its reliance on traditional classic cookery with its cream sauces, herbed butter, and roux.

That is not to suggest that such ingredients are abandoned entirely; if anything, the menu has been supplemented with a contemporary influence. Where shrimp from an older menu might have been prepared, for example, in a butter sauce, now they are hickory smoked instead of sauteed. A rémoulade accompaniment is still cream enriched, but the sauce can be forgone if one is watching one's waistline or cholesterol.

Natural juices and reduced essences are seen among main-course selections, though a house classic, tournedos of beef Chez Paul, still comes with the required béarnaise sauce, pale yellow in color, creamy rich in texture and flavor. Roast rack of lamb, another house favorite, is always available. Fresh seafood varies from day to day.

The restaurant is housed in an old mansion, offering the sort of elegance not found in today's more trendy bistros, with their bare brick walls and loft ceilings. If a certain formality still reigns, I think it is all for the better.

# CHICAGO BRAUHAUS
KR 17.5/20
Decor 3.5/4   Hospitality 5/5   Food 7/9   Value 2/2

- **German**
- **Chicago/Mid-North**
- **$$**

4732 N. Lincoln Ave.
Chicago
(312) 784-4444
**Troubleshooters:** Harry and
Guenther Kempf (owners)

**Hours:** Sun-Fri 11-2 am, Sat
until 3 am
**Cards:** AE, DINERS, MC,
VISA
**Reservations:** Suggested
**Bar:** Full, specializing in
German beers and wines
**Parking:** Street or nearby lots
**Party Facilities:** For 75-250
Tuesdays only

Chicago Brauhaus is rather large and open, as one might expect of a brauhaus. The beer flows amply from spigots behind the long bar. A band plays most nights, offering tunes that can range from the "Beer Barrel Polka" or "Lili Marlene" to soft rock. On warm summer nights, it is not unusual for one of the musicians to pick up his trumpet and lead a couple of hundred people or more out the front door of the restaurant in a sort of Teutonic conga line up and down the Lincoln Mall, like some modern Pied Piper.

As for the food, one finds such typical German cooking as kassler rippchen, assorted sausages, and sandwiches. Full dinners include soup or salad, potatoes, vegetable or applesauce depending upon entree, and one of the better bread basket selections you will find anywhere. In fact, the temptation is to keep nibbling away at the delicious pumpernickel or other breads that come your way. Something similar can be said for the liver dumpling soup that is offered with dinners. The broth is clear, the small dumplings lightly seasoned.

Among dinner choices, sauerbraten is curiously more like a Yankee pot roast – it lacks the spicy bite one usually gets from this marinade of crushed gingersnaps, bacon, and vinegar. Still, the meat is tender and tasty, if not all that flavorful. Wiener schnitzel is a better choice, to my way of thinking. The crust is golden and succulent, the veal moist and tender. Roast duckling gets traditional treatment with a side of spaetzle that tastes homemade. As with other entrees, you could choose a plump potato dumpling instead. From specials in addition to what is on the menu, roast goose is crisped to a golden color and the skin pulls away easily from the meat. The bird comes with a brown gravy, but it tastes so good as is that no embellishment is needed.

From a selection of desserts, apple strudel is a fine finish to the evening's offerings.

# CHICAGO CHOP HOUSE
KR 16.5/20
Decor 3.5/4  Hospitality 4.5/5  Food 6.5/9  Value 2/2

- **American**
- **Chicago/Near North**
- **$$$**

60 W. Ontario St.
Chicago
(312) 787-7100
**Troubleshooter:** Henry Norton (owner)

**Hours:** Mon-Fri 11:30-12:30 am, Sat-Sun 5 pm-1 am
**Cards:** All majors, house accounts
**Reservations:** Suggested
**Bar:** Handsome long bar and piano bar evoke nineteenth-century Chicago
**Parking:** Valet
**Party Facilities:** For up to 85, lunch only

**C**hicago Chop House is splashed with antique photographs and etchings of the city's history. The first floor is occupied by one of the best-looking bars in the city, a serpentine affair that wraps its way around, just inviting conversation. The main dining room is on the second floor, up a flight of stairs lined with more photographs.

Chicago Chop House's menu is straightforward. Beef is the big item here. I use the word "big" deliberately, since the restaurant actually serves a 64-ounce Porterhouse steak (or a 48-ounce version for a few dollars less).

The still large but by comparison considerably more modest T-bone or smaller cuts of filet mignon and the tried and true New York strip are all featured, as is traditional roast prime rib and assorted chops.

Seafood includes swordfish, Dover sole and french-fried jumbo shrimp in a beer batter, as well as a few other choices. The restaurant is a big favorite with conventioneers and other tourists. Diners are allowed plenty of time to linger between courses and even after dinner, which is a positive note about hospitality.

# THE CHICAGO DINER

KR 15/20

Decor 3/4   Hospitality 4/5   Food 6.5/9   Value 1.5/2

- **Vegetarian**
- **Chicago/Mid-North**
- **$**

3411 N. Halsted St.
Chicago
(312) 935-6696
**Troubleshooters:** Mickey
Hornich and Jo Kaucher
(owners)

**Hours:** Mon-Fri 11 am-9:30
pm, Sat-Sun 10 am-10 pm
**Cards:** AE, DISCOVER, MC,
VISA
**Reservations:** For 8 or more
**Bar:** Organic wines and
naturally produced beers
**Parking:** Valet in evening
**Heart-Healthy Menu:**
Selections

Though the Chicago Diner is less than 10 years old, it can trace its roots to the hippie days of the 1960s, so the period decor seems more real than affected.

The menu is a fairly standard one for vegetarian restaurants, and specials change regularly. You can always count on some freshly squeezed fruit juices; cantaloupe juice was recently being offered. Among appetizers, an order of potato skins and a platter of raw vegetables come with a delicious garlic cream dip. The potatoes, really more than just skins, have plenty of filling and are topped with a layer of melted cheese. Tucked inside each potato half you'll find a bit of chopped tomato and onion as a nice little surprise. The potato skins are served with guacamole, which needs a bit more seasoning zip.

Soups are made each day, and they vary. So too do the entree choices. Usually there is an omelette of some variety, and always a rice dish. Vegetable fried rice is a large portion of chewy brown rice with a mix of vegetables in a light soy sauce, with a topping of tempeh strips. Tempeh is a texturized soy protein substance that can be fried easily or otherwise cooked to add a bit of meat-like texture to a recipe. Our waitress suggested a topping of honey and tamari on the rice for added flavor. Certainly, some saucing is needed, because otherwise the fried rice is too dry.

One recent choice for dinner was couscous and barley loaf. Perhaps it was the celery sauce, but this dish tasted like the stuffing served with turkey on Thanksgiving. The couscous came with sliced steamed carrots on a bed of kale, all rather prosaic.

Things get a bit tastier with dessert. Pear and lemon zest pie is delicious.

# CITY TAVERN

KR 16.5/20

Decor 3.5/4  Hospitality 4/5  Food 7.5/9  Value 1.5/2

- **American/Eclectic**
- **Chicago/Loop**
- **$$**

33 W. Monroe St.
Chicago
(312) 280-2740
**Troubleshooter:** Manager on duty

**Hours:** Mon-Fri 7 am-9 pm, Sat 11 am-8 pm
**Cards:** All majors
**Reservations:** Suggested
**Handicapped:** Accessible
**Bar:** Full
**Parking:** Valet, show nights only
**Party Facilities:** Available
**Heart-Healthy Menu:** Selections

No one in Chicago talks seriously anymore about the Loop's being dead at night, not as long as there are places like City Tavern. Located right across the street from the Shubert Theatre, it is perfect for that pre- or after-theatre supper. Of course, since the restaurant is open from breakfast on, it is a rather handy refectory for Loop workers and shoppers too.

City Tavern is just what its name implies. Favorites include fresh salmon from the wood-burning oven, several kinds of chicken, and a variety of pizzas, among other choices including seafood, salads, chops, and daily specials. The caesar salad is virtually a light meal, especially when topped with grilled shrimp.

# CLUB LUCKY
KR 18/20
Decor 3/4   Hospitality 5/5   Food 8.5/9   Value 1.5/2

- **Italian**
- **Chicago/Northwest**
- **$$**

1824 W. Wabansia Ave.
Chicago
(312) 227-2300
**Troubleshooters:** Robert L.
Paladino, Jim Higgins (owners)

**Hours:** Mon-Thurs 5-11 pm,
Fri-Sat until midnight, Sun 4-10
pm
**Cards:** AE, MC, VISA
**Reservations:** Not taken
**Bar:** Full
**Parking:** Valet and street
**Party Facilities:** For up to 35

If it's "retro" dining you want, then it's "retro" you get at Club Lucky. The look is right out of the '50s and '60s, including harlequin-design floor tiles, Formica table tops, wood slat back chairs, red vinyl booths, open ductwork, and deco-style lighting. The only thing missing is a lava lamp on each table.

Yes, Club Lucky is another Italian restaurant, but like its decor, the style is more throwback than cutting edge. You don't worry about eating pasta as a separate course here; there's no pecking order to the dining, just good food the way Italian restaurants used to be.

Well, maybe not quite, since there is an open kitchen and separate preparation area where salads and antipasti are arrayed to tempt diners. The menu is basically à la carte, but some courses are large enough to share a single order. For example, an antipasto platter includes smoked and rolled eggplant, Sicilian olives, a small slice or two of prosciutto, a little cheese, asparagus spears, and whatever else might be at hand, all in a light dressing that serves to underscore, not obscure. Other appetizers range from a cold fish salad to fried or grilled calamari and the standard Italian restaurant specialty, baked or fresh clams.

Sometimes, soup is a preferred starter. The Club Lucky version of pasta fagioli is not as two-fisted or hearty as some, but its basic stock provides the underpinnings for a good flavor.

The pastas number only a few. Among them, eight finger cavatelli (not the name of a wrestling opponent of Hulk Hogan) is a delicious extruded and chewy dough sauced in a thick marinara, to which a lavish amount of grated cheese is added. While cavatelli represents one extreme, the other is found in the light and delicate cappellini, known as angel-hair pasta. The thin noodles are delicately sauced with a chop of eggplant, sweet red peppers, olives, and capers in a slightly sweet tomato-based sauce.

Among entree selections, beef tenderloin is literally tender enough to be sliced with a fork. It is served with roasted red peppers and tomatoes, along with garlic and chives. Beef eaters will love this one. Other house specialties include a delicious version of chicken Vesuvio, eggplant parmigiana, veal Francese, which is lightly breaded and sautéed in butter, lemon, and white wine, plus a handful of other Italian standbys. Fresh fish is seen among the rotating daily specials and is usually served with a side of fresh vegetables.

# THE COTTAGE
KR 18.5/20
Decor 3.5/4    Hospitality 5/5    Food 8/9    Value 2/2

- **French**
- **Calumet City**
- **$$**

525 Torrence Ave.
Calumet City
(708) 891-3900
**Troubleshooters:** Gerald Buster (owner), Louis Paloma (maitre d')

**Hours:** Tues-Fri 11:30-2, dinner Tues-Sat 5-10 pm, Sun 4-8 pm
**Cards:** MC, VISA
**Reservations:** Suggested
**Handicapped:** Accessible
**Bar:** Service bar, 100 wines
**Parking:** Free lot
**Party Facilities:** Full restaurant available Sundays and Mondays, up to 20 semi-private other evenings

Featured selections have always included cottage schnitzel, duckling with orange sauce and chutney dressing, and steak Madagascar, but now the menu has greater depth and diversity. Selections remain within a framework of from eight to ten entrees nightly, augmented by fine appetizer and salad specials. Among dinner entrees, a splendid grilled sturgeon with napa cabbage and crumbled bacon comes with a capers-and-citrus-flavored sauce. Lamb sausages are grilled over coals, sauced with the juices of crushed sweet peppers, and served with minted lentils. Steamed sea scallops might come with a tarragon beurre blanc. Desserts usually include a fine white and dark chocolate mousse and rich chocolate cake with raspberry sauce.

# COURTYARDS OF PLAKA

KR 18/20

Decor 4/4   Hospitality 5/5   Food 7/9   Value 2/2

- **Greek**
- **Chicago/Near West**
- **$$**

340 S. Halsted St.
Chicago
(312) 263-0767
**Troubleshooters:** Chris
Liakouras (owner)

**Hours:** Sun-Thurs 11 am-midnight, Fri-Sat until 1 am
**Cards:** All majors, house accounts
**Reservations:** For 6 or more
**Handicapped:** Accessible
**Bar:** Full
**Parking:** Free valet parking

Unlike many other Greek restaurants in Chicago, Courtyards of Plaka is a genuinely sophisticated approach to Hellenic cuisine. True, you will still find such basics as moussaka and pastitsio, even gyros and saganaki. But, when the waiter ignites the Metaxa brandy to flame the saganaki, calling out "Oppa!" is strictly déclassé.

Diners can choose a combination dinner, but the real pleasure comes from ordering from the à la carte menu. This is where Courtyards of Plaka displays one of its primary differences from most of the other Greek restaurants along the Halsted Street strip.

To make your meal a feast, choose a variety of individual appetizers, creating your own personal mezedes. Your waiter will guide you through the choices. Be sure to order fried sweetbreads, which are silky smooth within, crusted on the outside. All you need do is splash on some fresh lemon juice to make these standouts even better. The Courtyards of Plaka version of taramosalata is as tasty as it comes, while spinach pie, called spanakotiropita, is a buttery phyllo crust wrapped around a filling of creamy cheese and fresh spinach.

Lamb comes in several varieties, as you might expect in a Greek restaurant. Kreatopita is a delicious casserole of lamb and beef baked together inside a domed pastry crust with a light cream sauce. Other lamb choices include double-cut chops with rice pilaf or a side of pan-fried Grecian-style potatoes, as well as a vegetable. Arni atomiko consists of sliced roast leg of lamb baked with spaghetti and tomato sauce, all simmered together in a serving crock.

Shish kebab may owe its origins more to Persia than Greece, but that does not diminish its popularity. Skewered chunks of lamb, chicken, or even whole shrimp or swordfish are flamed at tableside. Other seafood choices include stylish red snapper and sea bass, naturally flavored with oregano and lemon juice in Greek fashion.

# CRICKET'S

KR 18.5/20
Decor 4/4   Hospitality 5/5   Food 8/9   Value 1.5/2

- **American**
- **Chicago/Near North**
- **$$$**

100 E. Chestnut St.
Chicago
(312) 751-1900
**Troubleshooter:** Christopher Kievit (asst. manager)

**Hours:** Lunch Mon-Sat 11:30 am-2:30 pm, Sun brunch 11 am-2 pm, dinner daily 6-10:30 pm
**Cards:** All majors
**Reservations:** Mandatory
**Handicapped:** Accessible
**Bar:** Full, entertainment each evening
**Parking:** Valet
**Party Facilities:** For 15-300

This Chicago version of New York's 21 Club is a masculine, almost club-like, sort of restaurant. The place reminds me of taverns that used to be called "tack rooms." At Cricket's, instead of horse-racing memorabilia, the decor features artifacts of Chicago commerce, ranging from baseball, football, and newspaper paraphernalia to earth-moving toys suspended from the ceiling.

Food and service are exceptional. Waiters and captains seem to anticipate every need, from replenishing hot rolls to topping off a goblet of wine. The à la carte menu, which changes seasonally, holds some wonderful selections. Saucing is virtually perfect, with just the correct nap for meat and fish. Among early courses, crème Senegalese has become a signature soup for the restaurant.

Steak tartare is prepared and served as a classic. Among newer conceptions has been tuna seared on the grill and served with daikon radishes and Japanese-influenced wasabi mustard butter. Sea scallops come handsomely presented in a potato basket, while linguine has been paired with venison sausage in a tomato sauce kissed with sage and rosemary.

Entrees are highlighted by some American classics. Not the least of these is the formidable rack of lamb, seasoned with cracked coriander and sauced with a glaze of mustard seed and white peppercorns, all of which is accompanied by cheddared potatoes. Other selections include the restaurant's own 21-day dry-aged sirloin with American mashed potatoes and creamed spinach; salmon with pepper, ginger, and lobster oil; and old-fashioned steak Diane with shallots and mushrooms in bordelaise sauce, prepared tableside.

From seafood choices, black sea bass is steamed and served on a bed of crinkly leafed Savoy cabbage, with a head of herb-roasted garlic and a nap of tomato coriander sauce. Dover sole meunière goes back to the classical roots of French cookery, while chicken hash is a signature dish.

Desserts can be as involved as a triple chocolate terrine or pirouette cookies stuffed with Chambord-flavored white chocolate mousse, served with fresh fruits and strawberry sauce. More direct is Cricket's house-baked cheesecake and an old-fashioned hot fudge sundae.

# DAO THAI
KR 17/20
Decor 3.5/4   Hospitality 4/5   Food 7.5/9   Value 2/2

- **Thai**
- **Chicago/Near North**
- **$**

105 E. Ontario St.
Chicago
(312) 664-9600
**Troubleshooter:** D. Pannipa
(owner)

**Hours:** Sun-Thurs 11 am-10 pm, Fri-Sat until 11 pm
**Cards:** All majors
**Reservations:** Accepted
**Handicapped:** Accessible
**Bar:** Full
**Parking:** Street and nearby lots
**Party Facilities:** Carry-out and catering for up to 100

Thai restaurants in Chicago have become almost as ubiquitous as hot dog stands. They can vary from small storefront family operations to something more sophisticated and elaborate. Falling somewhere in the upper middle of that range is Dao Thai. The dining area is bright and modern, highlighted by polished blond woods.

Portions are large, but the selections are not too expensive, so you can order several to get a good tasting. Naturally, as with all Asian cuisines, the best way to go is with a group of six or eight people to share each dish. Thai spring rolls are a good way to start, with their light filling of bean sprouts, pieces of cucumber, tofu, and cooked eggs – all wrapped in a thin pancake and best when topped with a sweet plum sauce. You need not wait until dessert for a sweet-tasting appetizer: crispy rice noodles called mee krob, which is almost like candy on a stick, bound with a syrupy sauce that is both sweet and slightly sharp. Other appetizer selections include egg rolls with a deep-fried noodle crust and delicious fish cakes so mild you would never guess that's what they are. The Thai taste for hot sauces is evident with a spicy peanut and cucumber sauce that serves as a dip for these fritter-like finger foods.

Soup is a "must" course in Thai dining. Try tom kha kai, a chicken broth finished with sweetened coconut milk, spiced with crushed chili peppers, cilantro, and lime. Salad is a good course to follow the soup – a refreshing palate cleanser and cooler.

The menu devotes a full page to entrees and house recommendations. Stir-fried beef with fresh basil leaves is served in a hot sauce that leaves a tingle, but is not so fiery as to dominate. Ginger chicken is another good selection from the list of more than three dozen choices. Here again, a careful hand seems to be at work, restrained from overseasoning. The menu is filled out with several styles of curry, plus other preparations of meats and fresh fish.

Pad Thai, a benchmark by which to evaluate Thai restaurants, is off the mark. There is nothing to bind together the various ingredients of noodles, fried tofu, ground peanuts, and more. As for dessert, Thai custard, with its coconut underpinnings, is good, but not as memorable as elsewhere in town. Service is somewhat rushed, even on slow nights, though if you ask before you order, I suspect they can slow down the parade of foods.

# D.B. KAPLAN'S
KR 18/20
Decor 4/4   Hospitality 4/5   Food 8/9   Value 2/2

- **American/Delicatessen**
- **Chicago/Near North**
- **$$**

845 N. Michigan Ave. (Water Tower Place)
Chicago
(312) 280-2700
**Troubleshooter:** Manager on duty

**Hours:** Mon-Thurs 10 am-9:30 pm, Fri-Sat until 11 pm, Sun 11 am-9 pm
**Cards:** All majors
**Reservations:** Not taken
**Handicapped:** Accessible
**Bar:** Service bar
**Parking:** In building
**Party Facilities:** Available

This is the King Kong of delicatessens. The menu goes on and on, with scores of sandwiches, salads, drinks, and desserts. It is also riddled with outrageous puns. Sandwiches have names like "Bruce Springstongue," "Jack Pumpernickleson," "Just Bacon a Livin'." Well, you get the idea.

Despite the cutesy names, the sandwiches are all you could ever want between a couple of slices of bread, bagel, or roll.

The restaurant has been given a facelift recently, but still has its mainstay celebrity caricatures, which create a bright, kicky look. This is a fine place to go to rest your tootsies after a day of shopping along the Magnificent Mile. Kids especially will get a bang out of D.B. Kaplan's Delicatessen, which, by the way, has no relation to your author.

# DIANNA'S OPPA!
KR 17.5/20
Decor 3/4   Hospitality 5/5   Food 7.5/9   Value 2/2

- **Greek**
- **Chicago/Near West**
- **$$**

212 S. Halsted St.
Chicago
(312) 332-1225
**Troubleshooter:** Petros
Kogiones (owner)

**Hours:** Daily 11-1 am
**Cards:** All majors
**Handicapped:** Accessible
**Bar:** Full, specializing in Greek wines and beers
**Parking:** Free lot

The newer Halsted Street Greek restaurants may be more fashionable and look somewhat more elegant, but Dianna's Oppa! is like an older pair of shoes you would never want to discard. Certainly owner Petros Kogiones has much to do with the restaurant's vitality. Hardly a night goes by that he is not there greeting customers, kissing women's hands, shouting to waiters to move along more quickly. Sometime during the evening, he will take center stage and demand the attention of all within hearing. Then, Petros will proceed to welcome his guests as only he knows how, highlighting special gatherings and birthdays, graduations, and wedding anniversaries. As the music grows more rhythmic and anticipation builds, he will balance a full glass of wine on his head and begin to dance, as only Greeks can.

All of this is window dressing, of course, to the food and dining. With several people at your table, you could order family style, starting with a large Greek salad of tomatoes, feta cheese, and lettuce, then the flaming cheese called saganaki, which draws a shout of "Oppa!" as its bath of Greek brandy is flamed by your waiter.

As with most of the other Greek restaurants crowded into this three- or four-block strip called Greek Town, the best deal on the menu is a combination platter, which features most of the traditional favorites. When it gets down to some serious cookery, the lamb chops are always among the best offerings, perfectly char-grilled and tasty to the bone. Greek restaurants are known for their fish, particularly broiled red snapper and sea bass; Dianna's Oppa! is no exception.

Dianna's Oppa! has its regulars, but for first-time visitors, and especially out-of-town tourists, this is a destination that must be on your itinerary if you are to understand Greek Chicago at its most fun!

# DIETERLE'S
KR 17.5/20
Decor 3/4   Hospitality 4.5/5   Food 8/9   Value 2/2

- **German**
- **Elgin**
- **$$**

550 S. McLean Blvd.
Elgin
(708) 697-7311
**Troubleshooters:** Ulrich and
Edna Dieterle (owners)

**Hours:** Mon-Thurs 11:30
am-10 pm, Fri-Sat until 11 pm,
Sun noon-8 pm
**Cards:** AE, CB, DINERS, MC,
VISA
**Reservations:** Suggested
**Bar:** Full, with good selection of
German wines and beers
**Parking:** Free lot
**Dress:** No shorts or tank tops
**Party Facilities:** For 50-200

**B**lack Forest half timbers set the stage for some very good
German cooking, as well as some dishes that are not especially
Germanic.

You could start with an appetizer as prosaic as shrimp cocktail or
as traditionally German as pickled tongue. But the house relish tray
that comes with all dinners includes some of the tastiest liver pâté
you are ever likely to enjoy, making an à la carte choice superfluous.
Entrees include several American-style beef and seafood choices, but
the German portion of Dieterle's menu is the primary attraction.

One of the best selections is duck à la Deutsch. Half a duckling is
roasted to a golden crispness and served with a lavish portion of
Bavarian red cabbage and a near-tennis-ball-sized bread dumpling.
The duck is marvelously flavored, not too fatty. The red cabbage is
cooked gently with apples, which leaves a nice aftertaste mixed in
with just a hint of aromatics such as cinnamon and cloves.

Naturally, Dieterle's features schnitzels and other staples of the
German larder such as kassler rippchen, Thuringer sausage, brat-
wurst platters, and liver with German-fried potatoes. The liver is ten-
der and sweet and in ample portion. Desserts include apple strudel,
which is a commercial product, not made in the restaurant's own
kitchen.

# THE DINING ROOM AT THE RITZ-CARLTON

KR 17.5/20

Decor 4/4   Hospitality 4.5/5   Food 7/9   Value 2/2

- **French**
- **Chicago/Near North**
- **$$$**

160 E. Pearson
Chicago
(312) 227-5866
**Troubleshooter:** Graziano
Berto (maitre d')

**Hours:** Mon-Sat 6 am-11 pm,
Sun brunch seatings at 10:30
am and 1 pm, dinner 6-10 pm
**Cards:** All majors
**Reservations:** Required
**Handicapped:** Accessible
**Bar:** Full, excellent wine list
offers 500 selections
**Parking:** Valet
**Dress:** Jackets and ties
**Heart-Healthy Menu:**
Selections

What's in a name? A lot of reputation when the name is Ritz, as in Ritz-Carlton Hotel. The dinner menu offers different approaches to dining. There is the à la carte menu, with its listing of separate courses. Then there is the "alternative cuisine," meant for dieters whose concern for calories is coupled with a desire for fine dining. With a change of selections each evening, the alternative cuisine menu recently offered a choice of rabbit soup with root vegetables, or a handsome salad with several different greens in a sherry vinaigrette dressing. The main course included two choices. One was sauteed turbot in a spiced shellfish-and-carrot broth, plated with a small crab cake and an herbed rouille, along with a lattice of crisped potato. The other alternative cuisine selection was a double loin cut of rabbit filled with Savoy cabbage, plated with Moroccan couscous. The Ritz-Carlton maintains these dinners contain only 650 calories.

From the regular menu, without regard to calories, Chef Sarah Stegner has much wider latitude. Her preparations can range from roasted beef tenderloin with braised beef and potato pie, plus baby carrots and caramelized shallots with chives, to sauteed veal chop and sweetbreads accompanied by porcini mushroom strudel.

The Dining Room is one of the city's more elegant restaurants. Its wood-paneled walls are highlighted by selective lighting. Service is generally impeccable. Considering the diverse cuisine that is being attempted at the Dining Room of the Ritz-Carlton, the effort deserves its share of recognition.

# DIXIE-QUE
KR 18/20
Decor 4/4   Hospitality 4/5   Food 8/9   Value 2/2

- **American/Southern**
- **Chicago/Northwest**
- **$$**

2001 W. Fullerton Ave. (at
   Damen Ave.)
Chicago
(312) 252-5600
**Troubleshooter:** Mel Markon
(owner)

**Hours:** Mon-Thurs 11 am-11
pm, Fri-Sat until 1 am, Sun
10:30 am-11 pm (brunch until
3 pm)
**Cards:** AE, MC, VISA
**Reservations:** Accepted
**Handicapped:** Accessible
**Bar:** Full
**Parking:** Free lots
**Party Facilities:** For up to 75

After you have lunch or dinner at Dixie-Que, you probably will want to learn how to drive an 18-wheel semi-trailer truck. Yes, there are other places that have managed to put together a Southern-style menu, but none is as much of a "joint" as Dixie-Que. The place reeks of authenticity and nostalgia from old advertising posters and road maps, not to mention the red vinyl seating and laminated plastic table tops. In warm weather, you can eat outside and pretend that sultry Chicago is redneck country.

The food centers on barbecue, ribs, chicken, and brisket. There are two basic sauces. The primary one is more sweet than tangy. The other sauce is made with Kentucky bourbon and is listed on the menu only with a designated chicken dinner. But as sure as Elvis had hips, I reckon that your waitress might be willing to bring out a small cup of the bourbon sauce, which does have a readily identifiable flavor. Smoked turkey with cole slaw and spiced peach dressing comes as a sandwich, as does brisket and hickory-smoked ham with cheese.

By the way, you can ask for a bib and all the napkins you need. There's a smattering of seafood, including fried catfish with tartar sauce plus grilled salmon or other grilled fish of the day. Most dinner platters come with slaw and beans flavored with raisins and apples. The beans are pretty good, but a little bit goes a long way. There's nothing fancy about the food or the way it's served. Portions are generous. As for desserts, the chocolate pecan nut pie is a dandy. The banana pudding, however, is not really as good as Mom's – this pudding is too sweet and needs more bananas and lots more vanilla wafers. Dixie-Que does not take Confederate money.

# D & J BISTRO

KR 16.5/20

Decor 3.5/4   Hospitality 3/5   Food 8/9   Value 2/2

- **French**
- **Lake Zurich**
- **$$**

1st Bank Plaza, 466 S.
Rand Rd.
Lake Zurich
(708) 438-8001

**Troubleshooters:** Dominique and Jacqueline Legeai (owners)

**Hours:** Lunch Tues-Fri 11:30 am-3 pm, dinner Mon-Fri from 5:30 pm, Sat from 5 pm, Sun from 4:30 pm

**Cards:** AE, DINERS, MC, VISA

**Reservations:** Saturdays and holiday evenings

**Handicapped:** Accessible

**Bar:** Full

**Parking:** Lot

**Party Facilities:** Semi-private for up to 30

Tucked away in an ordinary strip shopping mall, D & J Bistro is pleasantly country French, though the vinyl trim on chair backs and seats hardly carries through on the theme.

The Japanese chef, Masato Suzuki, certainly knows his way around French cuisine. His cooking is not without a certain flair, and his talent is evident.

Diners may order à la carte or choose from the entire menu to build a five-course prix fixe dinner of appetizer, soup, salad, entree, and dessert.

From appetizer choices on a seasonally changing menu, recent selections have included black linguine, colored by squid ink with goat's cheese; polenta with pieces of freshly smoked salmon embedded inside; plus standards such as a selection of house pâtés or angel-hair pasta with shrimp and asparagus bathed in saffron broth.

According to the bible of French cuisine, the *Larousse Gastronomique,* steak tartare should be made of horse meat. D & J Bistro's is not exactly up to that standard but is more conventionally prepared, with prime ground steak.

When it is available, the terrine of seafood is a real find. Two large nuggets of fish, one salmon, the other lobster, are centered in a mild vegetable mousse, napped in a smooth saffron sauce. Snails in garlic butter and blue point oysters round out the rather extensive appetizer selection.

As for main-course cooking, D & J Bistro really shines. The bistro classic, steak and pommes frites, headlines the menu, followed by classic French preparations of chicken dijonnaise, a trio of sausages, lamb rubbed with garlic, and other culinary delights. Fresh seafood entrees change depending upon availability. There are also other nightly specials to consider.

Desserts can be as formal as an assortment of cheeses or as simple as caramel custard.

# DON JUAN
KR 19/20
Decor 3/4   Hospitality 5/5   Food 9/9   Value 2/2

- **Mexican**
- **Chicago/Northwest**
- **$$**

6730 N. Northwest Hwy.
Chicago
(312) 775-6438
**Troubleshooter:** Marie Josefa Concannon (owner)

**Hours:** Mon-Thurs 11 am-10 pm, Fri-Sat until 11 pm, Sun noon-9 pm
**Cards:** All majors
**Reservations:** Sun-Thurs
**Handicapped:** Accessible
**Bar:** Full, specializing in margaritas, Mexican beers
**Parking:** Lot across the street

For all their popularity, many Mexican restaurants are all about the same. When one comes along that is clearly above the rest, it's time for a celebration of sorts. Well, bring on the hats and horns for Don Juan.

The menu appears hardly different from most of the Mexican restaurants you already know. If you insist on burritos and enchiladas, you'll find them. But taste some of the specials prepared nightly by Chef Patrick Concannon, whose mother founded the restaurant and greets diners each evening. Enjoy a chicken mole or chili relleno for a change of pace. The chicken mole has a dark, mysterious flavor, almost bitter, but not repellent. This mole is a blend of unsugared chocolate and spices, thickened almost to a paste, which bathes the tender roasted chicken. The chili relleno could be stuffed with black trumpet and cauliflower mushrooms, some goat's cheese, and the herbaceous flavor of epazote. An evening special might bring together a platter of wild game, spilling over with grilled venison, roasted lamb, and squab with poblano peppers, wild mushrooms, and an infused chili pasilla sauce.

I have never had tastier beef in any Mexican restaurant than the carne asada at Don Juan, with its medley of flavors at work on the meat. Charred beef filet is presented with a four-pepper crust, tomatoes, marinated wild mushrooms, and a chili and port wine sauce. A baby rack of lamb could be served with a purée of Peruvian yellow potatoes, roasted shiitake mushrooms, and a chili pasilla sauce.

Among seafood, filet of red snapper and sea scallops can come with crisp fried sweet potatoes, blackened baby corn, trumpet mushrooms, and a spicy sweet corn coulis. fileted catfish is charred and accompanied by seasonal vegetables, as well as such traditional Mexican accents as avocado, jicama, and a chili sauce.

For dessert, do not miss the flan, the Spanish custard in slightly burnt caramel sauce. This is as refreshing as they come.

# DON ROTH'S IN WHEELING
KR 18.5/20
Decor 4/4   Hospitality 4.5/5   Food 8/9   Value 2/2

- **American**
- **Wheeling**
- **$$**

61 N. Milwaukee Ave. (just north of Dundee Rd.)
Wheeling
(708) 537-5800
**Troubleshooter:** Don Roth (owner)

**Hours:** Lunch Mon-Fri 11:30 am-2:30 pm, dinner Mon-Thurs 5:30-9:30 pm, Fri 5-10:30 pm, Sat 5-11 pm, Sun 4-8:30 pm
**Cards:** All majors
**Reservations:** Suggested
**Handicapped:** Accessible
**Bar:** Full
**Parking:** Free lot
**Party Facilities:** Semi-private for up to 25
**Heart-Healthy Menu:** Selections

You may be into spa cuisine, doing health-club workouts three times a week. Maybe you count calories, watch your cholesterol, are into aerobics, and really do like Richard Simmons! But tell the truth, now. Aren't there times when all you really want to eat is a big hunk of meat?

There . . . I've said it, and I hope that as you read this you are nodding your head and thinking about a thick cut of prime rib, or a tender eye of round filet, and maybe even a 16-ounce sirloin.

If you've stayed with me this far, then go a little further – and then go out to Don Roth's in Wheeling. Roth has been in the restaurant business forever. There isn't a thing he doesn't know about making hungry people happy. And one of his cardinal principles is that if you keep things simple and give good value for the money, folks will come back again and again.

Don Roth's in Wheeling is a homey place, with a huddle of smaller dining rooms clustered about. There's nothing trendy or modern about the art or other decor. In fact, a recent remodeling almost turned the place into a broadcasting museum, with its memorabilia of big band broadcasts going back to the 1920s and '30s at the original Blackhawk restaurant in the Loop. You can even ask the bartender for a Pink Lady or a Rob Roy, and he will know what you're talking about.

The menu is straight-ahead American, featuring steaks, ribs, chicken, prime rib, and fresh fish selections of the day. The onion soup is the genuine article, with a thick layer of melted cheese blanketing the crock in which the soup has been baked and is served.

As soon as diners are seated, the waiter or waitress will bring out some toasted buttered rye rounds, the kind that are virtually irresistible for snacking. You can get the standard house salad, complete with baby shrimp, or glide on over to one of the best salad bars around. There isn't a thing they haven't thought of for this salad bar.

As for those entrees, a filet comes cooked to your specifications. Though the restaurant's reputation is built on solid pilings of beefsteak and prime rib, the seafood choices also win high marks. Norwegian salmon with an herb butter sauce, or grouper fished from warm Caribbean waters, or whitefish from Lake Superior are regularly featured.

Desserts can include some real favorites such as pecan pie, cheesecakes, and really big ice cream sundaes with hot fudge sauce.

# DRAGON INN NORTH

KR 19/20

Decor 4/4   Hospitality 5/5   Food 8/9   Value 2/2

- **Chinese**
- **Glenview**
- **$$**

1650 Waukegan Rd.
Glenview
(708) 729-8383
**Troubleshooter:** Jeannette
Sih (owner)

**Hours:** Mon-Thurs 11:30
am-9:30 pm, Fri until 11 pm,
Sat 5-11 pm, Sun
noon-9:30 pm
**Cards:** AE, MC, VISA
**Reservations:** Suggested
**Handicapped:** Accessible
**Bar:** Full, tropical drinks
**Parking:** Free parking
**Party Facilities:** For up to 40

From the moment you drive up to the handsome pagoda-like exterior, you expect something special from Dragon Inn North. That feeling continues inside, where low ceilings and beautiful oriental art help to shut away the outer world.

The menu is extensive, as one would expect from a better Chinese restaurant. Diners will find familiar items. Kwoh te, those delicious morsels of steamed dumplings, are top notch, as is shrimp toast with its moist, creamy filling and flavorful, tender onion pancakes. Among soups, sizzling rice always brings warmth and pleasure to the table.

The best-kept secret about Dragon Inn North is that there is a secret menu. All you need do is ask, and virtually anything you might desire can be whipped up in the restaurant's kitchen. Among these secrets is General Tso's chicken, fast becoming one of the most popular dishes at Chicago-area Chinese restaurants. At Dragon Inn North, the chicken is more sweet than spicy hot, but make no mistake – the peppery underpinnings are there.

Among other dishes not found on the printed menu is vegetarian spring rolls, with a crisp, delicate wonton wrap. When shipments are available and fresh, Dover sole stir-fried with crunch oriental vegetables is a major treat.

The restaurant serves up its share of Cantonese cookery, if that is what you crave. But the Mandarin, Hunan, and Szechuan styles offer greater challenge and depth. Try an order of Hunan sizzling lamb, beef, chicken, or shrimp. The meat of your choice is grilled in the kitchen, then brought out to the dining room. There a waitress quickly transfers it onto a stove-hot metal platter with crispy white rice noodles. The meat instantly begins to sizzle, giving the dish its name. A somewhat spicy brown sauce tops the food.

For dessert, there are a couple of ice creams as well as the ubiquitous fortune and almond cookies.

# THE ECCENTRIC
KR 17.5/20
Decor 4/4   Hospitality 5/5   Food 6.5/9   Value 2/2

- **American**
- **Chicago/Near North**
- **$$**

159 W. Erie St.
Chicago
(312) 787-8390
**Troubleshooter:** Mark Kosanovich (general manager)

**Hours:** Lunch Mon-Fri 11:30 am-2 pm, dinner Mon-Thurs 5:30-10 pm, Fri-Sat until 11 pm, Sun 5-9 pm
**Cards:** AE, DINERS, DISCOVER, MC, VISA, house accounts
**Reservations:** Recommended
**Handicapped:** Accessible
**Bar:** Full
**Parking:** Valet
**Party Facilities:** For 50-75
**Heart-Healthy Menu:** Selections

The Eccentric is not as eccentric as its name would imply. That does not diminish nor intrude upon the fact that it is about as stylish a re-creation of a 1930s or '40s era nightclub as you are about to find this side of a time warp.

This is large-scale dining, with space for 350 or so eaters and another 120 seats in the long bar and its adjacent French café. Service is top notch and professional.

By now, anybody who cares knows that Oprah Winfrey is a key investor in the Eccentric. Though she might not be working one of the stoves, I am told that she really did take an intensive course to learn the business side of the restaurant business. At the very least, her culinary contribution includes the house signature dish – Oprah's mashed potatoes with horseradish.

Just so nobody misses the point that food is what the Eccentric is all about, full-length curtains that swag the stage on one large wall of the restaurant open to reveal the real star of the show, the kitchen.

The level of cooking seems to be directed to the high middle. There is nothing radical or challenging. Still, what is being done is good, if short of memorable.

Diners will find such readily recognizable fare as baked onion soup, caesar salad, shrimp cocktail, and smoked salmon among first courses. In a variation on snails in garlic butter, the Eccentric substitutes shrimp, though the menu's description sounds suspiciously like shrimp de jonghe.

You will not find anything too radical among entree selections, either. Roasted and grilled chicken, pepper steak, chops, and pastas are among regular selections. Several entrees rotate daily, especially fresh fish, which varies according to market and availability.

# ED DEBEVIC'S
KR 16.5/20
Decor 4/4   Hospitality 5/5   Food 5.5/9   Value 2/2

- **American**
- **Chicago/Near North**
- **$**

640 N. Wells St.
Chicago
(312) 664-1707
**Troubleshooter:** Manager on duty

## Other Locations
660 W. Lake-Cook Rd.
Deerfield
(708) 945-3242; Sun-Thurs
    11:30 am-10 pm, Fri-Sat until
    midnight; No reservations;
    Free parking lot

**Hours:** Mon-Thurs 11 am-midnight, Fri-Sat until 1 am, Sun 10:30 am-11 pm
**Cards:** All majors
**Reservations:** No
**Handicapped:** Accessible
**Bar:** Full
**Parking:** Valet and street
**Party Facilities:** Semi-private facilities available

**E**d Debevic's is a time warp into the 1950s. The goal was to re-create the diners that dotted America during that decade. They were all about the same: the food was secondary. Guys looking for girls, and vice versa, were not all that concerned with the cuisine. What was important was a jukebox with the latest by Elvis, the Everly Brothers, and Buddy Holly. That, by and large, is what Ed Debevic's is all about. There may not be carhops, but it's still a teenage hangout for grownups, and maybe for those among us who don't want to grow up.

The restaurant is probably larger than most hangouts of the '50s. The seats are covered with that sickly blue plastic that was someone's idea of interior decoration in the days before Golden Arches and Whoppers. The food is good enough for what it is. The meat is ground fresh for the hamburgers. And the chicken-fried steak tastes just as chicken-fried steak should. The fried chicken is like what we had in those good old days decades ago when pimples were of more concern than cholesterol. The malts are thick and flavorful – no, "yummy" would be a better word. Chances are you won't find a better malt or shake anywhere.

If you really insist on watching what you eat, there is a salad bar with a full array of greens, toppings, nibbles, soup, and even a casserole-style hot entree or two, recently priced under $6.

# Elbo Room
KR 18/20
Decor 3.5/4   Hospitality 5/5   Food 8/9   Value 1.5/2

---

• **American/Eclectic**
• **Chicago/Mid-North**
• **$$**
2871 N. Lincoln Ave.
Chicago
(312) 549-5549
**Troubleshooter:** Hugh Haller (manager)

**Hours:** Tues-Thurs 5-10 pm, Fri-Sat until 11 pm, Sun 5-10 pm (late-night menu served in bar until 2 am weeknights, 3 am weekends)
**Cards:** AE, MC, VISA
**Reservations:** Suggested
**Bar:** Full, entertainment
**Parking:** Street
**Party Facilities:** For 50-75

---

Though bare brick walls and open ductwork were more the restaurant design cliché of the 1980s, something about the Elbo Room has a special sort of appeal. Maybe it is the eclectic, rummage sale style of the furnishings. You cannot help but notice the closeness of the tables, which on busy nights can certainly demonstrate why the Elbo Room is named as it is.

Customers are genuinely made to feel welcome, even as newcomers. Though surrounded by the harsh environment of a semi-industrial neighborhood, the Elbo Room is as cozy as a tea room, and a lot more hip!

The primary culinary focus is on rôtisserie meats and seafood. Offerings are not limited to that manner of preparation, as a quick glance at the fairly short menu reveals. Among appetizers, a platter of clams and mussels comes in a seafood stock, garlic and herb sauce so delicious that you will want to use pieces of crusty bread to soak up every drop. Or have a go at grilled calamari, radically different in appearance and texture from the fried variety served elsewhere.

For total immersion in rich flavors and heady textures, take an order of Italian bow-tie noodles with dark strips of duck meat, luxuriant with pine nuts. It's wonderful self-indulgence. Pastas get other good treatment at the Elbo Room, which otherwise really has no pretense of being an Italian restaurant. The primary effort is not so much a search for subtle combinations of flavors and textures as it is for sharp contrasts. Elsewhere on the menu, rôtisserie chicken comes in a deliciously sweetened honey-mustard sauce, which really serves virtually as a glaze. Contemporary regard for good health usually dictates that chicken skin be removed before eating. Yet even when that accommodation is made, there remains a light infusion of the fragrant, flavorful underpinnings of the sauce. Incidentally, the chicken is served with sweet potato fries, also available as an à la carte side order and not to be missed in any circumstance.

At the Elbo Room, New York strip sirloin is not conventionally grilled, but given the same kind of rôtisserie cooking that a larger standing rib roast might be given. When served, the steak is cut across the grain, as if slices of roast prime rib were being offered. Recently, the meat was given a gorgonzola butter sauce. Deliciously extravagant, a little sauce goes a long way for flavor. The menu is fleshed out with a handful of other meat and chop selections, as well as at least one daily fish offering. Desserts include a wonderfully chewy pecan tart.

**Note:** This spot is considering opting out of the restaurant business in favor of music only. Call before heading over.

# EL CRIOLLO
KR 18.5/20

Decor 3.5/4   Hospitality 5/5   Food 8/9   Value 2/2

- **Argentinean/Mexican /Puerto Rican**
- **Chicago/Mid-North**
- **$**

1706 W. Fullerton Ave.
Chicago
(312) 549-3373
**Troubleshooter:** Margarita
Porto (owner)

**Hours:** Tues-Fri noon-midnight, Sat-Mon 2 pm-midnight
**Cards:** All majors
**Reservations:** Accepted
**Bar:** Full
**Parking:** Street
**Party Facilities:** For up to 50

**E**l Criollo offers some of the best Argentinean food around, as well as Mexican and Puerto Rican.

As soon as diners are seated, a large basket of nacho chips and two dipping sauces are brought to the table. One sauce is red and fairly hot. The salsa verde, the green sauce, is not peppery at all. This is El Criollo's famous parsley garlic sauce. Minced parsley in olive oil and vinegar is liberally flavored with crushed garlic. As good as this sauce is on nacho chips, it's even better on the Argentine empanadas, for which it is really meant. An empanada is the Argentine version of wrapped pastry. It is also known as gaucho pie, implying that this is the food the Argentine cowboys would pack in their knapsacks for a day out on the pampas. The empanadas are just about as tasty as can be. Other appetizers include Puerto Rican blood sausage, Mexican queso fundido, sweet fried plantains, ceviche, and other choices. There's no question that El Criollo is covering a lot of culinary territory.

Argentinean entrees, as might be expected, emphasize beef. A traditional parrillada is the kind of mixed grill that might be served in Buenos Aires: short ribs, two kinds of sausage, and sweetbreads, all given treatment on the charcoal grill. A bit more conventional is churrasco, a charcoal-broiled beefsteak. Its culinary genealogy also goes back to the gauchos.

Among a list of Puerto Rican choices is a delicious roasted chicken with a variety of island spices and pepper seasonings. Steak Caribe is beef marinated in spices, pan fried, and served with fried onions. The menu headliner is a skirt steak stuffed with bacon, onion, and tomatoes, among other ingredients.

The Mexican offerings at El Criollo include those seen at most Mexican restaurants. A combination platter gives you a slice of skirt steak along with an enchilada and some guacamole. Seafood includes traditional red snapper Veracruzana. The fish comes out whole, head to tail, slathered in slices of onion and peppers. It's really something special. But so is just about everything at El Criollo.

# ELDER'S MILL
KR 18/20
Decor 3.5/4   Hospitality 5/5   Food 7.5/9   Value 2/2

- **American**
- **Richmond**
- **$$**

5604 Mill St. (U.S. Rte. 12)
Richmond
(815) 678-2841
**Troubleshooter:** Harold Elder
(chef/owner)

**Hours:** Wed-Sat lunch 11:30 am-2 pm, dinner Wed-Thurs 5:30-8:30 pm, Fri-Sat until 9:30 pm, Sun noon-3 pm
**Cards:** AE, CB, DINERS, MC, VISA
**Bar:** Full, Fri-Sat live jazz
**Parking:** Free lot
**Party Facilities:** For up to 50 in adjacent art gallery or on outdoor terrace

The country restaurant today is much more than ham hocks, fried potatoes, and green beans washed down with soda pop. American dining has taken a route well traveled in French cookery, the establishment of fine restaurants in smaller towns.

Elder's Mill is a worthy addition to this genre. Chef/Owner Harold Elder has combined some of the concepts of French bistro cooking with a natural and American menu that would taste good no matter where served.

An onion tart for appetizer is representative of Elder's approach. It is somewhat brawny: the onions – in this case, red Spanish – are seasoned with ample garlic and, to a lesser extent, fresh thyme. The onions appear to have been caramelized and then finished in a fairly thin, but not particularly delicate, pastry shell. Other appetizers include smoked salmon with tarragon mustard, a creamy chicken liver pâté, as well as soups and composed salads. In one case, thin asparagus spears are arranged on a platter with greens and drenched in vinaigrette. Unfortunately, our waiter failed to disclose that a house salad comes with the entree, so when ordering a composed à la carte salad, be forewarned you will also get the regular house salad.

At Elder's Mill the entrees continue in a decidedly American manner, though some international accents can appear. Recently salmon has been served with an Indian-influenced fruit chutney glaze, while duck legs get a more French-style treatment in a confit.

Though often associated with bistro dining, steak and french fries strikes me as appropriate in the setting of Elder's Mill, as does its counterpart, roast chicken with fries. The chicken is well herbed and served with vegetables. These are not the delicate juliennes or purées of nouvelle cuisine, but rather the robust and flavorful common stock found in any Midwestern garden. Vegetables are prominent in Chef Elder's approach to lamb shank. The meat is braised in red wine, the finished shank kissed with a pale green basil aioli. A collection of root vegetables is roasted and served with caramelized onions.

Desserts are similarly substantial and range from berry tarts with custard to chocolate mocha torte and other such concoctions. There is a good, fairly priced wine list, and service is attentive. The restaurant takes advantage of the old mill building in which it is housed; dining rooms occupy three floors, though even on busy nights there is little sense of a crowd.

# ELI'S THE PLACE FOR STEAK
KR 17/20
Decor 3/4   Hospitality 5/5   Food 7.5/9   Value 1.5/2

- **American**
- **Chicago/Near North**
- **$$**

215 E. Chicago Ave.
Chicago
(312) 642-1393
**Troubleshooter:** Marc
Schulman (owner)

**Hours:** Lunch Mon-Fri 11:30 am-2:30 pm, dinner daily 4-10:30 pm
**Cards:** All majors
**Reservations:** Suggested
**Handicapped:** Accessible
**Bar:** Full, piano lounge
**Parking:** Special rate in building garage
**Dress:** Jackets requested
**Party Facilities:** For 20-100

These days Eli's cheesecake is probably more famous than the restaurant. But this is where it all began. Though founder Eli Schulman has passed away, his son Marc and a fairly constant staff over the years have kept this Chicago landmark as good as it has always been.

No one would ever call Eli's the Place for Steak an especially modern or imaginative restaurant. But at a time when restaurants come and go, this has always been a major draw on Chicago's Near North Side. Sure, the interior is glitzy, even garish by today's restaurant standards. But the quality is enduring.

Though "steak" is part of the restaurant's name, my favorite dish has always been Calves Liver Eli. It's as sweet and tender as you can imagine, the kind of dining that might even make a liver lover out of someone who usually refuses to touch the stuff. Thin slices are sauteed with sliced onions, green peppers, and mushrooms. It's decidedly untrendy, but what a treat it can be!

Among steaks, you will find all the cuts. There is even a dégustation of sorts, which includes portions of liver, black peppercorn sirloin steak, a huge "garbage" salad, potatoes, and cheesecake.

In the last couple of years, as dining tastes have evolved, Eli's the Place for Steak has also become a place for seafood. The selections are not numerous, but they are prepared with the same fastidious care that marks the restaurant. That most meaty of seafood, swordfish, gets a garnish of red bell peppers in a tarragon vinaigrette, while salmon is almost made trendy with pesto.

All dinners include Eli's lahvosh bread and matzo basket, a relish tray, salad, and potato. And, of course, for dessert there is the famous cheesecake, served exactly as it always has been and where it all began.

# EL SOL
KR 18/20
Decor 3.5/4   Hospitality 4.5/5   Food 8/9   Value 2/2

| | |
|---|---|
| • **Mexican** | **Hours:** Tues-Sun 10 am-11:30 pm |
| • **Chicago/Mid-North** | **Cards:** None |
| • **$** | **Reservations:** Accepted |
| 1363 W. Fullerton Ave. | **Bar:** Service bar |
| Chicago | **Parking:** Street |
| (312) 929-8120 | **Party Facilities:** For up to 80, Monday only |
| **Troubleshooter:** Carlos Bermudez (owner) | |

**E**l Sol may be the only Mexican restaurant anywhere with a Marilyn Monroe poster on display. Of course, that's not the only decoration in a restaurant that is not so much eclectic in decor as it is multilayered. Artwork ranges from an Aztec prince to tropical murals, and even an occasional Christmas decoration hanging from the ceiling, no matter the time of year.

But make no mistake about it: amidst the red Naugahyde seating and haphazard ornamentation is some of the very best Mexican cooking found in Chicago.

The menu ranges from breakfast through dinner. Appetizers include the classic vuelve a la vida ("come back to life") seafood cocktail, simple nachos, and similar nibbles. The guacamole, though expensive at $5 a portion, is the kind that makes you think of warm summer days. And the margaritas cannot be beat!

El Sol presents much of the standard repertoire of Mexican restaurants, though its selection is wider than might be expected. Classic tripe soup, called menudo, is there, as are Mexican chicken soup with corn and several seafood-based broths. Diners will also find whole fish served with a variety of cooked vegetables, or breaded and deep fried. There is also a refreshing seafood salad.

The typical Mexican enchiladas, tacos, and their relatives, the tostadas and flautas, come with a variety of delicious fillings. A combination of taco, tostada, and enchilada might be more than you can eat in a sitting.

The chilies rellenos are faultless. The pepper has just the right bite and texture; the filling is spiced and peppered, but not too much so. When ordered with a cheese stuffing, the creamy smoothness contrasts with a companion beef-filled pepper.

The carne asada, or skirt steak, is given a delicious marinade at El Sol, though it is not an especially tender cut of meat. The restaurant serves only one dessert, flan, which is brought in from an outside purveyor; more of a burnt caramel sauce flavor would make this a better flan.

Service is convivial and helpful, but you won't be able to rush through dinner unless you specifically ask.

# EMILIO'S
KR 19/20
Decor 3.5/4   Hospitality 5/5   Food 8.5/9   Value 2/2

- **Spanish**
- **Hillside**
- **$$**

4100 W. Roosevelt Rd.
Hillside
(708) 547-7177
**Troubleshooters:** Emilio Gervilla, Ann Marie Gervilla (owners)

**Hours:** Mon-Thurs 11:30 am-10 pm, Fri until 11 pm, Sat 5-11 pm, Sun 5-10 pm
**Cards:** AE, MC, VISA
**Reservations:** For 6 or more Sun-Thurs
**Handicapped:** Accessible
**Bar:** Full, specializing in Spanish vintages
**Parking:** Free lot
**Party Facilities:** For 50 or more Sunday afternoons

Tapas, the featured commodity at Emilio's, are Spanish appetizers, which, when eaten in sufficient quantity, can comprise an entire lunch or dinner. Savor the Spanish café atmosphere, with its mosaic tile floor, floral print curtains, and whimsical Iberian mural dominating one large, expansive wall. Then get down to the savory part of tasting.

Be sure to order potato salad, plentifully flavored with garlic. Have a platter of marinated octopus, perfectly tender, bathed in olive oil with onion and a light tomato vinaigrette. Roasted eggplant is another tantalizing tidbit, with small chunks of goat's cheese and fresh mozzarella sprinkled on top. More substantial might be cold roasted veal, the meat stuffed with a force of olives, sun-dried tomatoes, and a light sherry dressing. This one is so very good you might want to order enough for a full meal. But resist the temptation and continue with more tapas.

Several are listed as house specialties, including grilled shrimp in garlic butter, simple and delicate. The Spanish answer to Buffalo chicken wings might be spicy wings with a sherried mayonnaise. The mayonnaise adds a richness that the spiced wings really do not need. For all the excellence of the tapas, the only disappointment we found came with an order of grilled oysters coated with cracked peppers and served on a bed of leeks. The somewhat spongy texture of the oysters made them less than perfect.

If perfection is your goal, order paella, the great rice casserole that is Spain's gift to the culinary world. Saffron rice is simmered in chicken broth, absorbing the liquid. Cooked along with the rice are whole shellfish, including clams, mussels, shrimp, and lobster; in another version, Spanish sausage, ham, and chicken are added to the seafood.

Desserts include a version of crème brûlée laced with raspberries, a flan with strawberry sauce and mint, as well as other choices.

# EVEREST ROOM
KR 20/20
Decor 4/4   Hospitality 5/5   Food 9/9   Value 2/2

- **French**
- **Chicago Loop**
- **$$$**

440 S. La Salle St. (One Financial Place)
Chicago
(312) 663-8920
**Troubleshooters:** Jean Joho (chef), Mark Tormey (managing partner)

**Hours:** Dinner Tues-Thurs 5:30-8:30 pm, Fri-Sat 5:30-10 pm
**Cards:** AE, DINERS, DISCOVER, MC, VISA, La Salle Club membership accounts
**Handicapped:** Accessible
**Bar:** Full
**Parking:** Free in building garage
**Party Facilities:** For 75-100, 150 for cocktails only

**N**ever mind that the latest topological measurements may reveal that the Himalayan peak K2 is taller than fabled Mt. Everest. Everest remains the metaphor for the pinnacle of greatness. Besides, who would go to a restaurant named K2? That sounds like a spot remover!

The Everest Room showcases Chef Jean Joho's cooking in a handsome blend of rich furnishings, chandelier lighting, and even suggestions of big-game hunting. The chef first made his mark on the city at the late and fabled Maxim's, where he was literally cooking in a basement. Now, 40 floors above the city, diners are entertained by a vista outside the windows as they await each dinner course.

As is the case with virtually all great restaurants, the menu changes quite often. Chef Joho's native Alsace region is a prime influence on his cooking, which brings together only the best and freshest of ingredients.

In addition to the regular menu, a multicourse dégustation dinner is available each evening at fixed price. As proposed by the chef on a given evening, the meal could begin with a taste of cauliflower mousse topped with tiny beads of black caviar. The first course might be followed by a mosaic of leek, foie gras, and woodland mushrooms in terrine. Next would come a fish course, such as a Maine lobster pot-au-feu in a light, almost clear broth, whose color belies its taste intensity. A meat or poultry course, such as goose prepared in the Alsatian manner, could be next, followed by a course of fine cheese and a grand dessert.

The garniture of platters is especially handsome, showcased on the oversized dinnerware. One recent and truly exotic highlight was escargot mousse with escargot caviar – the roe of the snail – which should make curious even the most jaded tastes.

Service is excellent, and presentations are positively sensual.

# FEEDING FRENZZY
KR 19.5/20
Decor 4/4   Hospitality 5/5   Food 8.5/9   Value 2/2

- **American**
- **Chicago/Mid-North**
- **$$**

3255 N. Halsted St.
Chicago
(312) 929-9960
**Troubleshooter:** Mark
Donaway (chef/owner)

**Hours:** Tues-Thurs 6-10 pm,
Fri 6-11 pm, Sat 5-11 pm, Sun
5-10 pm
**Cards:** None
**Reservations:** None
**Bar:** No liquor, but may bring
own
**Parking:** Valet or street
**Party Facilities:** Up to 50
**Heart-Healthy Menu:**
Designations and special
preparation available

I do not think I have ever come across a restaurant like Feeding Frenzzy. As for the decor, it's like eating inside Carmen Miranda's hat. There's a little bit of everything to look at, from art on the walls to gimcracks hanging from the ceiling; there are even drawings by first-grade school children in the bathrooms.

The menu is just as eclectic, under the direction of chef and co-owner Mark Donaway. Donaway seems to have thrown away convention; where else would you find a stuffed onion appetizer served atop a glass brick! Donaway has a fanciful eye when it comes to platter art. His arrangements go right to the core of abstract design as he combines, for example, a variety of raw vegetables at one side of his platter with an inverted baked potato on the other, some sliced whole poblano peppers elsewhere, and in the center a large tuna steak, cross-hatched with a spicy Cajun tomato sauce. In the process, it all tastes pretty good.

Yet, with so much going on, there is the danger of contrivance, sometimes at the expense of good taste. An entree of Thai-spiced seafood casserole comes in a large soufflé dish. As handsome as it looks, the seasonings seem somehow askew, leaving a soured, salty flavor where I suspect exotic was intended. In another entree, curried chicken pot pie, there is no trace of curry flavor. But what is left is more than interesting. Visually, the pot pie is more like a large, flattened pop tart. Inside the pastry crust are potatoes, gravy, and chicken.

That is about the worst that can be said for Feeding Frenzzy. Order an appetizer such as Vietnamese escargot, and out comes a platter with two red bell peppers. Cut inside and you will find the tasty, tangy snails; meantime the platter creates the kind of eye-catching excitement that is at the heart of Chef Donaway's whimsical sense of presentation. Another entree, pasta with venison sausage, brings a serving bowl, about a foot across, loaded with tri-colored rollatini and slices of tangy venison sausage. There is not much in the way of a sauce save for the barest hint of marinara. Nonetheless, it works.

When Donaway is on the mark, his preparations are just about the match of his presentations. Recent appetizers have included delicious lobster pancakes, a creamy soup he calls chicken Vesuvio chowder, and an elaborate and truly delicious presentation of turnips stuffed with peppered goat's cheese. All entrees are served with your choice of a variety of sauces, or none if your prefer, and a selection of side dishes, which arrive at the whim the the chef.

Desserts are equally surreal, whether a chocolate piano or white chocolate box filled with strawberry mousse, a luscious carrot cake, or even apple pie with cinnamon ice cream. Here, the pie and ice cream come on a platter dusted with ground cinnamon that has been checkered with a stencil; the look is country kitchen!

# FERNANDO'S

KR 18/20

Decor 4/4   Hospitality 4.5/5   Food 7.5/9   Value 2/2

- **Mexican**
- **Chicago/Mid-North**
- **$**

3450 N. Lincoln Ave.
Chicago
(312) 477-6930
**Troubleshooters:** Carmen and Mario Gonzales (owners)

**Hours:** Mon-Thurs 2:00 pm-10:30 pm, Fri-Sat until 11:30 pm, Sun 3-10 pm
**Cards:** AE, MC, VISA, house accounts
**Reservations:** Accepted
**Handicapped:** Accessible
**Bar:** Full
**Parking:** Street
**Party Facilities:** For 20-80

It's refreshing to find a Mexican restaurant that breaks the mold. Fernando's menu features many of the traditional dishes to be expected at any Mexican restaurant – tacos and enchiladas, burritos and chilies rellenos – but a few regional specialties and one or two recipes seem to come more from kitchen inspiration than tradition. For example, while a Mexican seafood classic, snapper Veracruzana, gets due attention, so does rainbow trout sauteed in butter and topped with a sprinkling of fresh coriander leaves and sliced cucumbers. True, coriander is a typical Mexican seasoning, but trout is not usually seen within the confines of a Mexican restaurant. It is such a touch of originality that makes Fernando's stand out.

As for that snapper Veracruzana, it is one of the best I've ever tasted. The large serving platter on which the fish comes is laden with a virtual garden of rice, tomatoes, avocado slices, carrots, broccoli, and cauliflower with a mild cheese sauce. It is one of the most beautiful presentations I've ever seen in a Mexican restaurant. A recent remodeling has spruced up what already was a handsome restaurant and bar.

A selection of appetizers, soups, and desserts can round out dinner; and for dessert, don't miss flan and crisp, sugared sopapillas to go along with your coffee.

# FROGGY'S
KR 18.5/20
Decor 3.5/4   Hospitality 5/5   Food 8/9   Value 2/2

- **French**
- **Highwood**
- **$$**

306 Green Bay Rd.
Highwood
(708) 433-7080
**Troubleshooters:** Gregg Mason (owner), Thierry Le Feuvre (chef)

**Hours:** Lunch Mon-Fri 11:30 am-2 pm, dinner Mon-Thurs 5-10 pm, Fri-Sat until 11 pm
**Cards:** CB, DINERS, DISCOVER, MC, VISA
**Reservations:** For 6 or more
**Bar:** Full, small lounge, more than 50 California chardonnays
**Parking:** Street or nearby lot
**Party Facilities:** For up to 54

Though Froggy's is no longer the novelty it once was, this pioneering French bistro has held up well over the years and continues to draw a loyal dining audience. No wonder, considering the imaginative presentations and reasonable prices.

As with most good restaurants these days, the menu changes quite often, so what you read about today may not be what is served tonight. But, you can be sure that the quality will be consistently good.

The cooking leans toward the nouvelle style, though with a link to traditional bistro fare. Among featured entrees, diners might find chicken sauteed with tomatoes, onions, and peppers, country style. Sliced filet of beef gets a traditional handling with a red wine sauce and bouquet of herbs. Roast duckling, so often seen in a creamy black peppercorn sauce, might get a trio of red, green, and black peppercorns. Deliciously prepared sweetbreads, that genuine delicacy of French provincial dining, are braised in a casserole with bacon, mushrooms, and onions, then simmered in a red wine reduction. On the other hand, there is no dabbling with rack of lamb, presented in rather straightforward fashion with a fresh mint sauce.

Seafoods are seasonal. Whitefish, so prosaic on many menus, is treated at Froggy's to a fruity papaya and vanilla sauce. Lobster, on the other hand, gets almost regal treatment, bedded down with a mound of wrapped noodles in a saffron sauce, underscoring a Mediterranean influence.

Appetizers can include sauteed snails with applejack brandy and slices of apple; it's quite a change from traditional snails in garlic butter sauce. Freshly made terrines and pâtés are a mark of the house. Consider yourself fortunate if a veal and wild mushroom terrine is being served the night you visit.

As for desserts, take a look at what is offered and let your taste-buds, not your waistline, be your guide!

# FRONTERA GRILL
KR 18.5/20
Decor 3.5/4  Hospitality 4.5/5  Food 9/9  Value 1.5/2

- **Mexican**
- **Chicago/Near North**
- **$$**

445 N. Clark St.
Chicago
(312) 661-1434
**Troubleshooters:** Rick and
Deann Bayless (owners)

**Hours:** Lunch Tues-Fri 11:30
am-2:30 pm, brunch Sat 10:30
am-2:30 pm, dinner Tues-Thurs
5:20-10 pm, Fri-Sat 5:30-11 pm
**Cards:** AE, CB, DINERS,
DISCOVER, MC, VISA
**Reservations:** Only for 5-10
**Handicapped:** Accessible
**Bar:** Service bar
**Parking:** Valet, public lot
across street
**Party Facilities:** For 45-65,
Sundays and Mondays only

Frontera Grill is like no other Mexican restaurant in Chicago. Forget about border food. Chef/owner Rick Bayless and his wife, Deann, have chosen instead to explore the multiplicity of Mexican cuisine possibilities. The restaurant is crowded, noisy, and on the cutting edge of fashion in contemporary dining. You might even say there is a certain boisterous character. It isn't rowdy, but there's just enough hubbub to suggest a cantina.

Diners will see some familiar items on the Frontera Grill menu, but any similarity to conventional Mexican cooking stops there. The guacamole is thick and chunky, with the full flavor of avocado and a hint of seasonings. Chicken taquitos are thin fingers of crisp dough around a filling of seasoned, minced chicken, topped with dollops of a fresh sour cream unlike any I've tasted before.

Try the appetizer platter, which brings with the taquitos and guacamole some small quesadillas and ceviche tostadas. The ceviche is cooling, with the raw bite of lime juice. A bit of cilantro and other herb seasonings make this a distinct winner. By the way, you might also want to sample a platter of sopes if your party is large enough. Sopes are cornmeal tarts, each with a different filling or topping. Frontera Grill serves them with plantain and sour cream, guacamole, chorizo, and chicken in mole sauce. Among past entrees has been duck breast in a green pumpkin seed mole. As in fashionable French restaurants, pieces of the duck breast are slightly pink, bathed in a thick, but not heavy, sauce that complements the flavor of the poultry. The platter also comes with Mexican rice, small rings of zucchini, and chayote. Among other entrees is split game hens. Here, the small birds are grilled over charcoal, which seals in a marinade of garlic and spices. Dinner choices also include an unusual turkey breast steak with a red mole, fresh fish, chilies rellenos, and specials of the evening. The dessert list replaces familiar flan with a different style of fruit custard, fresh ice creams, and other sweets.

# GANDHI INDIA RESTAURANT
KR 17/20
Decor 2.5/4   Hospitality 4/5   Food 8.5/9   Value 2/2

- **Indian**
- **Chicago/Far North**
- **$**

2601 W. Devon Ave.
Chicago
(312) 761-8714; fax orders
   (312) 761-4167
**Troubleshooter:** Sham Hans
(owner)

**Hours:** Lunch (buffet) daily 11:30 am-3:30 pm, dinner Sun-Thurs 5-10 pm, Fri-Sat until 11 pm
**Cards:** All majors
**Reservations:** Only Fridays and Saturdays
**Handicapped:** Accessible
**Bar:** Service bar
**Parking:** Street or city lot across street

**M**ore than many other cuisines, Indian depends upon a bouquet of spices and seasonings for its very substance. It is the restaurant's handling of these seasonings – turmeric, cardamom, saffron, and others – which makes a firm statement on what Gandhi is all about. The menu explains most of the dishes, which makes this a welcome stop for beginners or those more experienced in the Indian way of dining.

Start with a combination platter of appetizers for a preview. Much of Indian cooking can be picked up and eaten out of hand if you choose. Try the deep-fried pakoras and samosas. Pakoras are made with spiced chickpea flour, formed into hollow dumplings into which is stuffed a mix of vegetables. The samosas are potato-based, deep-fried, and savory. Then pick up a piece of the chicken tikka, roasted in the tandoori ovens, which have become standard equipage for Indian restaurant kitchens. Similarly tasty are the Indian shish kebabs – cubes of lamb given a deep charcoal roasting.

Diners can order a selected combination dinner or à la carte; let your own tastes and instincts be your guide. Incidentally, curries can be mild or hot; those at Gandhi seem to be somewhere in between. There is no paucity to seasonings here, nor is there a sameness.

# GAYLORD INDIA
KR 19/20
Decor 4/4   Hospitality 5/5   Food 8/9   Value 2/2

* **Indian**
* **Chicago/Near North**
* **$$**

678 N. Clark St.
Chicago
(312) 664-1700
**Troubleshooter:** I. Puri
(general manager)

**Hours:** Lunch Mon-Fri 11:30 am-2:30 pm, Sat-Sun noon-3 pm, dinner nightly 5:30-10 pm
**Cards:** AE, MC, VISA
**Reservations:** Accepted
**Handicapped:** Accessible
**Bar:** Full
**Parking:** Street or lot across street
**Party Facilities:** For up to 50

Gaylord India was Chicago's first important Indian restaurant, and though many others have sprung up as the city's Indian population has grown, it remains a favorite. The restaurant features a northern style of Indian cuisine, with striking Moghul influences. Much of the cooking is characterized by the use of tandoors, large clay urns used as ovens. Hot coals line the bottom, generating intense heat. Meats are set over the coals, or laid along the sides of the urn, sealing in flavor and juices. A mark of the tandoori style of cooking is the bright red color of the grilled meats or seafood. The coloration comes not from the cooking itself, but from a marinade of yogurt, spices, and a coloring dye.

No beef is served at Gaylord because of the Hindu prohibition, but delicious chicken, lamb, prawns, and vegetables are regular menu items. Naturally, because vegetarianism is so prominent in Indian dietary culture, vegetables get wonderful treatment, usually in full-flavored and heavily spiced sauces. À la carte dining gives you a free hand with selections, but combination platters offer newcomers to the cuisine a good assortment of textures and tastes. At the conclusion of your meal, take a cup of steaming hot and fragrant tea and one of the delectably sweet desserts.

# GEJA'S CAFE

KR 16/20

Decor 4/4   Hospitality 3.5/5   Food 7.5/9   Value 1/2

- **Spanish/Fondue**
- **Chicago/Mid-North**
- **$$$**

340 W. Armitage Ave.
Chicago
(312) 281-9101
**Troubleshooter:** Russell
Rehberg (general manager)

**Hours:** Mon-Thurs 5-10:30
pm, Fri to midnight, Sat to
12:30 am, Sun 4:30-10:00 pm
**Cards:** All majors
**Reservations:** Sunday
through Thursday only
**Bar:** Full, extensive wine list
**Party Facilities:** For up to 50

Geja's Cafe is one of Chicago's most romantic restaurants – small,
quiet, and intimate. Couples can order fondue selections from the
fairly abbreviated menu and then cook and dip to their hearts'
content.

Even with today's emphasis on healthy dining, fondue cookery re-
mains popular. Meat, chicken, or seafood is cooked at the table in
hot peanut oil. Fondue cookery can be as elaborate or simple as you
choose. At the top of the menu choices is the connoisseur fondue,
which consists of aged beef tenderloin, lobster tail, and large, fresh
shrimp. Other individual or combination dinners might include
shrimp, scallops, or chicken.

For something lighter, though certainly no less caloric, a cheese
fondue might be the way to go. Melted cheese of your choice bub-
bles in the pot, into which are dipped crusty chunks of French bread.
The cheese is blended with white wine and seasonings and is truly
delicious. The standard house dessert is – what else? – chocolate
fondue, flamed with orange liqueur and served with apples, melon
chunks, pineapple, sliced bananas, pound cake, and marshmallows.

Adding to the romance is a flamenco guitarist and one of the bet-
ter wine lists in town.

# GENE & GEORGETTI

KR 15.5/20

Decor 2/4   Hospitality 4/5   Food 8/9   Value 1.5/2

- **American/Italian**
- **Chicago/Near North**
- **$$$**

500 N. Franklin St.
Chicago
(312) 527-3718
**Troubleshooter:** Ida
Michelotti (owner)

**Hours:** Mon-Sat 11 am-
midnight
**Cards:** AE, CB, DINERS, MC,
VISA, house accounts
**Reservations:** Mandatory
**Handicapped:** Accessible
**Bar:** Full
**Parking:** Valet and private lot
**Party Facilities:** For up to
100

No matter that surveys show dining tastes and trends are moving
away from red meats to chicken, fish, and vegetables. There remain
large numbers of people who still like nothing better than a huge
prime cut of beefsteak, often the larger the better.

At Gene & Georgetti, the specialty is prime aged steaks, along
with large-portion asides of cottage-fried potatoes and an old-fash-
ioned head lettuce salad dressed with nothing more exotic than oil
and vinegar or French dressing.

Gene & Georgetti is one of the more clubby restaurants in Chi-
cago, where it probably pays to know someone in charge. Real fans
of the restaurant swear by its excellence, which explains why this has
traditionally been one of the more difficult restaurants to get into on
a last-minute reservation.

Once you're seated, service can be as good as it gets. Many of the
waiters look as if they have been on duty since the day the restau-
rant first opened its doors, sometime back in Chicago's early history.
In fact, Gene & Georgetti is a part of Chicago's history, so whatever
inconveniences may be involved in obtaining a table here are proba-
bly tolerated better than they would be elsewhere.

# GENNARO'S
KR 19/20
Decor 3/4   Hospitality 5/5   Food 9/9   Value 2/2

- **Italian**
- **Chicago/Near West**
- **$$**

1352 W. Taylor St.
Chicago
(312) 243-1035
**Troubleshooter:** John
Gennaro (owner)

**Hours:** Thurs 5-9 pm, Fri-Sat until 10 pm, Sun 4-9 pm
**Cards:** None
**Reservations:** Accepted
**Bar:** Full
**Parking:** Valet

**W**hen Chicago diners think about the old style of Italian cooking as it used to be done on Taylor Street, Gennaro's is probably the first place that comes to mind. To its regulars it is akin to a private club, an idea the locked front door and buzzer entry does nothing to dispel.

The menu is typical Italian-American, without the extravagances of fashion which mark newer restaurants. In the kitchen are large cauldrons of sauces and the preparation tables for fresh pastas. Order the homemade gnocchi – little potato dumplings which are as pleasurable a way to enjoy Gennaro's as there can be. Veal receives excellent treatment, from basic parmigiana to country-style with sausage. Everything is cooked to order, and dining is not to be rushed.

# GIANNOTTI STEAK HOUSE
KR 20/20
Decor 4/4    Hospitality 5/5    Food 9/9    Value 2/2

- **Italian**
- **Norridge**
- **$$**

8422 W. Lawrence Ave.
Norridge
(708) 453-1616
**Troubleshooter:** Vic
Giannotti (chef/owner)

**Hours:** Lunch Mon-Fri 11 am-3 pm, dinner Mon-Thurs 3-11 pm, Fri until midnight, Sat 5 pm-midnight, Sun 2-10 pm
**Cards:** AE, DINERS, DISCOVER, MC, VISA
**Reservations:** Suggested; for parties of 3 or more Fridays and Saturdays
**Handicapped:** Accessible
**Bar:** Full, live entertainment Tues-Sat, karaoke Monday after 10 pm, dance floor
**Parking:** Valet
**Dress:** No shorts or gym shoes
**Party Facilities:** For up to 30

Even considering the abundance of new Italian restaurants that are part and parcel of fashionable dining in and around Chicago, Vic Giannotti remains the best Italian chef, bar none! He's certainly had enough practice; he learned the restaurant trade when his parents ran a small West Side eatery, which led to a larger restaurant some years ago.

Giannotti took over the operation himself, then sold the restaurant, and its name. During the early 1980s, he cooked at a variety of other restaurants. Finally, he reopened his own place and brought the family name back into the restaurant business.

Though the name suggests that this is a steak house (and steaks are featured), it is the sublime array of Italian, and especially Neapolitan, cooking which makes this such an outstanding restaurant. I confess that each time I visit, I order the same things. It is a dinner selection that I think is unbeatable.

Begin with the merluzzi, a delicious cold seafood salad with the tang of lemon juice. Counter that with stuffed rolled eggplant. The pulp is fashioned into a crêpe-like patty, floured and fried to the color of gold. Then it is filled with a rich tomato sauce and ricotta cheese, rolled up, and baked, to be finished with a drizzle of red sauce.

For pasta, the very best is eight-finger cavatelli with marinara sauce. The cavatelli, handmade nuggets of pasta dough, also can be had with fresh broccoli, olive oil, and plenty of garlic. If your taste leans toward other kinds of pasta and saucing, you will not be disappointed.

Among entrees, I have never failed to order veal piccante. The meat is lightly floured, sauteed in butter and lemon juice, then topped with toasted pine nuts. This is as good as it gets! Seafood lovers will savor swordfish Vesuvio, which takes the popular Chicago-Italian chicken recipe and puts it to work with meaty seafood, in the interest of conserving both calories and cholesterol.

Among desserts, the cheesecake is light and sweet. A cup or two of cappuccino or espresso, and nothing could be better. For anyone who loves Italian food, Giannotti's is a must visit!

# THE GOLDEN OX
KR 19/20
Decor 4/4   Hospitality 4/5   Food 9/9   Value 2/2

- **German**
- **Chicago/Mid-North**
- **$$**

1578 Clybourn Ave.
Chicago
(312) 664-0780
**Troubleshooter:** Fred P. Greif (owner)

**Hours:** Mon-Sat 11 am-11 pm, Sun 3-9 pm
**Cards:** All majors
**Reservations:** Preferred
**Handicapped:** Accessible
**Bar:** Full, German beers
**Parking:** Valet
**Party Facilities:** For up to 80

Several years ago, when I first reviewed the Golden Ox, I called it the best German restaurant in Chicago. I still keep that opinion of a restaurant which improves with the passage of time. Visually, the Golden Ox is stunning. This is not just some Black Forest kitsch. The Old World charm is refreshing at a time when newer restaurants are little more than storefronts or warehouses where industrial-tech passes for atmosphere.

Soup is an excellent yardstick for measuring a kitchen's abilities. The liver dumpling broth is ample testimony to the capabilities at work here. The broth is dark golden, with dumplings afloat in a lake of plenty.

The German dinner entrees are so abundant and tempting as to make it difficult to pick any single one. If you choose the delicious sauerbraten, with its tangy bite of vinegar marinade and gingersnaps, you can't miss.

The restaurant wanders away from its German roots with several choices of chops and seafood. Dover sole almandine is as good as fish can get.

Desserts tend toward the rich end of the spectrum, and of course include fruit strudels and Black Forest cake drenched in kirschwasser. Service is efficient, not overbearing.

# GOOSE ISLAND BREWERY
KR 16/20
Decor 4/4   Hospitality 4/5   Food 6/9   Value 2/2

- **American**
- **Chicago/Mid-North**
- **$$**

1800 N. Clybourn Ave.
Chicago
(312) 915-0071
**Troubleshooter:** John Hall (owner)

**Hours:** Mon-Thurs 11-1 am, Fri-Sat until 2 am, Sun 10 am-midnight
**Cards:** All majors, house accounts
**Reservations:** For 8 or more
**Handicapped:** Accessible
**Bar:** Full, featuring draft beers brewed on premises
**Parking:** Free lot
**Party Facilities:** For 10-250, up to 500 for cocktails

Goose Island Brewery has become a very popular gathering spot for the young, trendy residents who frequent its neighborhood for shopping, dining, and recreation. Its primary appeal lies with the variety of beers brewed on the premises. This was probably the first of the boutique breweries in Chicago, and its beers deserve their accolades.

The food tends to the casual, running the gamut of snacks, appetizers, salads, and sandwiches. Heading up the menu is a pizza, which uses salty and pungent gorgonzola cheese instead of the milder mozzarella; it's a perfect combination with the house brews, especially one of the stout lagers.

Other snacks range from blue corn chip nachos to the house version of Buffalo wings, in this case dubbed "goose wings." Most of the salads are small, to accompany an entree, but dinner-sized platters of caesar, spinach, calamari, and grilled chicken salads will satisfy lighter appetites.

In addition to its sandwich selection, Goose Island Brewery serves a basic, though limited, array of entrees. They include a couple of steaks, smoked baby back ribs, and a mixed vegetarian stirfry.

# GORDON
KR 19.5/20
Decor 4/4   Hospitality 5/5   Food 8.5/9   Value 2/2

* **American**
* **Chicago/Near North**
* **$$$**

500 N. Clark St.
Chicago
(312) 467-9780
**Troubleshooter:** Gordon Sinclair (owner)

**Hours:** Lunch Mon-Sat 11:30 am-2:00 pm, Sun brunch 11 am-2 pm, dinner Sun-Thurs 5:30-9:30 pm, Fri-Sat until 12:00 am
**Cards:** All majors, house accounts
**Reservations:** Required
**Handicapped:** Accessible
**Bar:** Full, extensive cognacs and ports, wine list one of best in country
**Parking:** Valet or lots across street
**Dress:** Jackets required, ties optional
**Party Facilities:** Private rooms for dining or as many as 225 for stand-up cocktails and hors d'oeuvres

Gordon has probably changed chefs more often than almost any other major restaurant in this book. It is a testament to the restaurant's quality that so many former chefs have gone on to positions of even greater prominence. Despite the revolving door at the Gordon kitchen, the food remains remarkably consistent.

The menu changes regularly and reflects American and other world cuisines which have influenced ours, which is to say, all of them. One might find smoked salmon for an appetizer, given unusual treatment with the addition of thin pasta noodles fashioned with bits of black caviar and a touch of chive. The restaurant's nod to the popularity of pasta also extends to another appetizer, homemade ravioli filled with a purée of wild mushrooms and served in an exquisitely delicate tomato broth. Another menu features grilled portobello mushrooms with duck in a stylized sandwich, coupled with a bit of tabbouli, the Middle Eastern salad of parsley, bulghur wheat, tomatoes, and lemon.

Gordon, for all its hedonism, wisely offers diners the opportunity to order half-portion entrees, at half the cost of the whole-portion entree plus one dollar. It's a good way to trim calories and the budget, or have a more rococo go at things by ordering double entrees.

Choose from pan-roasted halibut, roasted loin of lamb, or perhaps poached breast of chicken, all excitingly garnished and served. The large L-shaped dining area sets a sybaritic mood, swathed in swag draperies, with bold flesh- and earth-toned murals. It is a restaurant that speaks of self-indulgence and fashion, characteristics manifest in the foods that come from the Gordon kitchen.

# GREEK ISLANDS

KR 17/20

Decor 3/4   Hospitality 4/5   Food 8/9   Value 2/2

- **Greek**
- **Chicago/Near West**
- **$$**

200 S. Halsted St.
Chicago
(312) 782-9855
**Troubleshooter:** Gus
Couchell (owner)

## Other Location
(not reviewed)

300 E. 22nd St.
Lombard
(708) 932-4545

**Hours:** Sun-Thurs 11 am-
midnight, Fri-Sat until 1 am
**Cards:** All majors, house
accounts
**Bar:** Full
**Parking:** Free valet parking
**Party Facilities:** For 30-200
**Heart-Healthy Menu:**
Selections

The rustic Greek fisherman's look at Greek Islands makes this an appealing restaurant to while away a couple of hours when neither time nor budget permits a journey to the Aegean. During the height of the lunch and dinner hours, this is one of the more bustling stops on the Halsted Street strip. As with its shoulder-to-shoulder competitors, the food is abundant and fairly cheap.

Though at least one experience here some years ago was less than satisfactory, more recent dining has changed my opinion. Broiled sea bass is served with lots of oregano and fresh lemon. The fish is deftly de-boned at tableside, after your waiter proudly shows you the entire fish from head to tail.

In addition to the seafood, Greek Islands serves the usual array of Hellenic fare: braised lamb, loin and leg of lamb, Greek-style skewered pork, called souvlaki, plus the casserole standbys, pastitsio, moussaka, and all the rest. As with the other Greek restaurants in the neighborhood, the combination platter may not be the most delicate dining, but it is a best buy for price-conscious or bargain-seeking diners.

# GULFPORT DINER
KR 18.5/20
Decor 4/4   Hospitality 5/5   Food 7.5/9   Value 2/2

- **American/Southern**
- **Calumet Park**
- **$$**

12401 S. Ashland Ave.
Calumet Park
(708) 385-3100
**Troubleshooter:** Charlie
Taylor (chef/owner)

**Hours:** Brunch Sun noon-3:45
pm, lunch Tues-Fri 11 am-3
pm, dinner Tues-Thurs 4-9 pm,
Fri-Sat until 10 pm, Sun 5-9 pm
**Cards:** AE, MC, VISA
**Reservations:** For 5 or more
**Handicapped:** Accessible
**Bar:** Full
**Parking:** Free lot
**Party Facilities:** Private
section in dining room
**Heart-Healthy Menu:**
Selections available

**W**hen the taste strikes for old-fashioned Southern cooking,
Gulfport Diner is the place to be. This really is a diner, with a long
counter plus booths and tables scattered about. Chef/Owner Charlie
Taylor trained as a French chef, but when it came time to open his
own restaurant, he returned to his roots.

Specialties such as ham hocks or red beans and rice, deep-fried
catfish, and shrimp jambalaya are all the rage here. Though some
spiciness appears in New Orleans-style jambalaya, the influences are
more deep Dixie than Creole or Cajun Louisiana. It is not unusual to
find a fine shrimp étoufée or blackened steak or chicken as an eve-
ning special. But it is with something like smoked rib tips and corn-
bread that old Southern style shines.

But there is a touch of modernity on the menu. Vegetarians are
now catered to with a platter that includes whatever is fresh and
good, especially okra, when it's available. And you can bet the sea-
sonings will be delicious.

# GUSTO ITALIANO
KR 18/20
Decor 3/4   Hospitality 4.5/5   Food 8.5/9   Value 2/2

- **Italian**
- **Glenview**
- **$$**

1470 Waukegan Rd. (Carillon
  Square)
Glenview
(708) 729-5444
**Troubleshooters:** Ciro
Esposito and Debbie Dubin
(owners)

**Hours:** Mon-Thurs 11 am-10
pm, Fri-Sat until 11 pm, Sun
4-9 pm
**Cards:** AE, DINERS, MC,
VISA
**Reservations:** For 5 or more
**Handicapped:** Accessible
**Bar:** Full
**Parking:** Lot
**Party Facilities:** For 20-125

**R**eaders of earlier editions of this book may remember Seven
Hills. Although it went out of business a few years ago, its influence
is still being felt at Gusto Italiano, where family members are continu-
ing some culinary traditions. The influence of Seven Hills becomes
immediately apparent as soon as you are seated and a basket of din-
ner rolls is brought to the table. These are crusty hard rolls with a soft
doughy center, all buttery and studded with bits of fresh-roasted gar-
lic. There's not a better dinner roll anywhere.

Fight off the temptation posed by the rolls and think about a selec-
tion of appetizers. If the choice is too tough, which it could be, order
a house platter. You'll get delicious baked clams, hot spinach bread,
deep-fried mozzarella cheese with a crumb coating, and a buttery ar-
tichoke with a light breading. If that's not enough for the trencher-
men at your table, try an order of fried calamari, or scungilli salad.
The restaurant will even take a dinner-size portion of eggplant roll-
atini and cut it down to appetizer size. That rollatini is scrumptious,
pancake-thin layers of pounded eggplant rolled around a filling of
ricotta cheese and spinach, topped with mozzarella and a tangy
tomato sauce.

The Gusto Italiano dinner menu is otherwise rather conventional
on first reading. But the cooking belies anything prosaic. Consider
chicken Vesuvio, with its crisp skin over a quarter of a fryer, sauteed
in garlic butter, served with roasted potatoes, the meat pinpointed

with bits of garlic. There is nothing greasy or oily about this chicken Vesuvio.

The pastas are excellent. Linguine with clam sauce is another classic, with most of the liquid drained away, leaving the bits of clam meat clinging to the fresh cooked pasta.

Be sure to save room for desserts. A house special not listed on the menu is a double chocolate Italian torte. Other choices include four kinds of cheesecake, some ice creams, torte Inglese, and a luscious Grand Marnier torte.

# HANS' BAVARIAN LODGE
KR 19/20

Decor 3.5/4   Hospitality 5/5   Food 8.5/9   Value 2/2

- **German**
- **Wheeling**
- **$$**

931 N. Milwaukee Ave.
Wheeling
(708) 537-4141
**Troubleshooter:** Jane
Berghoff (owner)

**Hours:** Lunch Tues-Fri 11:30 am-4 pm, dinner Tues-Thurs 4-10 pm, Fri-Sat until 11 pm, Sun noon-9 pm
**Cards:** All majors
**Reservations:** Suggested
**Handicapped:** Accessible
**Bar:** Full, specializing in German beers and wines
**Parking:** Free lot
**Party Facilities:** For up to 125

**H**ans' Bavarian Lodge looks and feels right for a German restaurant, without too much kitsch. Waitresses bustle about in their dirndl costumes, shuttling back and forth from bar or kitchen to dining areas. The menu offers some surprises for a German restaurant, such as crab cakes as a hot appetizer, and even shrimp de jonghe. Try a combination platter that includes the crab cakes, stuffed hot mushrooms, and rounds of deep-fried onion rings. A large stein of Berghoff beer is the perfect accompaniment.

Even without an à la carte appetizer, the full dinners are prodigious. A cold relish platter is the first thing set out on your table. The dinners also include salad, delicious warm light rye bread by the loaf, even soup or juice. The liver dumpling soup is a flavorful, semi-clear broth with a tasty dumpling settled at the bottom of the bowl.

The restaurant features a handful of nightly specials, but the regular menu is tempting enough. Consider any of the veal schnitzels; egg-battered and fried wiener schnitzel; natur schnitzel Berghoff sauteed in butter with mushrooms, white wine, and lemon juice; schnitzel à la Bremen, with mushrooms and Marsala; or the cream-enriched rohm schnitzel. A combination platter will bring a large portion of the wiener schnitzel, plus delicious beef rouladen, which is steak wrapped around a filling of bacon and seasoned breading, all in a dark natural gravy. Sauerbraten, slices of beef marinated in spices, red wine, herbs, and ginger for added bite, is a genuine favorite.

Other entrees include roast duck with sage stuffing, Hungarian goulash that gives new meaning to stew, German pot roast, lamb and pork shanks, plus fresh fish, steaks, and chicken. Desserts include such classics as apple strudel and kirschwasser torte.

# HARRY CARAY'S
KR 17.5/20
Decor 4/4   Hospitality 4/5   Food 7.5/9   Value 2/2

- **American/Italian**
- **Chicago/Near North**
- **$$$**

33 W. Kinzie St.
Chicago
(312) H-O-L-Y-C-O-W
**Troubleshooter:** Manager on duty

## Other Location

933 N. Milwaukee Ave.
Wheeling
(708) 537-2827; Lunch Mon-Fri 11 am-4 pm, dinner 4-10 pm, Fri & Sat until 11, Sun until 9; party facilities for up to 60

**Hours:** Lunch Mon-Fri 11:30 am-4 pm, Sat-Sun (bar only) noon-4 pm, dinner Mon-Thurs 5-10:30 pm, Fri-Sat until midnight, Sun 4-10 pm
**Cards:** All majors
**Reservations:** Preferred for lunch, taken for dinner for 8 or more
**Handicapped:** Accessible
**Bar:** Full bar 60'6" long (the distance from the pitcher's rubber to home plate)
**Parking:** Valet, street, and lot
**Party Facilities:** For 15-500

**J**ust for the record, Harry is more inspiration than restaurateur. But the restaurant that bears his name is run by competent professionals and must be judged on that basis.

The menu is a mix of meat, fish, and some Italian specialties. Service is cordial, with just the right amount of personality. Right out of the batter's box, from a selection of appetizers including carpaccio, shrimp cocktail, roasted peppers, and fresh or baked clams, try an excellent seafood salad. The portion is large enough for two to split, fresh with cold squid, perhaps some codfish, shrimp, and other seafood, all in an oil and vinegar herbed and seasoned dressing. Less successful is toasted ravioli. Toasting defeats the whole purpose of the pasta, which is meant to be tender, not crisp.

Things get back to high ground as you begin to round the bases of entrees. From a list of pastas and other Italian specialties, spaghetti carbonara is a solid hit. Linguine is bathed in a full-flavored sharp cheese sauce that clings to each strand. Bits of bacon are tossed into this classic recipe. A couple of turns of fresh cracked pepper, and it's better than a seat in the bleachers.

If you like lamb, you'll love a trio of lamb chops oreganato. These are simply broiled chops, meaty, with little or no fat, and the kind of flavor for which you'd trade away your best shortstop.

Among meat selections, veal piccante is a major leaguer on any team. This veal can be a bit light on buttery sweetness, though it's tender enough to be a two-bagger. Batting cleanup at Harry Caray's are the steaks and chops, a full lineup from porterhouse to peppered.

Rounding third and heading for home are desserts, piled high on a three-layer cart, just waiting to be picked for your all-star team. They range from apple tarts to chocolate tortes and pumpkin cheesecakes.

# HA SHALOM
KR 19/20
Decor 3/4   Hospitality 5/5   Food 9/9   Value 2/2

---

- **Middle Eastern/Israeli/Moroccan**
- **Chicago/Far North**
- **$**

2905 W. Devon Ave.
Chicago
(312) 465-5675
**Troubleshooter:** Jacques Zrihen (owner)

**Hours:** Mon-Thurs noon-9 pm, Sat-Sun 4-10 pm, closed Fridays
**Cards:** None
**Reservations:** Taken
**Handicapped:** Accessible
**Bar:** No liquor, customers may bring their own
**Parking:** Street

---

For all its ethnic diversity, Chicago has not given diners much in the way of Moroccan food; not, that is, until Ha Shalom. In the neighborhood one can find Russian groceries, Indian food stores, a Croatian cultural center, Hasidic Jews, and even a Thai restaurant, all on the same block. Ha Shalom closed down for a time, then re-opened about a block from its original location. Its menu has stayed largely intact – a spectrum of offerings ranging from an Israeli-style breakfast of tomatoes, peppers, and cheeses, to American-style pancakes and omelettes, sandwiches, and salads, to Moroccan couscous (served only on Saturday nights).

The couscous alone is worth a special visit! Couscous begins with steamed millet that serves as a bed for a variety of tastes. At Ha Shalom, the couscous is made with chicken, although some people prefer lamb because its fat adds flavor that chicken cannot. In any event, vegetables such as carrots, garbanzo beans, tomatoes, and turnips may find their way into the mix. Seasoning often includes the likes of cinnamon and cloves, with perhaps some saffron, cumin, and other aromatics.

Perhaps even tastier, and available every day, is stuffed Cornish hen. The hen is split, its cavity stuffed with a mixture of almonds, raisins, apricots, and rich seasonings. There's turmeric and saffron, to be sure, as well as other tastes in the blend, all bound together in sticky honey that glazes the roasted bird and all its stuffing. This is sybaritic, self-indulgent dining at its best.

Dinners can begin with a choice of à la carte appetizers; our waitress suggested a platter of hummus and pureed smoked eggplant, deep-fried balls of ground chickpeas called felafel, and a refreshing coarse chop of cucumber and tomato with just a hint of coriander for added zest. Desserts range from Levantine baklava to a simple fruit compote.

# HAT DANCE
KR 18.5/20
Decor 3.5/4  Hospitality 5/5  Food 8.5/9  Value 1.5/2

- **Mexican/ Contemporary**
- **Chicago/Near North**
- **$$**

325 W. Huron St.
Chicago
(312) 649-0961
**Troubleshooter:** John Buchanan (managing partner)

**Hours:** Lunch Mon-Fri 11:30 am-2 pm, dinner Mon-Fri 5:30-10 pm, Sat 5-11:30 pm, Sun 5-9 pm
**Cards:** All majors
**Reservations:** Accepted
**Handicapped:** Accessible
**Bar:** Full, plus juice bar
**Parking:** Valet evening hours
**Heart-Healthy Menu:** Selections available

**H**at Dance appeals to the sophisticated tastes of people who delight in the unexpected. Much like the neighboring art galleries in River North, the restaurant is a showcase for intriguing images and textures – in this case, white on white or white on silver, suggestive of Mexican or Aztec designs. There is a great deal of bustle, and hardly any effort to cut down on the conversational noise of a busy restaurant that seats more than 200. That doesn't include the bar, with room for another 150 or so.

Of course, it is the food that sets Hat Dance apart. In addition to traditional dishes, Mexican cuisine is reinterpreted with fresh approaches, from the classic pollo en mole to Mexican pizzas, as well as smoked chicken, seafood, and crab-cake quesadillas. Among appetizers, try queso fundido, not made with traditional Chihuahua cheese, but with velvety smooth goat's cheese. It comes out in a small skillet in which the cheese and a tingling, but not burning, hot pepper sauce have been warmed. Spread on a bit of tortilla, it is fantastic. The restaurant offers several different ceviches, and even some Japanese-influenced sashimi, plus steak or salmon tartare. Both of the latter are a bit on the bland side.

That's hardly the case with some of the entrees. Tuna asada is unforgettable. A good-sized cut of tuna steak is grilled, but left rare in the center, then napped with a chili sauce and papaya relish. The fish is as mild and clean as can be. Blindfolded, one might mistake this for rare beefsteak. For anyone who loves seafood, this is not to be missed.

Other standout entrees include carne asada, a tender strip steak in a mole-style sauce, or whole wood-roasted chicken with a trimming of assorted vegetables and a rubbing of ground chilies and other seasonings for flavor accent.

Do not ignore dessert. Cinnamon pudding has a light citrus-flavored underpinning. And, if offered, the chocolate tostada should not be missed. Two granola-like cookies simulate the tostadas, with a center filling of white chocolate mousse, all resting in a pool of mango sauce.

Hat Dance is always busy, but if you come for dinner before 6:30, you should be able to waltz right in. Otherwise, prepare for a long wait.

# HATSUHANA
KR 20/20
Decor 4/4   Hospitality 5/5   Food 9/9   Value 2/2

- **Japanese**
- **Chicago/Near North**
- **$$$**

160 E. Ontario St.
Chicago
(312) 280-8287
**Troubleshooter:** Poshifumi Mukai (manager)

**Hours:** Lunch Mon-Fri 11:30 am-2 pm, dinner Mon-Fri 5:30-10 pm, Sat 5-10 pm
**Cards:** AE, DINERS, MC, VISA, JCB
**Reservations:** Suggested
**Handicapped:** Accessible
**Bar:** Full, sake and Japanese beers
**Parking:** Public lots
**Party Facilities:** For up to 50

**H**atsuhana manages to offer a serenity present in only one or two other Japanese restaurants in the city. The restaurant is decorated with white walls accented with blond wood trim. Individual tables accommodate small groups, and a 25-seat sushi bar lets diners watch the sushi masters at their culinary artistry.

Sushi can be ordered à la carte or in fixed-price combinations that offer samples of several different styles. Should you find the idea of eating raw seafood unpleasant, start with something easy, such as chopped tuna and scallions. This is much like a seafood version of steak tartare, but with mild oriental seasonings adding to the flavor. Then work up to other choices, usually served in bite-sized pieces on a wedge of vinegared rice and wrapped in a sheet of dried seaweed. Or you might try something more open-faced, seasoned with a dab of hot green wasabi horseradish and a bit of pickled ginger, sliced paper thin.

In addition to the selections of sushi and sashimi, Hatsuhana serves complete lunches and dinners with soup, pickled vegetables, rice, and tea. À la carte selections will raise your tab, but they will also give you the chance to work through the menu and try some of the more exotic fare. More conservative diners may want to stay with tempura, lobster, or steak, but whatever you choose, Hatsuhana is the best of its kind in Chicago.

# THE HELMAND
KR 18.5/20
Decor 4/4   Hospitality 4.5/5   Food 8/9   Value 2/2

- **Middle Eastern/ Afghan**
- **Chicago/Mid-North**
- **$$**

3201 N. Halsted St.
Chicago
(312) 935-2447
**Troubleshooters:** Abdul Karzai and Fozia K. Royan (owners)

**Hours:** Mon-Thurs 5-10:30 pm, Fri-Sat until 11:30 pm, Sun 4-9 pm
**Cards:** AE, CB, DINERS, MC, VISA
**Reservations:** Recommended
**Handicapped:** Accessible
**Bar:** Full
**Parking:** Street
**Party Facilities:** Weeknights for 20 or more

I knew we were in for something special at the Helmand when our waiter poured a steaming cup of tea, then sprinkled what looked like pepper into the cup. He quickly explained it was ground cardamom, a fact readily proved by its pungent aroma and taste.

Though Afghan food is suggestive of Indian and Middle Eastern cuisines, it soon becomes apparent that this cookery really stands on its own. One will find things on the menu that suggest neighboring countries, but this only brings to mind the crosscurrents of history that have shaped these lands over the centuries. Thus, what Mogul conquerors brought to India may have come from Afghanistan or neighboring Persia. Where Indian seasonings may be more complex, there is a purity of flavors that runs through the Afghan foods offered diners at the Helmand.

The restaurant is handsomely furnished and decorated, with patterned wallpapers, white napery, and chandelier lighting. Though wines and mixed drinks are offered, the hot, cardamom-spiced tea is a perfect beverage. Dinner portions are such that it is probably a good idea to order appetizers. All are tantalizing. Kaddo borawni is sugared cubes of baby pumpkin, pan fried and served with a mild yogurt and garlic sauce. The same yogurt sauce also appears in a fried eggplant appetizer that tastes entirely different. Add an order of fried ravioli-style pastries called aushak, filled with leeks and accented with yogurt and mint. This comes served in a lightly flavored meat sauce.

Soups and salad courses may also be ordered, any of which are typically exotic and aromatic. Entrees stress meats, especially lamb, though beef and chicken are also offered. Typical might be kabuli, a deliciously seasoned platter of lamb tenderloin on a bed of flavored rice lavished with raisins and sweet-glazed julienne carrots. Dwopiaza, a saute of lamb with yellow peas and onions, seems somewhat under-flavored compared to many of the other dishes. But murgh challow, a saute of two pieces of chicken on rice with a seasoning of mixed spices and pepper in a lush red gravy, is more assertive. Other entrees include an Afghan version of shish kebab and dinner-sized portions of a few of the appetizers.

Dessert choices include sweetened ricotta cheese with ground pistachios, as well as a thin custard, which our waiter said was made without eggs.

# HIMALAYA
KR 17.5/20
Decor 2.5/4   Hospitality 4/5   Food 9/9   Value 2/2

- **Indian**
- **Chicago/Far North**
- **$**

6410 N. Rockwell
Chicago
(312) 761-5757
**Troubleshooter:** Tikka Ram
Sharma (owner)

**Hours:** Lunch (buffet) daily
11:30 am-3:30 pm, dinner Sun-
Thurs 5-10 pm, Fri-Sat until
11 pm
**Cards:** AE, MC, VISA
**Reservations:** Accepted
**Handicapped:** Accessible
**Bar:** Service bar, featuring
Indian beers
**Parking:** Street and city lot
**Party Facilities:** Entire
restaurant available

**H**imalaya is only a storefront, but the cooking by Chef/Owner
Tikka Ram Sharma is on a level that speaks of something substan-
tially more interesting. Service may not be up to quite the same
level, due more to inexperience, perhaps, than indifference. But for
those who have a working familiarity with Indian dining, there
should be no real problems.

The menu features most of the usual appetizer finger foods common on an Indian menu in Chicago, including the fried dumplings
known as pakoras and samosas. We passed them up in favor of
what the menu simply calls the Himalaya appetizer. The platter holds
bites of various styles of lamb and chicken in a delectable and satisfying gravy. Indian food depends upon aromatic seasonings such as
cardamom, poppy seed, ginger, saffron, and fenugreek. These
should not be combined haphazardly but should establish an identity
that contributes to the whole. I think Himalaya comes as close to
achieving that goal as any Indian restaurant I know in Chicago.

We found this to be true in a trio of entrees, particularly the vegetables. Since so many millions of Indians live on a vegetarian diet, it
should come as no surprise that the culture treats vegetables so well.
Thus, a purée of chickpeas comes in one small container, comple-
mented with another that holds mixed vegetables in a smooth sauce
enriched with an Indian version of cottage cheese and butter. A third
has a mildly seasoned eggplant.

Himalaya features the usual array of tandoor-roasted meats and
chicken, though portions tend to be rather small. Among curries, a

tomato sauce gives its red cast to chicken that has been cooked down with other ingredients to a near pulp. While some dishes are hot, the seasonings in this version are fairly mild, though hardly timid. Other dishes include a splendid version of rogan josh, a stew-like lamb in a sauce that speaks of many influences.

The point is that there is an astute hand and palate at work with the seasonings and spices in the Himalaya kitchen. Though the restaurant offers nothing distinctive in atmosphere, and service seems to have a mind of its own, the food is so commendable that the restaurant deserves praise.

# HOME
KR 18.5/20
Decor 3.5/4   Hospitality 5/5   Food 8/9   Value 2/2

- **American**
- **Chicago/Near North**
- **$$**

733 N. Wells St.
Chicago
(312) 951-7350
**Troubleshooter:** Joan Kurlan (owner)

**Hours:** Breakfast Mon-Sat 8-11 am, Lunch Mon-Sat 11:30 am-3:00 pm, no dinner (coffee, tea, and scones are served daily, 9-11:30 am)
**Cards:** AE, MC, VISA
**Reservations:** None
**Handicapped:** Accessible
**Bar:** Full, unusual selection of beers
**Parking:** Nearby lots or street
**Party Facilities:** Entire restaurant available

Its name suggests that Home is the kind of place where Mom's apple pie sits out on the back windowsill to cool and where checked gingham tablecloths are the major decor. But more about Home is revealed by its address – in the upstart gallery district of River North, where fashion and clubs go hand in hand.

Bare brick walls and scuffed, wood-planked flooring set the decor, though the food is not as minimalist as its surroundings suggest. The menu, which changes almost daily, leans toward contemporary cookery, without any particular limitations. One day could bring a richly flavored garlic flan at rest in a cream-enriched herb sauce. The same menu might include a fairly simple chicken-and-vegetable soup thickened by the likes of chopped carrots and tomatoes, with whole beans amidst the chunks of chicken. The idea does not seem to be simplicity for its own sake, but rather a free hand at recipe preparation, which may or may not involve certain complexities.

Consider an entree such as steak au poivre, in a mild-flavored mushroom cream sauce. Accompanying the meat is a version of soufflé potatoes, which the menu designates as custard potatoes, and a flourish of fresh broccoli, which adds color to the plating.

Escolar, a warm-water fish much like grouper in taste and fleshiness, shows up with a collection of sauteed orange bell peppers, a Niçoise olive sauce, peas in the pod, and yellow squash, plus lightly oiled garlic fettuccine. Nothing is overwhelmed or overwhelming, but the combination makes for satisfaction. Even better is sand dab, which, on a recent menu, had been dredged in crushed almonds and sauteed to a golden light crispness, then served along with a couple of shrimp, saffron rice, and French-style green beans.

No restaurant worth its menu cover ignores pasta. At Home, fettuccine has been served with a boned grilled chicken breast and bacon along with goat's cheese, spinach, and scallions. Though it sounds excessively rich, everything is kept in balance. Other entrees might include a vegetarian platter, which combines a red bell pepper stuffed with spinach and corn custard, napped in a mushroom sauce and plated alongside pinto-bean chili and snap peas in the pod.

# HONDA
KR 16.5/20
Decor 4/4   Hospitality 4/5   Food 7/9   Value 1.5/2

- **Japanese**
- **Chicago/Near North**
- **$$$**

540 N. Wells St.
Chicago
(312) 923-1010
**Troubleshooter:** George de la Garza (manager)

**Hours:** Lunch Mon-Fri 11:30 am-2 pm, dinner Sun-Thurs 5-10 pm, Fri 5:30-10 pm, Sat 5-11 pm, closed holidays
**Cards:** All majors
**Reservations:** Suggested
**Handicapped:** Accessible
**Bar:** Full
**Parking:** Free valet parking
**Party Facilities:** For up to 300, private tatami rooms for small gatherings

**H**onda is one of the most elaborate and traditional Japanese restaurants in Chicago. Housed in a large pagoda, or temple-like building, the restaurant covers two floors of dining and bar space that includes two sushi bars, private tatami rooms, and conventional seating arrangements. The atrium lobby towers up to a third level and is highlighted by an indoor waterfall that cascades into a traditional Japanese pool and garden. Traditional as are the setting and food, service people speak perfect English, so there is no confusion about how or what to order. At the same time, I suspect that visitors from Japan would feel as comfortable at Honda as they might in Tokyo or Osaka.

The tradition begins with a welcoming hand towel, steam-warmed and refreshing. After drink orders are taken, menus are presented that list a variety of à la carte and special dinner choices. Sushi and sashimi selections are as varied as any in Chicago. Presentations reflect the Japanese concern for artistry and balance. A combination platter will have an artful arrangement that might include various fish, roes, and vegetables ranging from pickled radish roots to avocado, cucumber, or seasoned tofu. Other appetizer or entree choices include lightly battered tempura, yakitori, and teriyaki, plus soups and side vegetables.

Honda is one of the few Japanese restaurants here that serve shabu-shabu. This elaborate dinner is traditional for festive occasions. A large silvered cooking pot is brought to the table and set over a gas burner. Water flavored with pieces of kelp is brought to a rolling boil. Then, carrots, scallions, tofu, enoki, and shiitake mushrooms, spinach leaf, and other ingredients are cooked for a few minutes. Finally, the heart of shabu-shabu, thin slices of marbled prime beef, are presented on a platter. The idea is to take a slice of beef with chopsticks and quickly swish it through the boiling broth. The meat should be just barely cooked when it is dipped into either a soy base or sesame sauce, then eaten. Finally, the cooked vegetables themselves can be taken from the boiling liquid and eaten either alone or on top of a bowl of rice.

Honda is definitely a restaurant for special occasions, yet even newcomers to Japanese dining will come away with a sense of refreshment, and maybe even tranquility.

# IT'S GREEK TO ME
KR 18.5/20
Decor 4/4   Hospitality 5/5   Food 9/9   Value 1.5/2

• **Greek**
• **Chicago/Near West**
• **$$**

306 S. Halsted St.
Chicago
(312) 977-0022
**Troubleshooter:** Victor
Salafatinos (owner)

**Hours:** Daily 11 am-midnight
**Cards:** All majors, house accounts
**Reservations:** Suggested
**Handicapped:** Accessible
**Bar:** Full, large selection of Greek wines
**Parking:** Free valet parking
**Party Facilities:** For up to 65

The saying "it's Greek to me" is used to designate confusion or ignorance. But at this restaurant there is no confusion at all about the good cooking and festive air. The restaurant is as handsome as any on the Greek Town strip, and more so than many. Its terraced, spacious dining area, bright and airy, gives one the feel of outdoors. All that is missing is the feel of the Mediterranean sun and its warmth overhead.

The fact is that many of Chicago's Greek restaurants are about equal, doing a generally good job, even though some cater more to tourists than others. It's Greek to Me is one of the few that seem determined to win and keep an ethnic Greek-American business.

The menu is somewhat more expansive than a lot of other Greek restaurants', presenting specialty dishes beyond the usual pastitsios, moussakas, gyros, and the like. If you want to try a bit of this and that as you sit down for dinner, order a combination of appetizers. Within minutes, a platter laden with tidbits will be brought forth from the kitchen. There will be some fish roe spread called taramosalata, and its garlic-laden cousin, skordelia. Both are fantastic when spread like cream cheese on hard-crusted bread. Savor the spinach pie with the jaw-breaking name spanakotiropita in its oiled phyllo crust. Some dolmades, grape leaves stuffed with ground meat and rice, are great when eased down with a bit of wine. For more gusto, taste the melitzanosalata, an eggplant salad like a French country concasse. Then there are simple little delights like lima beans and wedges of feta cheese with tomatoes.

You could order a combination dinner platter, too, for a taste of the staples. But try something more adventurous. Lamb exohiko stuffs the meat with artichoke hearts, pine nuts, feta cheese, tomatoes, and peas. Try it as souvlaki, shish kebab style. Or order lamb gemisto for about $7.95, stuffed with a forcemeat of ground beef laden with pine nuts and raisins in a wrapping of the lamb itself.

Seafood is a natural for Greek restaurant cooking. Among several choices of soft and shellfish, shrimp Mediterranean is a delicious blend of seasonings in a cream-based wine sauce, the whole shrimp absorbing all the flavors. Desserts range from baklava to custards.

Service is courteous and on the mark, although sometimes it can be just a little rushed.

# JACKIE'S

KR 19/20

Decor 4/4   Hospitality 5/5   Food 8/9   Value 2/2

- **American/Eclectic**
- **Chicago/Mid-North**
- **$$$**

2478 N. Lincoln Ave.
Chicago
(312) 880-0003
**Troubleshooter:** Jackie Shen
(chef/owner)

**Hours:** Lunch Tues-Sat 11:30 am-1:30 pm, dinner Tues-Thurs 5:45-8:30 pm, Fri-Sat 5:30-9:30 pm
**Cards:** All majors
**Reservations:** Mandatory
**Handicapped:** Accessible
**Bar:** Full
**Parking:** Valet
**Party Facilities:** Sunday and Monday

The cooking of Chef/Owner Jackie Shen is opulent, matching the stylized richness of her restaurant. One-half of the restaurant is draped in heavy earthtone swags, while the other half creates a more open, though no less comfortable, setting. A pianist provides music – not so much cocktail-style tinkling, but more the likes of Beethoven or Schumann.

The fairly short printed menu is expanded by a large selection of daily offerings. These are recited almost lovingly by a waiter whose familiarity with good food speaks of polished professionalism.

The cooking strikes a graceful balance between East and West. An appetizer of Chinese sauteed wontons may be served with shredded cabbage, shiitake mushrooms, and a mild ginger butter sauce. The fillings might also be influenced by contemporary food fashion, a mix of sun-dried tomatoes, goat's cheese, and snails with fresh bits of garlic and shreds of basil leaf. Or consider Jackie's approach to a seasonal delight, soft-shell crabs. In this version, the crabs receive the expected butter saute. In an appetizer portion one crab comes on an oversized platter, at the top of which is a cupped leaf of radicchio, serving as nest to Szechuan peppers fettuccine. A round of goat's cheese and small portion of salmon caviar are at the center of the platter, which is completed with asparagus spears and small shrimp.

Composition is at the heart of each presentation. In an appetizer of large morel mushrooms and snails, the key ingredients are set clockwise around the plate. At center is a mound of delicate basil linguine flavored with sun-dried tomatoes, garlic, the bite of scallions, and a truffle sauce for flavor depth, perhaps to complement the earthy morels.

Among choices from the printed dinner menu, Dover sole has been offered with scallop mousse. The sole rests on a puff pastry bed and julienne leeks. The mousse is wrapped inside twin rounds of the fish, napped by a yin and yang contrast of tomato butter and lemon butter sauces. The combinations, however, are without enough flavor intensity to be of great interest.

For dessert, a chocolate fudge tart topped with fresh raspberries demonstrates how perfect these flavor combinations can be. Service is slow, so be prepared for long waits between courses.

# JILLY'S CAFE
KR 18.5/20
Decor 3/4   Hospitality 5/5   Food 8.5/9   Value 2/2

- **Continental/American**
- **Evanston**
- **$$**

2614 Green Bay Rd.
Evanston
(708) 869-7636
**Troubleshooter:** Erich Rauch
(owner)

**Hours:** Lunch Tues-Fri 11:30 am-2 pm, Sun brunch 10:30 am-2 pm, dinner Tues-Thurs 5-9 pm, Fri-Sat until 10 pm, Sun until 8 pm
**Cards:** AE, MC, VISA
**Bar:** Full, 80 wine selections
**Parking:** Street
**Party Facilities:** Entire restaurant available

Jilly's Cafe is hardly bigger than a tiny storefront; tables place diners almost elbow to elbow. But as its name suggests, Jilly's is a café; if an air of informality exists, so be it. To say the cooking is notches above the ordinary is to damn with faint praise. Some choices are exceptional; virtually all are imaginative.

The menu changes regularly, always taking advantage of seasonal availability. The influence is contemporary, though without regard to national boundary. Thus morels, thought of as a French mushroom, fill out an Italian pasta as appetizer. Barbecued quail sounds quintessentially American, though it is matched with an oriental-style, sesame-flavored slaw of napa cabbage. Maryland's soft-shell crabs are also given an oriental spin, fried tempura-style and served with ponzu, a soy and citrus juice dipping sauce usually found at sushi bars. An American influence might be brought to bear in an appetizer pizza topped with Iowa's Maytag blue cheese and apple slices, an exciting contrast of flavors.

Entree offerings are equally imaginative. A dinner-sized Thai salad might be presented one evening. A deep bowl is filled with various Asian greens, ground peanuts, and the unmistakable flavors normally found at a Thai restaurant. Another entree might present grilled loin of lamb cut into small slices, fanned out on its platter with a mixed salad and a dressing that brings goat's cheese into the blend of oil and mild vinegar.

Jilly's Cafe will feature traditional French bistro-style steak and fries, but also something as interesting as grilled sturgeon with an anchovy sauce, or a risotto of roasted garlic and vegetables. Desserts are tempting to even the most selective of diners. Custards, fruit tarts, chocolate cakes, ice creams, and other indulgences are satiating selections.

# JIMMY'S PLACE
KR 19/20
Decor 4/4   Hospitality 5/5   Food 8.5/9   Value 1.5/2

- **Continental/American/ Eclectic**
- **Chicago/Northwest**
- **$$$**

3420 N. Elston Ave.
Chicago
(312) 539-2999
**Troubleshooter:** Jimmy Rohr (owner)

**Hours:** Lunch Mon-Fri 11:30 am-2 pm, dinner Mon-Sat 5-9:30 pm
**Cards:** CB, DINERS, MC, VISA, DISCOVER
**Reservations:** Suggested
**Handicapped:** Accessible
**Bar:** Full, excellent wine list
**Parking:** Free lot
**Party Facilities:** For 12, Greenhouse for up to 40 weekdays

**A**t first glance it would appear that fine dining at Jimmy's Place and heart-healthy dining are diametrically opposed. The menu seems almost awash with cheese, cream sauces, butter, and meats. But like the truly good restaurant it is, Jimmy's Place can accommodate just about any dining request.

Of course, if there is no reason to restrain yourself, an appetizer of wild mushrooms terrine, bound with cream, stuffed with dabs of goat's cheese, and bell peppers, then served with a curried mayonnaise would be luscious temptation indeed. Or, from the selection of entrees on the often-changing menu, there are sweetbreads with thin slices of chestnuts and a coating of fried brioche crumbs bedded on fresh spinach with a reduced Madeira wine sauce. Or consider filet of beef with an accompanying horseradish mousse, a stylized Bordelaise sauce, and the richness of bone marrow. Medallions of veal are paired on the menu with customized ravioli filled with Teleggio cheese, buttery and mild, served with bits of pancetta and pine nuts in a red pepper cream sauce. Unfortunately, in the only culinary flaw of a recent evening, a portion was overcooked.

A nightly special could bring slices of duck breast fanned out on the platter, bathed in a syrupy wine sauce, a pairing of fried and filled won tons with a bit of ginger soy and a mélange of cooked vegetables. The flavors are full and satisfying.

Because everything is made to order, Chef Kevin Shikami is able and willing to meet specialized needs and still display his talents. Tuna tartare needs no adaptation; it is splendidly flavored with ginger, bound with a crush of vegetables. Nor need there be revision for shrimp in a light, clear broth garnished with tomato pieces, slivers of scallion, celery, even an oyster for richness, and a crisp rice cake for balance. It is a typical example of the East-meets-West concept that has guided the cooking at Jimmy's Place since its opening 15 years ago.

As for specialized requests, steamed halibut came with a light stock, instead of the creamy lobster sauce it would otherwise be served with. An array of freshly cooked vegetables, still with texture and crunch, filled out the platter. Similarly, an order of steel eye salmon and swordfish are twinned, two very different fish in a preparation that would meet virtually any heart-healthy menu requirement.

Service is accommodating, almost to a fault. My request for milk with coffee instead of heavy cream created a delay of several minutes. When the milk came, I realized why: it had been heated.

# J.P.'S EATING PLACE
KR 17/20
Decor 3/4   Hospitality 5/5   Food 7/9   Value 2/2

- **Seafood/American**
- **Chicago/Mid-North**
- **$$**

1800 N. Halsted St.
Chicago
(312) 664-1801
**Troubleshooter:** Jorge Perez
(owner)

**Hours:** Mon-Thurs 11:30 am-10:30 pm, Fri-Sat until midnight, Sun until 10 pm
**Cards:** All majors
**Reservations:** Suggested
**Bar:** Full
**Parking:** Valet
**Party Facilities:** None
**Heart-Healthy Menu:** Designations

At first blush, J.P.'s Eating Place seems to be a somewhat upscale Mexican restaurant. The decor reflects such stylistic accents, as do some of the menu choices. But J.P.'s Eating Place is more the restaurant for fresh and varied seafood. "Varied" may really be the operative word. As soon as diners enter, they are confronted by a chalkboard listing that looks like a transoceanic guidebook.

You name the fish, and J.P.'s Eating Place probably has it. You can have it grilled, sauteed, sauced or not as you choose. And if a single choice is too difficult, considering the options, you can custom design a combination platter that brings a trio of choices.

One such tasting might include a selection of shrimp étouffée, tilapia, and grouper. The tilapia is sauteed to a golden glow, flaky and sweetly fresh. The grouper is meaty and firm, a good contrast to the tilapia. Shrimp étouffée is a variation of a spicy New Orleans specialty. Shrimp or crayfish is served with a highly seasoned and flavorful rice.

J.P.'s Eating Place also serves a version of paella that is as complex and savory as one could ask for. The restaurant offers a variety of steaks and chops, and even J.P.'s version of ribs.

# KATSU

KR 18.5/20

Decor 2.5/4   Hospitality 5/5   Food 9/9   Value 2/2

- **Japanese**
- **Chicago/Far North**
- **$$**

2651 W. Peterson Ave.
Chicago
(312) 784-3383
**Troubleshooters:** Katshishi
and Haruko Imamura (owners)

**Hours:** Daily 5 pm-1 am,
closed Tuesdays
**Cards:** AE, DINERS,
DISCOVER, MC, VISA
**Reservations:** Suggested
**Bar:** Full, Japanese beers, sake
**Parking:** Street
**Party Facilities:** For up to 40

**M**idway up the wall behind the sushi bar at Katsu are strips of parchment embellished with ornate calligraphy. What at first glance appears to be some kind of oriental art is in fact a menu of the various kinds of sushi or sashimi available on a given night.

Katsu draws a predominantly Japanese following. It also happens to be a very welcoming place even for the newcomer to Japanese foods. The sushi and sashimi, raw fish with or without vinegared rice, may seem intimidating at first. So start out with something easy, such as tomago, which is nothing more than a wedge of cooked egg on a mound of rice wrapped in seaweed. Move on to kappa makki, chopped cucumber in the center of a rice roll, again bound with seaweed.

Of all the sushi, shrimp and tuna are probably the easiest to start with. Both are meaty, clean tasting, and familiar. A mixed selection of sushi is prepared at an immaculately clean counter by the sushi chef. Take a seat at the sushi bar to watch, and converse as each piece is hand crafted in an age-old fashion. The finished pieces are presented on a decorative wood board with a mound of green and very hot wasabi mustard, plus thin slivers of pickled ginger. Use the wasabi and a little soy sauce to perk up your taste buds, and nibble on the ginger as a palate cleanser between each piece.

The sushi and sashimi can be ordered in combinations. Unfortunately, Katsu does not sell them by the piece, which makes it difficult to order one or two additional selections as an afterthought.

Katsu also offers some standard versions of cooked Japanese dinners. From among appetizers, take small beef roll-ups around sliced asparagus with sesame seeds. Or try delicious fried dumplings stuffed with ground beef and vegetables, called gyoza.

Grilled chicken, salmon, or beef choices are always tasty, as is the traditional Japanese one-pot meal, sukiyaki, a steaming broth filled with cooked leafy greens, slender translucent noodles, and thin strips of beef. Other selections include the house namesake, a deep-fried pork cutlet, plus various noodle soups and chowders.

Katsu could use a little cosmetic sprucing up; the paint has become scuffed, and the furnishings are nothing special. But service is as cheerful as can be, and a conversation with the sushi chef is a delight.

# KIKI'S BISTRO
KR 19.5/20
Decor 4/4   Hospitality 5/5   Food 8.5/9   Value 2/2

| | |
|---|---|
| • **French/Bistro** | **Hours:** Lunch Mon-Fri 11:30 am-2 pm, dinner Mon-Thurs 5-10 pm, Fri-Sat until 11 pm |
| • **Chicago/Near North** | |
| • **$$** | **Cards:** All majors |
| 900 N. Franklin St. | **Reservations:** Suggested |
| Chicago | **Handicapped:** Accessible |
| (312) 335-5454 | **Bar:** Full bar and lounge |
| **Troubleshooter:** Georges Cuisance (owner) | **Parking:** Valet |

One of the buzzwords on the restaurant scene of the early 1990s is "bistro." This comfortable French concept, which denotes a casual café setting, has been beautifully realized at Kiki's Bistro.

The menu appears complex and is rather extravagant by most bistro standards. But the basics are there, whether steak and wispy curls of crisp french fried potatoes, the rich aroma and presence of traditional baked onion soup, or the comfort of grilled calf's liver with tiny pearl onions, red cabbage, and the bite of a vinegared wine sauce.

However, Kiki's Bistro does not ignore contemporary tastes. Consider the bistro pizza topped with Niçoise olives, melted gorgonzola cheese, and roasted slices of red peppers. Goat's cheese makes an appearance in a ratatouille tart, while a traditional roasted duck and its confit gets the addition of a green peppercorn sauce.

The menu takes a somewhat different turn when a sturdy fish, such as grouper, is available. Recently the fish has been grilled in rather conventional manner, then unconventionally placed in an herbed fish stock which is drained off, leaving a bouillon with cooked vegetables. Herbs are used imaginatively in a version of roasted chicken, which is served with a side of old-fashioned mashed potatoes. Sliced leg of lamb is given an underpinning of eggplant compote bound with herbs and the seasoned juice from the roasting pan in which the lamb has been cooked.

Desserts include a delicious crème brûlée with chocolate center, as well as fresh berries, cream, and fruit tarts, and other pastries.

# KLAY OVEN
KR 16/20
Decor 4/4   Hospitality 4/5   Food 7.5/9   Value .5/2

- **Indian**
- **Chicago/Near North**
- **$$$**

414 N. Orleans St.
Chicago
(312) 527-3999
**Troubleshooters:** Pari and Brenda Gujral (owners)

**Hours:** Sun-Thurs 5-10:30 pm, Fri-Sat until 11:30 pm
**Cards:** AE, DINERS, MC, VISA
**Reservations:** Recommended
**Handicapped:** Accessible
**Bar:** Full, 30 imported beers, specialty drinks
**Parking:** Street and lots
**Party Facilities:** For 30-95, only afternoon hours
**Heart-Healthy Menu:** Selections

Aside from the fact that this is the most costly Indian restaurant in the city, from the moment you enter the Klay Oven it is apparent that this is an Indian restaurant different from virtually all others in Chicago. What with few exceptions has been storefront, neighborhood dining has been transformed into a more refined – and to be sure, more expensive – way of doing things. The restaurant is carpeted, and seating is at banquettes. Japanese shoji screens are illuminated from behind to add a soft, diffused light. It is a handsome surrounding, made even more so by the sweet, aromatic smells of Indian cookery.

The menu focuses on tandoor cookery, but not exclusively. The tandoor is a large clay urn in which foods are grilled, the heat generated by charcoal at the bottom. Tandoor cookery certainly is not new to Chicago, but Klay Oven's manner of service and presentation are. Oversized platters are set at tables; service is from rolling carts. Diners may choose from the list of à la carte appetizers or a combination platter that brings a pair of deep-fried prawns, skewered tandoori chicken, plus several deep-fried pakoras and samosas, Indian-style dumplings.

Klay Oven features two soups: traditional mulligatawny, a chicken-based broth with Indian seasonings, and a tomato soup highlighted by cumin. Neither is especially entrancing.

More than a dozen entrees are offered, most from the tandoor, some from the karhai, an Indian wok used for stir- or deep-frying. Virtually every entree we ordered was superbly seasoned and cooked. Rack of lamb from the tandoor and large prawns from the karhai were exceptional.

More traditional Indian selections, such as a lamb stew called rogan josh, or simple murgh chicken from the tandoor, were without fault. Rather than trying to overwhelm, the Klay Oven kitchen seems more intent on striking a flavor chord, only to let it dissipate naturally. It is certainly a more elegant, refined approach to Indian cuisine. All of this does not come without a price, sometimes excessive. For example, à la carte side vegetables range from $6 to $8, an amount that in many Indian restaurants can almost buy a full dinner. The wine list is similarly inflated, as well as pretentious.

# KONAK
KR 18/20

Decor 3.5/4   Hospitality 4.5/5   Food 8/9   Value 2/2

- **Turkish**
- **Chicago/Far North**
- **$**

5150 N. Clark St.
Chicago
(312) 271-6688
**Troubleshooter:** Art Akova
and Enver Ozbay (owners)

**Hours:** Tues-Sun 4-11 pm,
closed Mondays
**Cards:** AE, MC, VISA
**Reservations:** Weekends only
**Handicapped:** Accessible
**Bar:** Full
**Parking:** Street
**Party Facilities:** Entire
restaurant available for up to 50
except Fridays and Saturdays

The Ottoman Empire once ruled a vast stretch of the Near East, including Europe all the way to the gates of Vienna, so it was only natural that imprints of its culture were left behind. Traces of Ottoman cuisine can be found in central European strudels, with their phyllo crusts, or in eastern Europe's taste for ground lamb, as in Serbian cevapcici. But the current runs in both directions. Paprika from Hungary finds its ways into some Turkish recipes; wrapped grape leaves, hummus, and eggplant in any number of fashions are taken intact from the Levant and incorporated into the Turkish diet.

The crosscurrents that make Turkish cookery what it is are given delicious demonstration at Konak. A narrow room is festooned with rugs, handsome and eyecatching in their geometric patterns. Tables are covered in white, the light is dim; waiters wear white shirts and black bow ties. Their service is somewhat dilatory, but informative and friendly.

Dinners include a choice of soup or salad; à la carte appetizers deserve more than passing attention. Several feature a variety of stewed vegetables or legumes, glistening in olive oil, seasoned with subtle and often fragrant spices. A tart, but not sour, yogurt sauces both vegetables and meats as taste demands. Many appetizers are familiar Middle East staples. Hummus, the puree of ground chickpeas, is more pronounced in flavor than many others, though a fried zucchini pancake is rather dull, not the exciting little tidbit described on the menu.

Nonetheless, Konak is rich with inducements. A combination dinner platter offers tastes of beef and chicken in various forms: cubed, ground, char-broiled, some highly seasoned, some not. Any of the combination platter's ingredients can be ordered individually as an entree. My favorite is Konak kebabs, given an invigorating dose of ground peppers. Other entrees are more sybaritic. In two instances, your choice of chicken or lamb cubes is broiled in butter, cooked along with mild peppers and onions, wrapped in phyllo dough to form a large purse, which is then baked in an oven to a golden crispness. Inside the pastry, the meat simmers in the butter and its own juices and seasonings.

Konak serves beer and wine, but the aromatic Turkish tea seems a perfect accompaniment, exotically served from an ornamental platter suspended by three chains from the hands of your waiter. Desserts are syrupy and sweet.

# KUNI'S
KR 18/20
Decor 4/4   Hospitality 4/5   Food 8/9   Value 2/2

- **Japanese**
- **Evanston**
- **$$**

511 Main St.
Evanston
(708) 328-2004
**Troubleshooter:** Yuji Kunii
(owner)

**Hours:** Lunch Mon, Wed-Sat 11:30 am-2 pm, dinner Mon, Wed-Sun 5-9:45 pm
**Cards:** AE, MC, VISA
**Reservations:** For 6 or more
**Bar:** Service bar
**Parking:** Street; lot nearby charges $2
**Party Facilities:** Limited

The art of Japanese dining need not be confusing. The key is to find a restaurant that can serve as teacher and culinary guide. Kuni's fits that description. The experienced diner will find more than enough to enjoy, while the less experienced will find clear explanations at the sushi bar.

First off, Kuni's looks the way a Japanese restaurant should look. Handsome blond woodwork sets off the dining area and the sushi bar. You may choose a conventional table, though if you are a party of just two or three, I think the counter service at the sushi bar is more fun. For one thing, you can watch the sushi chefs at work as they delicately scribe patterns in vegetables and fish. When completed, the food is arranged and set out on a large scrubbed and polished wood block; view it as art, and then eat it. Diners may order sushi pieces à la carte or choose from a list of combination platters.

"Sushi" is any raw food served on a mound of rice, often, but not always, wrapped in an edible sheet of dry seaweed. "Sashimi" is the raw fish served with only wasabi horseradish and paper-thin slices of pickled ginger. Finally, there is chirashi, an assortment of sashimi served over a bowl of rice.

As for types of fish, they range from tuna to mackerel to eel, octopus, fluke, and many others. The fish served at Kuni's is fresh, firm-fleshed, without sponginess, and immaculately clean. As a general guideline, never accept any sushi or sashimi that has even the faintest odor of fishiness, which could indicate the start of spoilage.

Cooked entrees include tenkatsu, a breaded pork tenderloin that is as common on Japanese dinner tables as is chicken-fried steak in an American Southern diner.

Some people like to make complete meals of tempura, the deep-fried vegetables and shrimp brought to Japan in the sixteenth century by Portuguese traders. The best tempura should be pale in color, without any greasy residue; this is tempura at Kuni's. A trio of teriyaki dishes, grilled meat, or seafood is offered, as is the Japanese recipe best known in the West, sukiyaki. At Kuni's sukiyaki is created in a noticeably sweet broth, a flavor common to much Japanese cookery. Thin slices of steamed beef rest atop a mélange of cooked, but not soggy, oriental greens and other vegetables.

# LA BOHÈME
KR 19/20
Decor 3.5/4   Hospitality 5/5   Food 8.5/9   Value 2/2

- **French**
- **Winnetka**
- **$$$**

566 Chestnut (The Laundry Mall)
Winnetka
(708) 446-4600
**Troubleshooter:** Chris Skafidas (owner)

**Hours:** Lunch Tues-Sat 11:30 am-2:30 pm, dinner 6-10 pm
**Cards:** AE, CB, DINERS, MC, VISA, house accounts
**Reservations:** Required
**Handicapped:** Accessible
**Bar:** Service bar
**Parking:** Free lot
**Party Facilities:** For up to 25
**Heart-Healthy Menu:** Available at lunch

Since it opened in 1979, La Bohème has been one of the handsomest restaurants on the North Shore, with its French Provincial country warmth, its brick wall facings, copper cookware, and tapestry. But because food and service sometimes were hit and miss, I never considered the restaurant among the top rank. Not, that is, until the last couple of years, when a succession of chefs brought a new culinary freshness to the kitchen.

The menu changes with the seasons and offers à la carte as well as four-course prix fixe dining. Appetizer selections might include a mild seafood sausage with baby vegetables and Dijon mustard sauce, chicken ravioli with quenelles of wild mushrooms, or perhaps a crayfish bisque studded with floating saffron profiteroles.

Entrees with the prix fixe dinner can include roasted leg of lamb with a stylized ratatouille; veal medallions sauteed with lemon butter sauce that has been flavored with fresh basil; or, as a seafood choice, grilled Pacific ono with roasted potatoes served in a soy vinaigrette and chives. A house salad is included with all entrees, as is a choice of three desserts. Recently priced at around $25, the fixed-price dinner has been quite the bargain.

As for the à la carte menu, the selection is deeper. Features have included roasted red snapper and Gulf shrimps in a warm curry vinaigrette. Duck breast is roasted and served with spinach mousse and a raspberry sauce, which is a little too contrived. But sauteed venison medallions, when offered, are right on the mark with an onion marmalade and natural juice from dried fruit cooked down into the confit.

Desserts range from sabayon with fresh fruits and chocolate sauce to an elegant plat du surprise for two, which offers a trio of choices from the nightly listing.

Where service in the past at La Bohème has been often confused, though never rude, it now is more structured and better informed. The wine list is impressive, with such a depth of age and sensitivity that cost must often be a factor.

# LAC VIEN
KR 19/20
Decor 3.5/4   Hospitality 4.5/5   Food 9/9   Value 2/2

- **Vietnamese**
- **Chicago/Far North**
- **$**

1129 W. Argyle St.
Chicago
(312) 275-1112
**Troubleshooter:** Paul Nguyen
(owner)

**Hours:** Sun-Thurs 10 am-10 pm, Fri-Sat until 11 pm
**Cards:** DINERS, DISCOVER, MC, VISA
**Reservations:** Accepted
**Bar:** Service bar
**Parking:** Street

The Lac Vien menu is as complete as one will find in a Chicago Vietnamese restaurant. Like most oriental menus, it is divided into the various courses that make up a complete meal. There are certain "don't miss" selections. First and foremost are the guo cuon, or spring rolls. A tissue-thin rice-paper pancake wraps a firm filling of shrimp and pork pieces along with bean sprouts, cucumbers, and other vegetable snips to hold things together. The logic of spring rolls, particularly considering the tropical climate of Vietnam, is inescapable.

There is poetry in the presentation of foods at Lac Vien. What the menu describes as "grilled marinated beef slices and bean sprouts, cucumber, lettuce served with rice paper" is too prosaic a choice of words. A platter layered with several sheets of rice-paper pancakes is set next to another large platter mounded with shards of crisp, fresh lettuce leaves, firm romaine highlighted among them. Beneath the lettuce are slices of the cooked beef and assorted vegetables, to which, like the lettuce, the words "crisp and fresh" certainly apply. The idea is to take a pancake and mound all the ingredients inside, using the pancake as wrapper. A sweet pepper sauce, or peanut-based dark sauce, works to complement the flavors and contrasting textures.

For dessert, we were urged by our friend to order Vietnamese coffee, whose presentation is almost a ritual. Sweetened condensed milk covers the bottom of a tall glass. A French-style coffee filter sits atop, into which hot water is poured. The water leaches through ground coffee into the sugared milk. When done brewing, the coffee is thoroughly stirred and the glass topped off with ice. The result is one of the most refreshing ways of serving iced coffee I have ever encountered.

# LA GONDOLA
KR 18/20
Decor 4/4   Hospitality 5/5   Food 7/9   Value 2/2

- **Italian**
- **Chicago/Mid-North**
- **$$**

2425 N. Ashland Ave.
Chicago
(312) 248-4433
**Troubleshooters:** Dominic and Luciano (owners)

**Hours:** Mon-Sun 4-11 pm
**Cards:** AE, MC, VISA, DINERS
**Reservations:** Suggested
**Handicapped:** Accessible
**Bar:** Full
**Parking:** Valet, lot, and street
**Party Facilities:** Available

La Gondola genuinely encourages people to dine in the Italian manner: let each course dictate the next. In other words, order a first course, and when that is done, a second, and when that is done, a third, and so on until the end of the meal.

Begin dinner with wine; a semi-dry Orvieto complements a large antipasto platter practically overflowing with bounty. It includes lightly breaded, deep-fried slices of zucchini, baked clams, deep-fried baby calamari, and stuffed whole calamari.

Having taken your time with the antipasti, choose a pasta course. Your waitress brings a platter, presented family style.

The logic to ordering course by course suggests that only a glutton could choose too much food. Having finished two courses, and steaming bowls of minestrone, take some time before main course selections. Though La Gondola's is a rather standard-issue Italian menu, you are certain to find several items that will please. The most difficult part is deciding which ones.

Having been moderate about main course selections, you can still look forward to dessert. Bisque tortoni and cannolis are the perfect finishing touches. I have yet to find the restaurant that makes its bisque from scratch; at least La Gondola has a good supplier. Although the shells come from outside, the kitchen does do the sweet filling for the cannolis.

# LA LOCANDA
KR 17.5/20
Decor 4/4   Hospitality 4/5   Food 8/9   Value 1.5/2

| | |
|---|---|
| • **Italian/Northern** | **Hours:** Lunch Mon-Fri 11:00 am-2:30 pm, dinner Mon-Thurs 5:00-10:30 pm, Fri-Sat until 11:00 pm, Sun closed |
| • **Chicago/Near North** | |
| • **$$$** | |
| 743 N. LaSalle | **Cards:** AE, CB, DINERS, MC, VISA, house accounts |
| Chicago | |
| (312) 335-9550 | **Reservations:** Suggested |
| **Troubleshooters:** Anthony Vespa, Traca Volpi (owners) | **Bar:** Full |
| | **Parking:** Valet, lots |
| | **Party Facilities:** None |
| | **Heart-Healthy Menu:** Selections |

**N**ow that Chicago has discovered Northern Italian dining, it seems as if any place that can put together something approximating risotto considers itself expert in the field. The fact is that really good Northern Italian restaurants are few and far between.

One of the better ones is La Locanda, which serves the best risotto I know of in a Chicago restaurant. It is creamy without being milky, chewy without being tough. In one of several versions, the risotto was prepared with spinach and radicchio. The flavor was sharp but short of bitter. In another modification, the rice was prepared with a quartet of cheeses and delicious porcini mushrooms.

The menu points to those choices that are vegetarian, as well as those that are available for restricted diets and can be made without cheese, butter, or salt. It's the kind of awareness that is characteristic of better, healthier dining at minimum sacrifice to flavor. For example, tagliatelle is presented in a mild tomato sauce, lightly coated without pooling. Garlic and fresh arugula add flavor. In another variation, delicate angel-hair pasta, called capellini, is served with a mix of lightly cooked vegetables in a tomato sauce.

The cooking is understated; it is rare that any one flavor overwhelms others. Another example of this approach to cooking is calamari, or squid. More often than not, when calamari is featured on a restaurant menu, the dish is fried. At La Locanda, it is marinated in herbs and olive oil, then grilled. The flavor has a freshness that is obscured by frying.

This direct approach to cooking similarly appears in some of the entree selections. Broiled swordfish, that meatiest of all seafood, is marinated in oil with fresh chunked tomatoes, basil, a bouquet of other herbs, and garlic, of course. Lamb chops can be delicious, simply treated with a brush of oil and a trio of thyme, rosemary, and garlic. Ossobucco, or veal shanks, is about as Milanese as you can get. The shanks are dressed with a fine chop of vegetables in a stylized gremalada.

Desserts include tiramisu, gelati, and pastries.

# LANNA THAI
KR 17/20
Decor 3.5/4   Hospitality 4.5/5   Food 7/9   Value 2/2

- **Thai**
- **Chicago/Far North**
- **$**

5951 N. Broadway
Chicago
(312) 878-1155
**Troubleshooter:** Temi Sesi
(owner)

**Hours:** Mon-Sun noon-10 pm
**Cards:** AE, MC, VISA
**Reservations:** Accepted
**Handicapped:** Accessible
**Bar:** Full, Thai beers
**Parking:** Street

Lanna Thai is brightly lit and modestly decorated with art and arti-facts from the owners' Thai homeland. This is a good restaurant for newcomers to Thai food because the seasoning tends to be on the less peppery side of the scale. The negative side of that is that if you really want your food hot, it's difficult to get the owners to go along, appar-antly out of fear that you really do not know how hot, hot can be.

Satay is typical of Thai restaurants, seasoned grilled pork or chicken served in a spiced peanut sauce as an appetizer. Among other choices are egg rolls and spring rolls, noodles, squid tempura, and deep-fried tofu. The spring rolls are lightly steamed, filled with a mix of vegetables and mild oriental sausage, all stuffed inside the dough wrapping, picked up, and eaten like a taco. A sweet, syrupy sauce is a usual accompaniment.

The best appetizer is mee krob, deep-fried noodles that must be seen and tasted to be believed. Rice noodles are quickly stir-fried with meat and seasonings. The temptation is to snack on these like potato chips; the satisfaction is far greater.

After appetizers, try one of the soups, such as tom yum koong, with shrimp in a spiced broth. The flavors of lemon grass and pep-pers are most predominant, though at Lanna Thai this soup is only moderately hot.

Thai restaurants usually serve a variety of curries, not always as hot as their Indian inspirations. All Thai curries are made with a base of coconut milk, its sweetness playing on the tongue and palate in counterpoint to the other flavors competing for attention.

To round out a dinner, you might want one of the beef dishes, such as larb noor, with a mix of roasted rice and pieces of vegetable.

The real specialty is a whole deep-fried fish. Priced at market, this may push your check average up a bit higher, but it is well worth the few extra dollars. Red snapper comes with either a spicy sauce (not as spicy as you might fear) or a sweet and sour sauce for topping.

Lanna Thai is a good bridge to the unique food of Thailand in a style and setting that could make the less adventurous eater comfortable with the exotic.

# LA STRADA
KR 17.5/20
Decor 4/4   Hospitality 4.5/5   Food 7.5/9   Value 1.5/2

- **Italian/Northern**
- **Chicago/Loop**
- **$$$**

155 N. Michigan Ave. (at Randolph)
Chicago
(312) 565-2200
**Troubleshooters:** Michael Mormando (owner), Paolo Capobianco (maitre d')

**Hours:** Lunch Mon-Fri 11:30 am-2:30 pm, dinner Mon-Thurs 5-10 pm, Fri-Sat until 11 pm
**Cards:** All majors, house accounts
**Handicapped:** Accessible via elevator
**Bar:** Full, wine list has 230 selections
**Parking:** Valet
**Party Facilities:** For 20-600 people on 38th floor (Top of the Plaza)

**W**hen red tomato sauce, meatballs, and veal Parmigiana were centerpieces of Italian dining in Chicago, the opening of La Strada more than a decade ago helped mine a rich new vein from the Italian larder. Since then, of course, Northern Italian dining has set a new standard of excellence.

While the restaurant serves foods from most regions of Italy, the emphasis is on the north. More complex saucing replaces tomato, and subtler seasonings are not overpowered by garlic. In its richly appointed surroundings, La Strada has joined the first rank of restaurants in and around Chicago. Service is lavish, with enough space between tables for a degree of privacy and for waiters and captains to do tableside preparation. Veal gets prominent treatment, as is fitting in better Italian dining. Veal piccata is the expected thin scallops finished in butter and lemon sauce. The house namesake, scaloppine di vitello della Strada, comes from Italy's middle regions. Scallops of veal are cooked with prosciutto, fontina cheese, and the bite of lemon.

The restaurant regularly offers four styles of risotto to supplement its pasta selections. Chicken, chops, and seafood make up a large selection of house specialties.

# LA TOUR
KR 16.5/20
Decor 4/4   Hospitality 3.5/5   Food 7.5/9   Value 1.5/2

- **French/Nouvelle**
- **Chicago/Near North**
- **$$$**

Park Hyatt Hotel, 800 N. Michigan Ave.
Chicago
(312) 280-2230
**Troubleshooter:** Pierre Lasserre (maitre d')

**Hours:** Sun brunch 11:30 am-2 pm, lunch daily 11:30 am-2 pm, dinner daily 6-10 pm
**Cards:** All majors, house accounts
**Reservations:** Required
**Handicapped:** Accessible
**Bar:** Full, extended wine list
**Parking:** Valet
**Heart-Healthy Menu:** Separate menu called "Cuisine Naturelle"

As good as it can be, La Tour offers some uneven service and a cuisine that, while inventive, is not always memorable. Servers are there when summoned, but only if you can catch their eye. Small details, such as bread basket and water refills, should be automatic. And there is a detached sort of style, not the kind of warm hospitality that is the difference between someone merely doing his job and someone doing his job with pleasure and enthusiasm.

With that said, the primary attention, aside from the splendid views out the spacious windows at the Water Tower and handsome neoclassic dining room of La Tour, remains Chef Charles Weber's cuisine. Weber cooks with flair tempered by restraint. When he is at his best, his dishes will not so much assault the senses as they will flirt and suggest.

Consider an appetizer, roast quail with noodles and curry oil. The small bird is easily broken apart, the meat mild, maybe even close to bland. The noodles add little flavor, and even the curry oil is hardly noticed. More assertive is well-spiced shrimp with a timbale of rat-atouille. Though zucchini is the base of the sauce, its contribution is more texture than flavor, which is given over more to the peppery seasonings. Other appetizers, all presented on handsomely com-posed platters, include smoked salmon with garnishes, duck confit with penne in a light glaze of sage and oregano butter or a platter of assorted caviars, another of kitchen-made terrines and pâtés, as well as a standard version of beef carpaccio. For an à la carte course, caesar salad is a visual delight, its dressing well balanced over pale green romaine.

La Tour's entree choices expand upon traditional ingredients and conceptions, but without the kind of excitement or adventurous pair-ing which their prices and setting might seem to suggest. Best of a recent evening's fare was medallions of grilled venison, served with sweet potato chips, a purée of slightly sweet root vegetables, and a peppery sauce combined with the meat's natural juicing. Rack of lamb was a similar success, though hardly unique. But a pair of fish entrees did show some imagination. Swordfish is roasted, then bed-ded on small lentil beans for texture and grilled onion for flavor, un-derscored with a subtle lemon and fresh thyme essence. Stronger-flavored red snapper was well matched with a coulis of red and yel-low sweet peppers.

Desserts are selected from a nightly cart array; the wine list is par-ticularly deep, though without any noticeable bargain.

# LAWRY'S THE PRIME RIB
KR 18.5/20

Decor 3.5/4   Hospitality 5/5   Food 8/9   Value 2/2

- **American**
- **Chicago/Near North**
- **$$**

100 E. Ontario St.
Chicago
(312) 787-5000
**Troubleshooter:** Dick Powell
(manager)

**Hours:** Lunch Mon-Fri 11:30 am-2 pm, dinner Mon-Thurs 5-11 pm, Fri-Sat until midnight, Sun 3-10 pm
**Cards:** All majors
**Reservations:** Suggested
**Bar:** Full
**Parking:** Valet
**Party Facilities:** For up to 120

A major redecorating job and facelift have not changed the substance of Lawry's the Prime Rib, which remains dedicated to exactly what its name indicates. The prime ribs are coated with a heavy layer of rock salt and then roasted in specially built ovens. The rock salt forms a hard shell, or cover. When the meat is done to the chef's specifications, the rock-salt cover is cracked open. The whole standing rib roast is placed onto a domed cart, from which it is cut and served to order.

Diners may choose one of four cuts, ranging from the extra thick Chicago cut, with the rib bone still in, to the smaller California cut, for lighter appetites. In between are the regular Lawry's cut and the thinner English slice.

Dinners include salad, with Lawry's dressing, of course, mashed potatoes whipped with milk, Yorkshire pudding, and cream horseradish sauce for the beef. Desserts are à la carte.

The luncheon menu includes several other, lighter choices besides the cuts of prime rib, including some seafood and salads.

# LE BISTRO
KR 19/20

Decor 4/4   Hospitality 5/5   Food 8/9   Value 2/2

- **Vietnamese**
- **Chicago/Far North**
- **$**

5004 N. Sheridan Rd.
Chicago
(312) 784-6000
**Troubleshooter:** Julie Mai
(owner)

**Hours:** Mon 4-10 pm, Tues-Thurs & Sun 10:30 am-10 pm, Fri-Sat to 11 pm
**Cards:** All majors
**Handicapped:** Accessible
**Bar:** Service bar
**Parking:** Street
**Party Facilities:** For up to 100

Though its name, Le Bistro, suggests French-style cuisine, the surrounding neighborhood is more reflective of the Vietnamese character of this handsomely appointed storefront restaurant. Located in the heart of Chicago's North Side Asian community, Le Bistro does offer a limited listing of French fare, but most of the menu leans toward Southeast Asia.

Cloth table coverings lend a continental atmosphere, it is true, as does the general coziness of the small dining room. While French onion soup is on the menu, the selection of Vietnamese broths, appetizers, and entrees is far more extensive. Like other Asian cuisines, Vietnamese stresses texture balances and contrasts.

To begin an evening's meal, try an order of spring rolls filled with scraps of vegetables and shrimp, topped with ground peanuts, a light plum sauce, and slivers of carrots more for color than flavor. As a contrast, taste Vietnamese egg rolls, which, like their Chinese counterpart, are wrapped in fried won ton noodles. But the similarity to Chinese cuisine ends there. The Vietnamese egg roll is crispier, less oily, its filling less reliant upon cabbage. Instead of mustard or sweet sauce, the Vietnamese use nuac mam, a fish sauce employed much in the way salt is used in Western dining and virtually as ubiquitous.

From among other appetizers, take an order of shrimp that has been char-broiled, wrapped in a sugar coating, and deep fried. The result is not nearly as sweet as it sounds. Noodle dishes also make good appetizer choices, though any of the pan-fried chewy noodles work equally well as accompaniments to main-course selections.

From among seafood entrees, a somewhat rubbery cuttlefish is served in a peppery garlic sauce, but not so hot as to overwhelm.

Other seafood includes deep-fried red snapper or flounder, each with distinctive saucing.

Among house specialties is the Le Bistro version of orange beef, abundant with orange peel cooked almost to caramelization, simmered with hot peppers for a challenging bite. It is one of the best orange beef recipes I have ever tasted. As for poultry, chicken with cashews is similar to the Chinese version of this tasty dish.

# LE FRANÇAIS
KR 20/20
Decor 4/4   Hospitality 5/5   Food 9/9   Value 2/2

| | |
|---|---|
| • **French** | **Hours:** Lunch Tues-Fri 11:30 am-2 pm, dinner Mon-Sat 6-10 pm |
| • **Wheeling** | **Cards:** All majors |
| • **$$$** | **Reservations:** Mandatory |
| 269 S. Milwaukee Ave. | **Handicapped:** Accessible |
| Wheeling | **Bar:** Service bar plus small lounge |
| (708) 541-7470 | **Dress:** Jackets required |
| **Troubleshooters:** Roland and Mary Beth Liccioni (chef/ owners) | **Party Facilities:** For up to 12 |

Chef Roland Liccioni is one of the finest cooks in the Midwest and arguably one of the best in the United States. When Liccioni and his wife, Mary Beth, left Carlos', where he was head chef and she pastry chef, to take over Le Français from the renowned Jean Banchet, the dining public and critics alike eagerly waited to see whether Liccioni could maintain the august stature to which Banchet had raised Le Français.

The Liccionis succeeded. Captains and waiters obviously respect the caliber of cooking that comes from Chef Liccioni's kitchen. That respect is warranted.

Dinner opens with a complimentary amusée, perhaps a vegetable mousse, barely a single bite or two on a small platter with an intense reduction of tomato cream sauce. Among à la carte appetizers, wild mushroom pâté binds the mushrooms in a mousse, accented with a morel cream sauce. Other appetizers include various cold seafood platters, some smoked, some sauced; hot duck pâté with pistachio and truffle sauce; platters of foie gras, beluga caviar, or elegant presentations of home-style charcuterie. Seafood ragout, consisting of shrimp, mussels, scallops, and a lobster claw, could be served in a lemon grass beurre blanc. This is just one example of how Chef Liccioni, whose heritage is Corsican and Vietnamese, balances Orient and Occident in his cookery.

Liccioni has a marvelous trompe-l'oeil touch. In one case he shaves thin threads of leek and gives them a quick fry, which creates the appearance of spun gold. In another instance, lotus root cut into thin slices looks like some sort of exotic fungi.

Liccioni pays tribute to Jean Banchet with Banchet's recipe for Dover sole stuffed with a salmon mousse, then napped with deeply flavored lobster sauce, and a lighter beurre blanc with chives. On one of the rolling display carts, an evening could bring a pairing of veal medallions, one wrapped in pastry and cloaked in foie gras, the other perfectly pink. The mushroom sauce is light, but not without substance; truffle sauce perigourdine in its own terrine is the essence of perfume.

Desserts in the capable hands of Mary Beth Liccioni are unassailable. To read the lengthy wine list is to take a course in enology. Le Français is as good as a restaurant can be and still be this side of mythology and legend.

# LE MIKADO

KR 19/20

Decor 3.5/4    Hospitality 5/5    Food 8.5/9    Value 2/2

- **French**
- **Chicago/Near North**
- **$$**

21 W. Goethe
Chicago
(312) 280-8611
**Troubleshooter:** Jacques
Barbier (owner)

**Hours:** Brunch Sat-Sun 11:30
am-2:30 pm, dinner Mon-Thurs
5-10 pm, Fri-Sat until 11 pm,
Sun until 9 pm
**Cards:** All majors
**Reservations:** Reservations
suggested Friday and Saturday
**Handicapped:** Accessible
**Bar:** Full
**Parking:** Validated parking
across street at 1250 N.
Dearborn
**Party Facilities:** For lunch
groups of 30-80

The conjunction of oriental techniques and accents with modern French cooking has gone beyond fad to become an accepted approach to fine dining. The theme is beautifully carried out at Le Mikado, its formality moderated by white butcher paper over tablecloths. Service is pleasantly gracious. Diners can choose from the à la carte menu or the very reasonably priced prix fixe. The latter includes appetizer, entree, and dessert, which, though listed on a separate card, usually includes choices from the full menu.

The melding of East and West is most apparent in the plating, where the chef's sense of design and color is displayed along with his culinary skills. Diners will see some unusual combinations, such as egg rolls filled with Italian goat's cheese, served with a light pesto-style mayonnaise and matchstick slices of jicama for garnish.

A ravioli might be made of sheets of Japanese dried seaweed and filled with roasted eggplant and red peppers, all in a saffron sauce. Spicy but cold Szechuan noodles are not unlike those found in Chinese restaurants, though the appetizer is served with the elegance more typical of French dining.

Among entrees, whole brook trout is roasted and served in a sauce whose flavor accents include ginger and scallions. Something as ordinary as a grilled chicken breast gets an accompaniment of shallots, fresh sage, and balsamic vinegar for a mild bite. Sea bass is sauteed French style but served with Chinese black bean and scallion sauce. More elaborate is free-range chicken, with a marvelous oriental glaze in which thyme, orange juice, and Chinese five spice powder are added to honey, with which the chicken is basted.

Though desserts are not prominent in oriental dining, they do figure in Western tastes. The flavoring of ginger shows up in ice cream-filled profiteroles napped with bittersweet and somewhat grainy chocolate sauce. Crème brûlée might be flavored with sake. On the other hand, flourless chocolate cake, a traditional Italian torte, can be served conventionally, perhaps with crème Anglaise. The special touches make Le Mikado a very special restaurant.

# LE PERROQUET
KR 19.5/20
Decor 4/4   Hospitality 5/5   Food 8.5/9   Value 2/2

- **French**
- **Chicago/Near North**
- **$$$**

70 E. Walton St.
Chicago
(312) 944-7990
**Troubleshooters:** Michael Foley (owner), Gerard Nespoux (maitre d')

**Hours:** Lunch 11:30 am-2:30 pm, dinner Mon-Sat 5:30 10 pm
**Cards:** All majors
**Reservations:** Mandatory
**Handicapped:** Accessible
**Bar:** Small bar, 120-bottle wine list
**Dress:** Jackets required at dinner
**Parking:** Discount parking in garage one door east
**Party Facilities:** For 8-60

**W**hen Le Perroquet suddenly closed its doors in January, 1991, the surprise and loss felt by Chicago's fine dining community almost registered on the Richter scale. Now, after an ownership reorganization, Le Perroquet is back in business.

The question is whether it remains on the leading edge. The answer is a qualified yes. Certainly Le Perroquet is as handsome, sophisticated, and warm as ever, with its plush red velvet seating, murals, tall vases of flowers, and outstanding service. This is a restaurant where customers are pampered.

From outward appearances, the transition has been a good one. The menu retains many signature creations, such as dodine of pigeon, with its intense sauce and forcemeat stuffing; veal sweetbreads in tarragon butter; and the seemingly prosaic beef tournedos with shallots in a demi-glacé.

There are newer selections, some on the printed menu, others featured as daily specials recited by a waiter. As always, diners are presented with a small platter of canapés. Next comes a complimentary amusée, such as a small quiche in a buttery smooth crust.

From among appetizers, a ragout of vegetables includes carrots, cauliflower, broccoli, and other vegetables cooked together in a light butter or oil, each flavor and texture distinct. Or consider a cross-section of lobster at the center of a seafood terrine, plated on a corn-flavored cream sauce, a decidedly American addition to an otherwise French menu.

More traditionally Gallic, though leaning toward today's lighter tastes, might be a pair of veal loin cuts sauteed in olive oil, presented in a light cream demi-glacé with thin strands of ginger. A puree of carrots reminds returning customers that Le Perroquet was perhaps the first restaurant in Chicago to use what at the time was such imaginative plating.

Roast squab is given due attention, with a natural reduction of juices from the cooking pan and a bouquet of herbs for panache. However, the forcemeat has the texture, if not the taste, of an inferior meat.

That said, Le Perroquet suffers only by comparison to other contemporary French restaurants. At one time unique, it now is one of several, set off more by its ambiance than by a distinctive style of cookery. Nonetheless, exceptional service, a wine list with extraordinarily low prices, and a genuine effort to lower fine-dining costs makes Le Perroquet a real value.

# LE TITI DE PARIS

KR 20/20

Decor 4/4    Hospitality 5/5    Food 9/9    Value 2/2

- **French**
- **Arlington Heights**
- **$$$**

1015 W. Dundee Rd.
Arlington Heights
(708) 506-0222
**Troubleshooters:** Chef Pierre
Pollin and Judith Pollin (owners)

**Hours:** Lunch Tues-Fri 11:30 am-2:30 pm, dinner Tues-Thurs 5:30-9:30 pm, Fri until 10 pm, Sat until 10:30 pm
**Cards:** All majors
**Handicapped:** Accessible
**Bar:** Full, wine list with more than 600 selections
**Parking:** Free lot
**Party Facilities:** For up to 45; entire restaurant Sundays and Mondays
**Heart-Healthy Menu:** No designations but most selections can be specially prepared on request

**D**espite its rather campy name, Le Titi de Paris has evolved into an outstanding French restaurant, on a par with the city's finest. Its handsome decor is tastefully restrained. Something similar is happening with the cooking. With today's emphasis on low cholesterol and fat content, dining concerns go far beyond how something tastes.

Consider what is being done with tuna carpaccio. Though the name suggests thin slivers, this tuna is rather fleshy, akin to what might be served in a Japanese sushi bar. Rounds of raw fish are laid up against a piling of matchstick cuttings of ginger-marinated jicama. Tastes are exceptional. Similarly, tuna tartare has a freshness underscored by dollops of ebony caviar and touches of smoked salmon, accompanied by an avocado vinaigrette.

The à la carte salads include a selection of greens with a round of warm goat's cheese and slices of poached pear with raspberry vinaigrette, an exceptional balance of flavors.

While diners will find such choices as rack of lamb, steak au poivre, and recently, wild boar, among entree selections, people concerned about healthy dining are also accommodated. Consider the outstanding grouper, coated with corn meal and quickly sauteed in olive oil. The fish tastes as if it had been caught that morning. Enticing lobster and shrimp are served with rice and crushed figs in a light vinaigrette, which substitutes for a rich cream or butter-based sauce without sacrificing taste. Venison, like most wild game, is lower in cholesterol than farm-raised meats. At Le Titi de Paris, venison has been served with a port wine sauce in an intensely flavored reduction.

I would be remiss not to mention the beautiful plating of virtually all dishes. Some are painted to suggest the fanciful visions of Miró, with dots of color from flavorful sauces or purees.

The handsomely contemporary dining room and attentive service make Le Titi de Paris as fine a dining experience as Chicago and its suburbs can offer.

# LE VICHYSSOIS

KR 17/20

Decor 3/4   Hospitality 3/5   Food 9/9   Value 2/2

- **French**
- **Lakemoor**
- **$$$**

220 W. Illinois Rte. 120
Lakemoor
(815) 385-8221
**Troubleshooters:** Bernard and Priscilla Cretier (owners)

**Hours:** Lunch Wed-Fri 11:30 am-2:30 pm, dinner Wed-Sat first seating at 5:30 pm, Sun at 4:30 pm
**Cards:** CB, DINERS, MC, VISA, house accounts
**Handicapped:** Accessible
**Bar:** Full, extensive wine list
**Parking:** Free lot
**Party Facilities:** For 20-50
**Heart-Healthy Menu:** On request

For lots of Chicagoans, a trip to the country means the Farm in the Zoo at Lincoln Park. But there is a real country out there beyond the city limits. One destination for food seekers is Le Vichyssois.

It's really too bad that service is not up to the mark set by Chef Bernard Cretier's wonderfully creative cookery. There is an inattentiveness to detail, though when service does come, it is friendly and effusive.

Chef Cretier grounds his wonderful cooking in French tradition. Though his menu rarely strays from tradition, he is willing to accommodate more contemporary tastes. When a recipe calls for a cream-based sauce, he is more than willing to prepare a wine sauce substitute. Le Vichyssois is really not a restaurant for calorie counters. Many selections come wrapped in buttery, delicate feuilletage.

Seafood is exquisite and always a good choice. Filets of Dover sole are prepared in a vermouth sauce. They and other fish listed on daily specials might come with other saucings, as well, based on fresh seasonal herbs. Tenderloin tips are a good choice for beef lovers, served in a classic and full-bodied Bordelaise sauce. Similarly, for those who like full-bodied dining, roast duckling in a red wine and vinegar sauce is delicious. The meat is roasted to a dark perfection, but still moist and flavorful. Even if you choose to peel away the skin in the interest of saving calories, the abundance of duck meat remains satisfying. From a selection of appetizers, any of the pâtés will be rewarding, as will soups, such as crayfish in a light bisque with chopped vegetables.

As for desserts, the classic tradition is continued with a bounty of Napoleons, tarts, and other examples of the pastry art.

# LITTLE BUCHAREST
KR 18.5/20
Decor 3.5/4  Hospitality 4.5/5  Food 8.5/9  Value 2/2

---

• **Romanian**

• **Chicago/Mid-North**

• **$**

3001 N. Ashland Ave.
Chicago
(312) 929-8640
**Troubleshooter:** Branko
Podrumedic (owner)

**Hours:** Daily 4 pm-midnight
**Cards:** AE, DINERS, MC, VISA
**Reservations:** Suggested
**Bar:** Full, Eastern European wines
**Parking:** Street
**Party Facilities:** For up to 100

---

Little Bucharest is the kind of earthy ethnic restaurant for which Chicago is justly famous. What draws people here are the bountiful platters of food, richly prepared, and at very reasonable cost.

Dinner centers around broiled, baked, and stewed meats, especially veal in any of several styles. The schnitzel is golden brown, dipped in a rich egg batter and so large that you might wind up taking half home for snacking the next day. A Romanian-style sauerbraten is quite different from the traditional German version, without the bite of gingersnaps and brine. This is more akin to a pot roast with olives, onions, and tomatoes in a red wine sauce, accompanied by a fresh vegetable, red cabbage, and spaetzle.

Baked chicken à la Bucharest is a house special. The chicken is filled with a liver dressing stuffed between the meat and skin, then baked in white wine basting. Be sure to order one of the soups, such as veal meatball with vegetables and dumplings or ciorba, a soup featuring fresh cuts of chicken, vegetables, and dumplings.

You will not want to ignore desserts, which is hard to do since they are displayed in a glass-door refrigerator in plain sight of diners. Tortes are a specialty, piled high with cream fillings, walnuts, perhaps mocha or chocolate.

# LITTLE ITALY
KR 15/20
Decor 3/4   Hospitality 3.5/5   Food 7/9   Value 1.5/2

| | |
|---|---|
| • **Italian/Sicilian** | **Hours:** Sun-Thurs 4-10 pm, Fri-Sat until 11 pm |
| • **Highwood** | **Cards:** MC, VISA |
| • **$** | **Reservations:** For 6 or more |
| 47 Highwood Ave. | **Handicapped:** Accessible |
| Highwood | **Bar:** Service bar |
| (708) 432-0070 | **Parking:** City lot or street |
| **Troubleshooter:** Sam Visconti (owner) | **Party Facilities:** For luncheons daily |

One mark of restaurant success is longevity. Little Italy has been around for at least seven years in its Highwood storefront. There has never been a night when I have visited over the years that owner Sam Visconti was not sitting at a table in the rear of the dining room, usually eating a helping of pasta and red sauce. When the boss eats there, the restaurant must be OK, right?

Little Italy may not always have the smoothest or best-informed service, but employees are always polite and cordial. While the food may not win culinary accolades, I always come away feeling that I have eaten in a friend's kitchen, rather than at a restaurant. In other words, while some Italian restaurants are shooting for trends in dining, Little Italy continues to serve good, home-style Italian-American dinners. Little Italy's spinach in garlic and oil is just about the best spinach I have ever tasted. The garlic is sweet and pungent, the spinach oily, but not oppressively so. If it seems a little strong for your taste, just sprinkle on some grated cheese, and it will be just about perfect.

Other appetizers, no less delicious, include fried calamari, excellent tortellini soup, and a terrific seafood salad with mussels, shrimp, baby squid, crisp greens, and a simple oil-and-vinegar dressing.

I suspect that most people who visit Little Italy order pasta not as a separate course, but as their entree. The presentations are certainly ample enough. Baked ravioli or tortellacci can be ordered with either a meat or cheese sauce. With cheese, it becomes a rich and creamy platter of food, best when shared with others. It's hard to pick a favorite pasta, but the pasta primavera is a candidate. The vegetables are almost stewlike, zucchini slices, broccoli, green beans in a meaty marinara with plenty of garlic for zest. This is not especially delicate dining, which makes it perfect for cold winter nights. Chicken Vesuvio would be better if served with the traditional accompaniment of roasted potatoes. Otherwise, there's lots of chicken cooked to perfection. The veal Parmigiana is basic home-style fare, a large cut of veal blanketed with melted Parmesan cheese, all served in a generously flavored meat sauce. Eggplant and chicken Parmigiana get similar treatment. Other entrees include several seafood and steak dinners, plus a country-style Italian sausage cacciatore.

Tortoni, spumoni, and a plump cannoli make up the trio of desserts.

# LITTLE SZECHWAN
KR 18/20
Decor 4/4   Hospitality 4.5/5   Food 7/5/9   Value 2/2

- **Chinese**
- **Highland Park**
- **$$**

1900 First St.
Highland Park
(708) 433-7007
**Troubleshooters:** Simon Lin, Phil Chiu, Robert Lin (owners)

**Hours:** Mon-Thurs 5-9:30 pm, Fri-Sat until 10:30 pm, Sun 5-9 pm
**Cards:** AE, CB, DINERS, MC, VISA
**Reservations:** Suggested
**Handicapped:** Accessible
**Bar:** Service bar
**Parking:** Free lot

**W**hite tablecloths set the tone amid decorative accents, including a large and handsome aquarium that adds a restful note. The menu is not all that extensive, which gives the kitchen an opportunity to concentrate on doing a few things well, rather than trying to re-create the entire 5,000-year history of the cuisine of China.

Among starters, chilled hacked chicken is a real favorite. Slices of the breast meat come on a bed of shredded lettuce with a peppery peanut sauce on top. It is a real appetite stimulant. Taiwanese chicken rolls are finger foods wrapped in a deep-fried skin of tofu, with shreds of chicken layered inside. The flavor is rather mild, but the texture is of more interest.

From among the main-course and chef's recommendations, it's hard to go wrong. Three treasures brings together tastes of beef, shrimp, and scallops along with stir-fried vegetables in a light black-bean sauce. Beef with orange peel has been one of my favorites in recent years. The version at Little Szechwan combines the sharp flavor of cooked orange skin with sauteed pieces of tenderloin and a cache of seasonings to make for exciting dining. In addition to the printed menu, the restaurant features a few nightly specials and will also prepare other dishes at your request, depending upon availability of ingredients.

# LOU MALNATI'S

KR 16.5/20

Decor 3.5/4   Hospitality 4/5   Food 7/9   Value 2/2

- **Italian/Pizza**
- **Chicago & Suburbs**
- **$**

439 N. Wells St.
Chicago
(312) 828-9800
**Troubleshooter:** Manager on duty

## Other Locations

85 S. Buffalo Grove Rd.
Buffalo Grove
(708) 215-7100
1050 E. Higgins Rd.
Elk Grove Village
(708) 439-2000
6649 N. Lincoln Ave.
Lincolnwood (original restaurant)
(708) 673-0800
1 S. Roselle Rd.
Schaumburg
(708) 980-1525

## Carry-Out Only at

1504 N. Elmhurst Rd.
Mount Prospect
(708) 590-1900
1324 Shermer Rd.
Northbrook
(708) 291-0250
3223 Lake Ave.
Wilmette
(708) 256-5780

**Hours:** Mon-Thurs 11 am-11 pm, Fri-Sat until 1 am, Sun noon-10 pm
**Cards:** AE, CB, DINERS, MC, VISA
**Reservations:** None
**Handicapped:** Accessible
**Bar:** Full
**Parking:** Public lots
**Party Facilities:** Monday to Thursday for 50-100

Is there anyone who grew up on Chicago's North Side who does not relish memories of Lou Malnati's? The original restaurant is still in Lincolnwood. Though Lou is gone, his son and family still watch over things. In recent years, the Malnati name has expanded to other Chicago and suburban locations. Many have sports themes. For example, at the one in Buffalo Grove, diners sit amidst showcases crammed with autographed baseballs and footballs, old uniforms, even Muhammad Ali's silk robe, prominently displayed near the entrance.

The menu at each restaurant sticks to the basic Lou Malnati's formula, which is centered around deep-dish pizza, a quartet of pastas, half-a-dozen sandwiches, plus salads and snacks. The pizza is the real draw for my money. The largest size will easily feed three people, or more if they order a couple of other entrees. The sauce has just the right bite, but what makes the pizza so special is the delicious crust. You can pay a little extra for the butter crust, but I think it's fine with the original crust.

A whole array of toppings can be ordered, from anchovies to mushrooms, sausage, and peppers if you really want to load down your pizza. Lou Malnati's can be a paradise for snackers who like to gorge on the delicious stuffed spinach bread and such assorted finger snacks as fried cheese, mushrooms, or zucchini sticks. As for the pastas, we are not talking trendy. The lasagna, spaghetti and mostaccioli come slathered in a thick meat and tomato sauce that, for my taste, is somewhat overburdened with chopped green peppers. It's kind of like the way Italian restaurants used to make spaghetti and meat sauce in the days before waiters were really out-of-work actors who tell you their first names and take orders for cutesy drinks and designer waters. In short, Lou Malnati's is the basic stuff, the kind of restaurant that is unique to Chicagoland.

# LOU MITCHELL'S

KR 18.5/20

Decor 3.5/4   Hospitality 4/5   Food 9/9   Value 2/2

- **American**
- **Chicago/Near West**
- **$**

565 W. Jackson Blvd.
Chicago
(312) 939-3111
**Troubleshooter:** Kathryn
Rentas (owner)

**Hours:** Mon-Fri 5:30 am-4 pm,
Sat 5:30 am-2:30 pm, Sun 7
am-3 pm
**Cards:** None
**Reservations:** For 6 or more
**Handicapped:** Accessible
**Bar:** None
**Parking:** Free lot weekends
only

**L**ou Mitchell's is in the breakfast business and serves just about the best there is in Chicago. Each year for about 60 years, literally hundreds of thousands of Chicagoans and visitors to the city find their way to what looks like just another coffee shop. There are two full-time bakers who do nothing but make fresh buns, breads, sweet rolls, and other pastries from scratch. Even the jams and jellies are kitchenmade. The French vanilla ice cream is 18 percent butterfat, which may not place it at the top of the surgeon general's healthy foods list, but you do have to splurge once in a while!

The restaurant's specialty is the enormous breakfasts served to Chicago's early risers. Light-as-air three-egg omelettes are made from double-yolk eggs. If the zoning laws would allow it, the restaurant probably would raise its own chickens behind the place. As it stands, the omelettes are spectacular creations, served in the individual pans in which they have been cooked.

Pancakes and waffles are among other favorites. Try rolled pancakes with apples, sour cream, and genuine pure maple syrup, or a fluffy-light Belgian waffle made with real malted milk. The breakfast specials are served all day, but if something more conventional is your preference for lunch, you might want the roast chicken in a barbecue-style sauce. Other choices include roast loin of pork with fresh sage dressing, broiled baby beef liver, or fried filet of sole.

But it really is the eggs, waffles, and pancakes that make Lou Mitchell's famous; if you don't try one of them, you will have missed what all Chicago talks about.

# LUPITA'S

KR 17.5/20
Decor 3.5/4  Hospitality 4.5/5  Food 7.5/9  Value 2/2

| | |
|---|---|
| • **Mexican** | **Hours:** Lunch Tues-Fri 11:30 am-2 pm, dinner Tues-Thurs 5-9:30 pm, Fri until 10:30 pm, Sat 11:30 am-10:30 pm, Sun 5-9:30 pm |
| • **Evanston** | |
| • **$** | |
| 1721 Benson Ave. | |
| Evanston | **Cards:** MC, VISA |
| (708) 328-2255 | **Reservations:** Accepted |
| **Troubleshooter:** Lupita | **Bar:** Full |
| Carson (owner) | **Parking:** Nearby city lots |

**I**f you are disappointed by the sameness of most Mexican restaurants, then welcome to Lupita's. The menu alone would not lead you to expect much difference. Nor does the decor, with its hanging piñatas, Mexican woven tapestry rugs, and other wall hangings.

But from the moment a platter of antijitos is placed on your table, Lupita's begins to show its style. Instead of ordinary corn taco chips, you receive deep-fried pastry puffed chips with a light and delicate feel and flavor. In the same bowl are small taquitos, folded-over tortillas stuffed with seasoned potatoes worked to a pulp. These are so good you might not even want to order an appetizer, but go ahead and do so anyway, for variety, if for no other reason.

Certainly, you would not want to pass up the delicious empanadas. Or order a combo that consists of three different kinds of finger snacks. Though you could choose a main course of chilies rellenos, you can also order them on the side. The stuffed peppers have had virtually all their bite cooked away and come filled with a mildly seasoned cheese or cheese-and-beef combination. Either way, these are the way stuffed peppers should be. Individual tacos, flautas, and tostadas can also be ordered, or you can enjoy them in dinner-size portions. Several combination platters give you a chance to mix and match tastes and textures.

Evening specials are particularly interesting. Recently sea scallops came in a mildly seasoned cucumber beurre blanc with slivers of vegetables quick-cooked to hold their texture. This is the kind of cooking that is far from routine Mexican restaurant fare. From among other selections, chicken or beef fajitas could use more in the way of flavor contrasts. The meat is overwhelmed by the peppers and onions. But one of a trio of steaks, bistec tampiquena, is right on the mark.

Spanish rice and refried beans, or frijoles, accompany some dinner platters, while delicious sliced zucchini in tomato sauce with a blanket of melted cheese comes with others.

Desserts include a house bread pudding with chocolate sauce and two cheesecakes.

# MAGGIANO'S LITTLE ITALY
KR 19/20
Decor 4/4   Hospitality 4.5/5   Food 8.5/9   Value 2/2

- **Italian**
- **Chicago/Near North**
- **$$**

516 N. Clark St.
Chicago
(312) 644-7700
**Troubleshooters:** Mark Tormey (vice president), Frank Conaty (general manager)

**Hours:** Lunch daily 11:30 am-2 pm, dinner Mon-Thurs 5-10 pm, Fri until midnight, Sat 11:30-11 pm, Sun brunch 9:30-2 pm, dinner 4:30-9 pm
**Cards:** All majors
**Reservations:** Suggested
**Handicapped:** Accessible
**Bar:** Full
**Parking:** Valet at dinner
**Party Facilities:** For 190

**M**aggiano's Little Italy may not seem unusual, but it is. For one thing, a bakery on the premises with a retail counter adds the kind of neighborhood ambiance you might not expect on this nightclub-dotted stretch of Clark Street. The restaurant is cavernous enough to seat 200 people, at red checker-clothed tables, of course. The floor is hand-laid mosaic tile that looks as if it has been in place since the early 1920s, not the '90s.

Maggiano's Little Italy serves up basic Italian comfort food in the kind of portions that encourage diners to take home plenty of leftovers. Many choices come in half or full orders; both are real bargains. An order of Maggiano's salad is easily enough to feed four, and at less than a couple of dollars per person.

Try an order of the crostini of the day as an appetizer. Crostini is basically thick-sliced Italian bread with a variety of toppings, such as caponata, the Italian version of ratatouille. Other appetizers are more conventional, though in portions that are anything but.

Next, in true Italian fashion, should come a pasta. Pasta comes in huge serving bowls, whether spaghetti in marinara, meat sauce, or with meatballs; rigatoni with a somewhat too-sweet eggplant and red tomato sauce, dubbed "country style" on the menu; or something a bit fancier, such as garlic shrimp with shell macaroni.

By the time you come to an entree, you might be ready to throw in the proverbial towel. But if you have paced yourself and have left some pasta to be taken home, you now can enjoy a continuation of some extremely contented dining. Entrees are not all that unusual, as befits the theme at Maggiano's Little Italy. But they are hardly dull. We took chicken cammarari, which I am sure, neither we nor our waitress ever managed to pronounce the same way twice. A cut-up roasted chicken is at the heart of the dish, its flavor enhanced by herbs and spices, garnished with fresh peas, mushrooms, and red peppers. As with previous courses, there is more than enough to go around. If you must have a side dish, try the crispy potatoes and onions, which are as delicious as they sound.

Other entrees include the usual suspects: steaks, lamb chops, various kinds of veal, and more than a casual nod to seafood, including swordfish and tuna steaks. After all this, if you still want dessert, it's there . . . and good luck.

# MAPLE TREE INN
KR 18/20
Decor 3.5/4   Hospitality 4.5/5   Food 8/9   Value 2/2

• **American/Creole/ Southern**
• **Chicago/South**
• **$$**

10730 S. Western Ave.
Chicago
(312) 239-3688
**Troubleshooter:** Charlie Orr (owner)

**Hours:** Daily from 5:30 pm, Sat-Sun from 5 pm
**Cards:** DISCOVER, MC, VISA
**Reservations:** Fridays and Saturdays for 4 or more
**Bar:** Full, jazz and blues lounge on second floor
**Parking:** Street
**Party Facilities:** For 30-40

There is a style of New Orleans cookery that shows its French roots, and there is a side that leans more toward the Cajun. The latter seems to hold sway at the Maple Tree Inn.

To get things off to a proper beginning, a combination plate of a dozen oysters is just right for a party of four. It offers a good taste of delightful oysters Rockefeller, with their blend of spinach, other greens, and a touch of absinthe. And you'll get the delicious oysters

Bienville; named for the founder of New Orleans, the tasty oyster in the shell is blanketed by the rich butter-and-cream sauce that is Bienville's trademark.

Among other delightful appetizers is a delicious crabmeat Remick, shreds of the meat in a remoulade-based pepper sauce. The andouille sausage combined with an order of grilled shrimp tastes like it comes straight from the Delta. If it is the peppery flavor you like, don't miss a platter of New Orleans boiled shrimp, perfect to tease the appetite for what's to come.

There are over a dozen entrees, ranging from something as simple as a strip steak to delicious shrimp or crawfish étouffée served in double portions for two. For simpler tastes, you might find pompano sauteed in black butter. It's a good presentation, with the fish boned and butterflied. Black butter is not burnt, by the way, and seems to add more color than flavor to the fish. In any event, it's a real pleaser. Ask owner Charlie Orr about the real house specialty, and he'll immediately propose the Cajun jambalaya. Laden with rice, chicken, and lots of ham, it's a classic of its kind. The barbecue platter gives diners the chance to taste a trio of New Orleans barbecued shrimp, ribs, and beef brisket.

For seafood lovers, the house version of bouillabaisse can't be beat. For "a bit o' dis and bit o' dat" another platter consists of catfish smothered with crushed pecans, a taste of crawfish étouffée, and stuffed mirliton, known elsewhere as chayote. This pear-sized fruit comes from the Mayan and Aztec cultures, adopted by European settlers in Louisiana who made it their own with a spicy stuffing to pep up the mirliton's otherwise bland taste.

Be sure to get dessert; the Mississippi mud cake and bread pudding with whiskey sauce are favorites.

# MAREVA'S

KR 19.5/20

Decor 4/4   Hospitality 4.5/5   Food 9/9   Value 2/2

- **Polish/Middle European**
- **Chicago/Northwest**
- **$$**

1250 N. Milwaukee Ave.
Chicago
(312) 227-4000
**Troubleshooter:** Irene Idzik (owner)

**Hours:** Sun, Wed-Thurs 5-10 pm, Fri-Sat until 11 pm
**Cards:** All majors, house accounts
**Handicapped:** Accessible
**Bar:** Full, extensive wine list
**Parking:** Free valet parking
**Party Facilities:** For up to 200
**Heart-Healthy Menu:** Selections

**P**olish and Middle European cooking are not noted for their light-ness. This is generally hearty food to fuel farmers and laborers. But Mareva's has transcended those old concepts. Step inside this gor-geously (though some might say overly) decorated restaurant and be whisked worlds away from dreary Milwaukee Avenue. It's like step-ping into a baroque painting. Brass chandeliers, forest green velvet covering for banquettes, starched white tablecloths and napery, and ornate artwork contribute to a setting in which tuxedoed waiters move about quietly between kitchen and tables.

In the kitchen is a style of cooking that seems light-years away from the tradition of Polish food. Diners who are calorie- and choles-terol-conscious can ask that skim milk be substituted for cream in sauces. Similarly, diners can ask that the mushroom sauce served over zrazy, a filet of beef stuffed with chopped veal, be prepared as a clear, not a cream, sauce.

Another light new menu item is the European salad. This alterna-tive to the usual American garden salad includes three vegetables, often sliced beets, cucumbers, carrots, and white radishes among them, topped with a lighter vinaigrette.

Lest anyone mistake Mareva's for a glorified health food restau-rant, the menu abounds with more traditional fare. Try an order of pierogis, the Polish version of ravioli, stuffed with a forcemeat of mushrooms. The house version of roasted duck is presented with your choice of orange, raspberry, or calvados saucing. Though chicken operaski is roasted and served in its natural juices, diners may also ask for one of the same sauces as for the duckling, at an additional charge.

Wonderful veal dishes include veal à la Kasimir the Great, in which a cream-and-cognac sauce bathes sauteed artichoke, truffle, shallots, and shiitake mushrooms. Kluski noodles are homemade; try an order primavera-style with fresh vegetables in a creamy Parmesan cheese sauce. More traditional is a hunter's stew of chicken, beef, lamb, and veal in a pastry crust, baked with vegetables and fresh herbs.

Mareva's is one of those restaurants in which reading the menu makes you feel like you can't wait to get started eating. A check of the desserts will make you feel like you can't wait for the finale!

# MARSI'S
KR 17.5/20
Decor 3.5/4   Hospitality 4/5   Food 8/9   Value 2/2

- **Italian**
- **Chicago/Northwest**
- **$$**

6352 W. Gunnison
Chicago
(312) 792-3322
**Troubleshooter:** Gabriel Sorci (chef/owner)

**Hours:** Tues-Thurs 4-11 pm, Fri-Sat until midnight, Sun until 10 pm
**Cards:** AE, MC, VISA
**Reservations:** For 4 or more
**Bar:** Service bar
**Parking:** Free lot
**Party Facilities:** Entire restaurant available for up to 50

From the outside, Marsi's looks like any other neighborhood carry-out pizza place. Inside is a different story. Black and white checkerboard floor tiles and neoclassic room accents set the mood of an Italian trattoria. Regular customers still come in to pick up pizzas, as they have for the past 13 years or so. But more and more diners are discovering Marsi's as an excellent, informal, sit-down restaurant.

The printed menu is supplemented by daily specials on a chalk-board. Recently, Chef and Owner Gabriel Sorci has been preparing baccala, salt codfish, in a manner associated with Venice. The fish is poached, but not with such intense heat as to dry it out. Then it is set on a bed of caramelized onions, whose luscious sweetness comes as a surprising complement to the flavorful codfish.

This is just one of any number of surprises at Marsi's, where traditional cooking gets the chef's personal touch. Consider a house specialty, vitellina pizzaiuola, in which scallops of veal are finished with potatoes and plum sauce.

No Chicago restaurant worth its garlic and oregano can ignore chicken Vesuvio. At Marsi's, the recipe is fairly traditional, though seasonings seem a bit more complex. Among appetizers, baked clams are perfect, with a stuffing of cheese, light garlic, and breadcrumbs.

Pastas are exceptional. Tagliatelle, a broad, flat noodle, is topped with a vegetable sauce that includes spinach, carrots, mushrooms, and tomatoes. Rigatoni might be combined with four cheeses in the manner of Roman cooking. The menu is fleshed out with other pastas, as well as a couple more chicken recipes. Chef Gabriel also likes to showcase shrimp, using large and fleshy prawns in a variety of presentations.

# MATSUYA
KR 18/20
Decor 3/4   Hospitality 4/5   Food 9/9   Value 2/2

- **Japanese**
- **Chicago/Mid-North**
- **$**

3469-71 N. Clark St.
Chicago
(312) 248-2677
**Troubleshooter:** Michie
Yokomori (owner)

**Hours:** Mon, Wed-Fri 5-11:30 pm, Sat-Sun noon-11:30 pm (closed Tuesdays)
**Cards:** MC, VISA
**Reservations:** No
**Parking:** Street

**M**atsuya has the kind of staying power and loyal following characteristic of Chicago's favorite ethnic restaurants. Its menu reflects not so much trendy Japanese cooking as it does a culinary way of life that outlasts fads.

Diners may order from an à la carte menu or choose combination dinners. The restaurant does a fine job with fish, especially when the dish is charcoal-broiled. Broiled eel is for more adventurous diners. Combination dinners offer a taste of this and that, including battered and fried tempura vegetables or shrimp, beef teriyaki, and a selection of sashimi or sushi. All dinners include a small cabbage salad, delicious miso soup, rice, light green tea with a delicate, woody fragrance, and dessert, usually a fruit sherbet.

# MAX'S DELICATESSEN
KR 18.5/20
Decor 3.5/4   Hospitality 5/5   Food 8/9   Value 2/2

- **American/Jewish**
- **Highland Park**
- **$**

191 Skokie Valley Rd.
Highland Park
(708) 831-0600
**Troubleshooters:** Bernard and David Katz (owners)

## Other Location

2301 N. Clark St. (at Belden)
Chicago
(312) 281-9100; Sun-Thurs 6:30 am-11 pm, Fri-Sat until 2 am; MC, VISA; No reservations; Handicapped accessible; Service bar; 90-minute free parking

**Hours:** Sun-Thurs 6:30 am-9:30 pm, Fri-Sat until 10 pm
**Cards:** None
**Reservations:** No
**Handicapped:** Accessible
**Bar:** None
**Parking:** Free lot
**Heart-Healthy Menu:** Bakery offers no-cholesterol and sugar-free items

**M**ax's Delicatessen bills itself as "Chicago's New York Deli." That's what they all aspire to; New York sets the standard for delis the way Chicago sets the standard for hot dogs. Max's Delicatessen goes so far as to import its own cured meats, corned beef, pastrami, and the like. It's rather tasty stuff, although the corned beef can have a bit too much fat. The pastrami, however, is lean and virtually perfect.

Max's Delicatessen is large, well lit, and bustling, the way a deli should be. Tables are crowded together, each table with a pot of half-done pickles for a centerpiece. What did you expect, a long-stemmed rose? Service is cheerful, considering how busy waitresses can be. The menu is packed with salads, soups, side dishes, sandwiches, dinners, and desserts. The deli dinners include soup or salad, a basket of bagels and rolls, your choice of a drink, and dessert.

In this day of lighter dining, skirt steak at **Max's Delicatessen** is large, practically spilling from the platter, cooked just the way you ask. It's not as tender as a filet mignon, but who would expect it to be? A side of potato pancakes, a "glass seltzer," and whooh, boy . . . that's eating!

For cold winter nights, one of the soup pots – beef, sweet and sour beef, or chicken – is hard to beat. Chicken soup broth for chicken in the pot is golden in color. The flavor is, believe it or not, delicate, very lightly seasoned; the huge matzo ball awash in the soup pot is lightly peppered with dill and perhaps other herbal seasonings. The pot also includes a kreplach (Jewish ravioli) and about a quarter of a chicken, its tender white meat just about falling from the bones. Other entrees range from meat loaf to roast brisket of beef, to stuffed cabbage served with mashed potatoes. I get hungry just writing about it! As for desserts, rolls, strudels, cheesecakes, and ice creams are among the choices. Max's rice pudding is as rich and creamy as cheesecake.

# MÉLANGE
KR 19/20
Decor 4/4   Hospitality 4/5   Food 9/9   Value 2/2

- **American**
- **Northfield**
- **$$**

305 Happ Rd.
Northfield
(708) 501-5070
**Troubleshooters:** David and
Cindy Jarvis (chef/owners)

**Hours:** Lunch Mon-Sat 11:30
am-2:30 pm, dinner Mon-Thurs
5-9:30 pm, Fri-Sat until 10:30
pm, Sun until 8:30 pm
**Cards:** AE, CB, DINERS, MC,
VISA
**Reservations:** Suggested
**Handicapped:** Accessible
**Bar:** Full, extensive wine list
**Parking:** Free lot
**Party Facilities:** For up to 65
sit-down, 80 cocktails
**Heart-Healthy Menu:**
Selections

When so many newer restaurants feature Italian/Mediterranean
themes, it is refreshing to discover the imaginative approach taken at
Mélange. A see-through fireplace separates a small sitting area and
bar from the expansive dining area. Bare brick and fieldstone walls
help create an atmosphere.

Chef David Jarvis has put together a menu that is more eclectic
than many, but not so exotic as to dissuade the less adventuresome.
He seems intent on using a wide variety of ingredients in differing
combinations to create unusual tastes and textures. In other words,
the effort is to create a "mélange" in fact as well as in name.

Look at what is being done with pastas, for example. In one case,
fettuccine noodles have a light saffron flavor, the dough rolled with
poppyseeds. The noodles are dressed with a tomato coulis, pieces of
arugula, and wild mushrooms cooked down into a mushroom ha-
zelnut sauce, which the menu describes as a "broth." No matter what
one calls it, the flavors are unique. In another pasta, Chef Jarvis stir-
fries fettuccine, this time with slivers of chicken, sweet peppers,
mushrooms, spinach, and fresh basil in a peppery combination of
flavors.

These and other selections often introduce an attention-grabbing
sharpness, whether it be the bitterness of field greens or the crisp tex-
ture contrast of a root vegetable. In the latter case, Mélange has re-

cently featured grilled tuna with jicama and carrot matchsticks in a complex sauce. Grilled lamb chops are rather sensuous, thanks to the essence of roasted garlic. The lamb is accompanied by haystack sweet potatoes so sweet and succulent that they melt on the tongue. Other entrees on the seasonal menu include filet of beef with wisps of onion slices in whiskey sauce and free-range grilled chicken given a Southwestern accent.

Though dinners include a tossed green salad, a quartet of à la carte selections is tempting. The chef likes to use field greens, both bitter and bland, to create fresh flavor and texture combinations. One salad brings together Granny Smith apples, frisé lettuce, walnuts, and a Maytag blue cheese dressing, while another combines field greens, wilted onions, and cracked pepper with warmed goat's cheese. Appetizers range from simple grilled vegetables or smoked salmon and caviar cream to an imaginative vegetable Napoleon napped in a tomato broth.

Desserts vary from day to day, but be assured that chocolate lovers will be well served.

# METROPOLIS 1800
KR 18/20
Decor 3.5/4   Hospitality 5/5   Food 8/9   Value 1.5/2

- **American**
- **Chicago/Mid-North**
- **$$**

1800 N. Clybourn Ave.
Chicago
(312) 642-6400
**Troubleshooters:** Erwin and Cathy Drechsler (owners)

**Hours:** Lunch Tues-Fri 11:30 am-2:30 pm, dinner Tues-Thurs 5:30-10 pm, Fri-Sat until 11 pm
**Cards:** All majors, house accounts
**Handicapped:** Accessible
**Bar:** Full
**Parking:** Free lot across street
**Party Facilities:** Sundays and Mondays

**M**etropolis 1800 occupies space in a renovated warehouse that has become home to shops, a theater, and the like. The menu changes nightly, save for a small core of popular choices. Dining begins from the à la carte menu with an appetizer or salad or both. A basic salad of mixed greens is a visually appealing study in mixed leaves and stalks that might include radicchio, arugula, mustard greens, or whatever else of interest is available from the green grocer on a given day.

Another salad has large slices of bright-red tomatoes, with spindly arugula, fresh basil, thin slices of swiss cheese, and fresh-tasting extra virgin olive oil for a light dressing. More substantial is smoked breast of duck served chilled with slices of yellow sweet peppers, frisé lettuce, pieces of walnut, and sliced fresh white figs in a light vinaigrette. Other appetizers might include ravioli pockets filled with forcemeat of capon, wild mushrooms, and peppers napped on a tomato basil sauce.

The point is that Chef Erwin Drechsler's cooking is stylish and up to the minute. For an entree, he might start with something as ordinary as halibut, which in most cases is good for little more than deep frying and slapping on a bun with tartar sauce. But at Metropolis 1800, the halibut comes steamed, a snowy white section of fish surrounded on its platter by an oriental stirfry of mixed veggies and sliced oyster mushrooms. What really adds zing is a snappy wasabi horseradish mayonnaise.

Other recent seafood choices have included a combination of tuna and salmon on a platter mounded with deep-fried parsnip chips. Walleyed pike has come out from the grill in a steak cut instead of the thinner cut more common with this freshwater fish. The pike holds up well to the searing heat of the grill and is offered with roasted peppers plus leek, an ear of roasted corn, and tiny grapes that can be eaten stalks and all.

From among recent meat choices, the calf's liver with a slight ginger underpinning to its mustard-shallot sauce comes with a side of bitter wilted mustard greens. Desserts are terrific, especially a date-filled tart with homemade cinnamon ice cream.

# MILL RACE INN
KR 20/20
Decor 4/4   Hospitality 5/5   Food 9/9   Value 2/2

- **American**
- **Geneva**
- **$$**

4 E. State St.
Geneva
(708) 232-2030
**Troubleshooters:** Rae
Ellsworth, Bonnie Rae Off,
Bobbie Smith (owners)

**Hours:** Daily 11 am-11 pm
**Cards:** AE, CB, DINERS, MC,
VISA, house accounts
**Reservations:** For 6 or more
Fridays and Saturdays
**Handicapped:** Accessible
**Bar:** Full
**Parking:** Valet and free lot
**Party Facilities:** For 10-175

**M**ill Race Inn has been a favorite dining spot for more years than I like to remember. It was listed in the first edition of this guide in 1977. But its history is much longer.

The restaurant traces its roots to a blacksmith shop built in 1842. That building remains the heart of Mill Race Inn, even after all the years and all the remodeling. The Fox River passes by outside, and in good weather diners can go outside to feed the ducks chunks of bread.

In fact, the ducks have become a sub-theme for the Mill Race Inn, which has an adjoining tavern called the Duck Inn, complete with fieldstone fireplace and a roaring blaze in colder weather, billiards, darts, even a Monopoly board. Yet another section of the restaurant complex houses Mallards, a post-and-beam sort of dining room, with undraped windows framing the view outside and entertainment each evening inside.

The menu has adapted over the years as tastes and dining habits have changed, but it still is basic American fare at core, though not without some interesting embellishments. Walleyed pike is a seafood favorite, made somewhat exotic with plantains and banana sauce. Grilled steaks and chops, an abundant selection of seafood, and several house specialties make this a superstar attraction for dining in the beautiful Fox valley.

# MIRABELL
KR 19/20
Decor 3.5/4    Hospitality 4.5/5    Food 9/9    Value 2/2

- **German/Austrian**
- **Chicago/Northwest**
- **$$**

3454 W. Addison St.
Chicago
(312) 463-1962
**Troubleshooter:** Werner and Anita Heil, Jeff Heil (owners)

**Hours:** Lunch Mon-Sat 11:30 am-2:30 pm, dinner Mon-Thurs 5-10 pm, Fri-Sat until 11 pm
**Cards:** AE, MC, VISA
**Reservations:** Suggested
**Bar:** Two full bars with German beers on tap
**Parking:** Street or nearby lot
**Party Facilities:** For up to 100

Though Austrian specialties are among the choices on the Mirabell menu, the atmosphere of this cozy restaurant is more along the lines of a hearty "oom-pah" band than the fragile refrains of a Strauss waltz. But however one might characterize the decor and ambiance, the hospitality offered here is wunderbar!

Naturally, the classic wiener schnitzel is on the menu, breaded to a golden turn in its rich egg batter; the veal is so tender it really can be sliced with a fork. One of Mirabell's distinctive features is that all the meats are cut and trimmed to the specifications of Chef/Co-owner Werner Heil.

There are several schnitzels offered, among them Parisian style with a puffy, almost soufflé-like crust. Diners will also find Zigeuner schnitzel, made with pork, rather than veal, then topped with a saute of peppers, mushrooms, and onions in a pronounced paprika sauce. Connoisseurs say this is the only legitimate way to prepare the dish.

Goulash, a heavily seasoned Middle European meat stew, is fine taken in a small portion as soup or in the hearty main-portion entree size. Another Austrian treat is wiener roastbraten, a prime sirloin quickly pan-sauteed in wine and its own juices and served with crisp, double-fried onions and mushrooms.

A number of German specialties, including traditional sauerbraten and assorted sausages, round out the menu. While this kind of dining does not particularly flatter waistlines, the restaurant has been featuring a variety of fresh seafoods prepared more simply than other entrees might suggest.

# MIRADOR
KR 17.5/20
Decor 3/4   Hospitality 5/5   Food 8/9   Value 1.5/2

- **French/Mediterranean**
- **Chicago/Near North**
- **$$**

1400 N. Wells St.
Chicago
(312) 951-6441
**Troubleshooter:** Amy Morton
(owner)

**Hours:** Lunch/brunch Sun 11 am-3:00 pm, dinner Mon-Thurs 6-10:30 pm, Fri-Sat until 11:30 pm, Sun 5-9:30 pm
**Cards:** All majors
**Reservations:** Suggested
**Handicapped:** Accessible
**Bar:** Full
**Parking:** Nearby lot or street
**Party Facilities:** For up to 50 sit-down, 150 cocktails
**Heart-Healthy Menu:** Most dishes are, though not listed as such

For all the talk about its revival, drab and dreary Wells Street remains drab and dreary. But there are pockets of interest, among them Mirador. This is bistro dining, though on the high end in both execution and cost. The restaurant is basically a long and narrow dining room with checkered flooring, a polished wood bar to one side, and seating extending the length of the restaurant. During warm weather, the back-door garden is open for outdoor dining.

A fairly short menu changes with the seasons. From among appetizers, good bets have been marinated eggplant glistening with oil, accompanied by slices of roasted red peppers and a small round of basil-herbed goat's cheese. This is simplicity at its best. A whole roasted artichoke is more earthy, the leaves peeled off until only the heart remains. A garlic-rich aioli tends the artichoke, with some saffron underpinning adding more color than flavor. One other recent selection has been a portion of linguine with some of the freshest clams I have ever tasted away from a seashore.

Diners at Mirador may opt for an à la carte salad or move right into the entree selections. Moroccan-style lamb is grilled over mesquite with a side of couscous. Though mesquite can impart a strong smoked flavor, the lamb is balanced in tang, set off by a couscous that holds an understated bouquet of flavors.

For the beefeaters still among us, prime rib-eye steak is served with a bed of greens and a hamhock reduction that is short of a gravy, yet not quite a sauce. Rib-eye is about the most flavorful steak cut there is, and it gets its justice in this version at Mirador.

From among seafood choices, the house version of bouillabaisse, a Mediterranean fish stew, is crammed with tiny squid, tender octopus, scallops, a prawn, and mussels in their shells ringing the bowl. The broth is intense, almost heady in its aromatic presence. For a poultry selection, the menu offers what has become rather standard bistro fare, free-range chicken, with a bouquet of herbs and a light onion confit. À la carte vegetables include somewhat ordinary roasted potatoes, more commendable sauteed spinach, and a satisfying wild rice.

For dessert, choices include a prune tart with armagnac ice cream, a date-nut tart with apricot compote, bread pudding, flourless chocolate cake, sorbet, and an elegant cheese platter with dried fruit and nuts.

# MORTON'S OF CHICAGO

KR 19/20

Decor 3.5/4   Hospitality 5/5   Food 9/9   Value 1.5/2

- **American**
- **Chicago/Near North**
- **$$$**

1050 N. State St. (Newberry
   Plaza)
Chicago
(312) 266-4820
**Troubleshooter:** Kevin
Weinert (maitre d')

## Other Locations

Columbia Center III, 9525 W.
   Bryn Mawr Ave.
Rosemont
(708) 678-5155; Lunch Mon-Fri
   11:30 am-2:30 pm, dinner
   Mon-Sat 5:30-11 pm, Sun
   5-10 pm; All major cards;
   Handicapped accessible; Full
   bar; Free valet parking;
   Troubleshooter John
   DosSantos (maitre d')
One Westbrook Corporate
   Center, 22nd and Wolf Rd.
Westchester
(708) 526-7000; Hours and
   details same as above;
   Troubleshooter Ron Parker
   (maitre d')

**Hours:** Mon-Sat 5:30-11 pm,
Sun 5-10 pm
**Cards:** All majors
**Reservations:** Required
**Handicapped:** Accessible
**Bar:** Full, more than 100 wines
**Dress:** Jackets required
**Parking:** Validated parking in
adjoining garage

**M**orton's of Chicago fancies itself an elegant saloon, which hardly does justice to what this restaurant really is all about. The restaurant is neither a saloon nor is it elegant. But it is convivial, comfortable, decidedly masculine, and American. Its brick dining room accents are softened by pastel art adorning the walls, stained-glass decorative windows, and starched white tablecloths and napery.

Steak and lobster are the major attractions, both in humongous portions. All the meat is prime, all the seafood as fresh as the morning air. Chalkboards placed strategically around the dining room offer listings of daily specials and prices. Those prices can be prodigious, especially when one tacks on the à la carte sides of salad and vegetables.

In addition to the grain-fed beef and fresh lobster, Morton's of Chicago serves a Sicilian-style veal chop, for which it is justly famous, rib lamb chops, whole roasted chicken, and daily fish specials. Among its tantalizing desserts are chocolate, lemon, and Grand Marnier soufflés, rich, but still light as air.

By the way, the Chicago Morton's is the prototype for what has become one of the most popular restaurant chains in the United States. Now you can tell your grandchildren that you were there!

# MOTI MOHAL
KR 18/20
Decor 3.5/4   Hospitality 4.5/5   Food 8/9   Value 2/2

- **Indian**
- **Chicago/Northwest**
- **$$**

2525 W. Devon Ave.
Chicago
(312) 262-2080
**Troubleshooters:** S.S.
Sikand (owner), Om Saini
(manager)

**Other Location**
(not reviewed)

1035 W. Belmont Ave.
Chicago
(312) 348-4392

**Hours:** Mon-Thurs noon-10
pm, Fri-Sun until 11 pm
**Cards:** AE, DINERS,
DISCOVER, MC, VISA
**Reservations:** Suggested
**Handicapped:** Accessible
**Bar:** Service bar
**Parking:** Street
**Party Facilities:** For up to
500

On a street almost overflowing with ethnic restaurants and food shops of many kinds, Moti Mohal stands out as something exceptional. This is a handsome restaurant, beyond the usual storefront simplicity. Service is knowledgeable, though it helps to have some familiarity with Indian dining. But even beginners will feel welcome and find fairly exact descriptions on the Moti Mohal menu.

You will know you are in for something beyond the ordinary with your first taste of appetizers. They can be ordered individually or on a combination platter. The two most widely eaten appetizers in Indian cookery probably are small finger foods called samosas and pakoras. Samosas are fried patties of flour often filled with mildly seasoned potatoes and green peas. Pakoras are more akin to fritters or dumplings. They are puffier and usually more varied than samosas. A combination appetizer platter brings delicious tastes of each, plus a bit of grilled lamb kebab, a tidbit called aloo-tikki, which is another fried and spiced vegetable patty, and grilled poultry, called chicken tikka. An assortment of chutneys, highly peppered or sweetened fruit preserves, can be brushed on as condiments.

It's a good idea to go with enough people to order several entrees, ranging from curries to seasoned rice platters to sauced and roasted meats. The curries can be hot or milder as you choose. The menu descriptions are mouthwatering and in most cases accurately reflect the flavorful dishes. Just think about how delicious this sounds: "Chicken cooked with spinach and nuts, seasoned with ginger, garlic and mild spices." It's enough to make you hungry just reading about it.

# MY PLACE FOR?
KR 19/20
Decor 4/4   Hospitality 4.5/5   Food 8.5/9   Value 2/2

- **Greek/American/ Seafood**
- **Chicago/Far North**
- **$$**

7545 N. Clark St.
Chicago
(312) 262-6765
**Troubleshooter:** Steve Dorizas (owner)

**Hours:** Daily 3-11 pm
**Cards:** AE, DINERS, MC, VISA
**Reservations:** Suggested, especially weekends
**Handicapped:** Accessible
**Bar:** Full, with nightly entertainment in lounge
**Parking:** Free lot across street
**Party Facilities:** For up to 100

**W**hat can you say about a restaurant that serves shrimp de jonghe as an entree and makes it seem like something new? Yes, you will find Greek standards such as saganaki, baklava, and taramosalata. But the menu also features Cajun-style chicken or fish, gyros sandwiches, and cheeseburgers.

It is not that My Place For? is all things to all diners. The specialty really is excellent Greek-style seafood. The Greek version of seafood stew, called psarosoupa, comes chock full of shrimp, scallops, cala-mari, cod, and lobster in an herbed tomato-and-fish stock. The wait-ress brings the stew out in a large cauldron. You might want to ask for extra bowls for others at your table; there's plenty to share.

My Place For? does not stop with only one kind of cookery. Fresh stuffed flounder, the kind featured in New England fish shanties, is often served, as is stuffed Idaho brook trout, so fresh the fish almost blinks at you.

All dinners include a small platter of the Greek fish roe spread called taramosalata. A green salad with a bit of feta cheese precedes the main course. Should you feel like going on a bit of a splurge, you will have no regrets about a caesar salad, with its crisp and cold shards of bright-green romaine lettuce, the bite of garlic and anchovy flitting across your tongue.

One big test of a seafood restaurant's quality is the raw bar. At My Place For? oysters on the half shell and cherrystone clams glide down the gullet, leaving their sweet liquor as an aftertaste. Delicious fried calamari has hardly a trace of oiliness, just a crispy batter, like the tender rounds of squid.

# NICK'S FISHMARKET
KR 20/20
Decor 4/4   Hospitality 5/5   Food 9/9   Value 2/2

- **Seafood**
- **Chicago/Loop**
- **$$$**

One First National Plaza
(Monroe St. at Dearborn)
Chicago
(312) 621-0200
**Troubleshooters:** Nick
Nicholas (owner), Steve Karpf
(managing partner)

## Other Locations

10275 W. Higgins Rd. (at
Mannheim Rd.)
Rosemont
(708) 298-8200

**Hours:** Lunch Mon-Fri 11:30
am-3 pm, dinner Mon-Thurs
5:30-11 pm, Fri-Sat to midnight
**Cards:** All majors, house
accounts
**Reservations:** Suggested
**Handicapped:** Accessible
**Bar:** Full, excellent wine list
**Parking:** Validated garage
parking from 11 am, valet after
5 pm
**Party Facilities:** For 22

When it comes to power dining, there's nothing like Nick's Fishmarket. Though the restaurant provides the perfect setting for business entertaining, it does not lack for romance. The oversized banquettes and big stuffed chairs are as comfortable as can be. Lighting can be individually adjusted at each table, turned up for you to see the menu or dimmed for a more intimate setting. An in-the-wall aquarium adds a touch of the nautical to what is otherwise a sophisticated urban setting.

The food remains nearly in a class by itself, as do the prices. But one is paying for the posh surroundings and impeccable service. Hardly a detail is missed, whether something as obvious as lighting a customer's cigarette, or refolding a napkin, or freshening goblets of water.

In a restaurant where little else has changed since its opening in 1988, there is a new menu. The à la carte vegetables are gone; now entrees include one or two vegetables. While seafood remains at the core of the fishmarket concept, diners will now find some contemporary Italian influences. Among them is a veal chop in Barolo wine sauce, a filet mignon carpaccio appetizer, and pasta Bolognese. Still, Italian restaurants are everywhere. Nick's Fishmarket shines on its whole finned fish presentations, which range from farm-raised catfish to exotic denizens of the Pacific. Blackened tuna might be served on a bed of lightly seasoned rice.

Desserts are as lavish as other courses, including several chocolate stylings that are knockouts.

# NUEVO LEON
KR 16/20
Decor 2/4   Hospitality 4/5   Food 8/9   Value 2/2

| | |
|---|---|
| • **Mexican** | **Hours:** Daily 8-midnight, Fri-Sat to 4 am |
| • **Chicago/South** | **Cards:** None |
| • **$** | **Reservations:** Taken |
| 1515 W. 18th St. | **Handicapped:** Accessible |
| Chicago | **Bar:** None, may bring your own |
| (312) 421-1517 | **Parking:** Street |
| **Troubleshooter:** Danny Gutierrez (owner) | |

**D**on't look for trendy atmosphere at Nuevo Leon. Located in the heart of the Pilsen neighborhood, this is the kind of Mexican restaurant that serves families with children in arms, young couples, and street people as well as the turista looking for something more authentic than cuisine served at glitzier emporiums.

The menu is typical of Mexican restaurants, emphasizing tacos, enchiladas, and the like. In fact, a neon sign out front notes that this is a taqueria, a place for snacks as well as meals.

You should do well with whatever you choose. The menu features a number of Mexican soups and stews, the kind with a deep homemade flavor. The real standout, however, is chicken mole. The sauce has the underpinnings of unsweetened chocolate, without which mole would not be mole. There is the essence of peppers, but not so hot as to upset the balance. One can almost imagine the breaking, cracking, and crushing of seeds and pods with a well-worn mortar and pestle, although more than likely a blender is used, a modern intrusion that is not out of place. Whatever the methodology, the sauce is exceptional. Nuevo Leon is quite the Mexican experience!

# OCEANIQUE
KR 18.5/20
Decor 3/4  Hospitality 5/5  Food 8.75/9  Value 1.75/2

| | |
|---|---|
| • **Seafood/Continental** | **Hours:** Mon-Thurs 5:30-9:30 |
| ⌐ **Evanston** | pm, Fri-Sat until 10 pm |
| • **$$$** | **Cards:** All majors |
| | **Handicapped:** Accessible |
| 505 Main St. | **Bar:** Full |
| Evanston | **Party Facilities:** For up to |
| (708) 864-3435 | 100 |
| **Troubleshooter:** Marc Grosz | **Heart-Healthy Menu:** |
| (chef/owner) | Preparations on request |

The name Oceanique suggests seafood with a French flair. That is precisely what Oceanique delivers. The tile flooring may be too stark, as if one were eating in a steam room rather than a fine French restaurant. But once you're seated and the attentive service begins, it becomes apparent that Oceanique is not just another French restaurant. There is a certain care that suffuses the dining experience. It is more than attentiveness; it is a sincere desire to explain, to suggest, to please.

Dining is à la carte. There are a dozen or so appetizers, salads, and soups from which to choose. Each is prepared with the same attention to detail, the same scrupulous perfection, that marks the service. For example, chilled Maine lobster and warm scallops were recently presented on a dinner-size platter with avocado and lemon, enhanced with a tarragon dressing. The sea scallops come right off the grill, as their hash marks attest. The lobster is abundant, considering that this is meant as an appetizer. The tarragon dressing is oil based. If you ask that no butter or cream be used, your request will be honored.

A composed salad of greens is given color and variety with grilled strips of calamari and delectable shrimp. Yet another salad may be centered around artichoke, with a round of warm goat's cheese, red, yellow, and green peppers, and a light vinaigrette.

Something as simple as lentil soup gets the same attention to detail that makes Oceanique such a wonderful dining experience. The soup is made with a lobster stock, not cream broth, underscored with pieces of fish. The flavors are subtle.

Among entrees, striped sea bass is exquisitely presented with a small mound of corn relish on one side of the plate, contrasted with a similar mound of sweet mango relish and a touch of cilantro. On the other side of the platter is a purée of herbaceous green vegetable. The fish filets harbor a clean, pure taste often masked in lesser kitchens by oversaucing. Even simple whitefish gets special treatment, sauteed with caramelized onions enhanced with a port-beaujolais sauce, putting to rest the notion that red wine sauces are inappropriate with seafood.

Only a linguine and mixed seafood failed to please completely. The linguine was in such small portion as to be merely a suggestion; the mix of soft and shellfish was good, but not up to the exceptional level of all else we tasted.

# THE OLD CAROLINA CRAB HOUSE
KR 18/20

Decor 4/4   Hospitality 5/5   Food 7.5/9   Value 1.5/2

- **Seafood**
- **Chicago/Near North**
- **$$**

465 E. Illinois St. (in North Pier) Chicago
(312) 321-8400
**Troubleshooter:** Manager on duty

**Hours:** Lunch Mon-Fri 11:30 am-2 pm, Sat until 3 pm, Sun brunch 11-2 pm, dinner Mon-Thurs 5:30-10 pm, Fri-Sat until midnight, Sun 4-10 pm
**Cards:** AE, MC, VISA, DINERS, DISCOVER
**Reservations:** None
**Handicapped:** Acceptable
**Parking:** Valet or nearby lots; 15 boat slips for nautical customers

The atmosphere here is not exactly fish shanty, though diners will find themselves in a fairly casual setting replete with advertising signs, open counters, and furnishings that appear simpler than they really are. But since the Old Carolina Crab House is at North Pier, there is also a glass-enclosed section that provides a full view of Chicago River traffic and combines the best of city and Southern dining.

Wherever you sit, you'll find generally good, if predictable, food. As the name suggests, crabs are a major offering served in various styles as appetizer, soup, and entree. Somehow, no one has yet figured out how to make a crab dessert. Speaking of dessert, be sure to save room for the peach cobbler, which comes in a heavy china bowl, topped with vanilla ice cream melting down into the warm peach glaze and cobbler pastry.

But this is putting the cart before the horse, or more accurately, the cobbler before the crabs. Begin with some appetizers such as fresh-made crab cakes. These are grilled, not fried. The crab cakes are full of flavor, though not overly seasoned. You can use some of the mild mustard mayonnaise to spice them up. If you don't mind using your pinkies, try an order of garlic crab claws. These come dripping with a powerful garlic butter. The fairly small claws yield their meat easily from the shells. Other selections include oysters, clams, and a heavily spiced, but too salty, platter of crayfish in the shell, which takes too much work for the meager amount of meat.

Entrees include larger portions of some appetizers as well as a range of other nauticals. Spicy shrimp are awash in butter but not interesting enough as a full entree portion. Something like red beans and rice, or New Orleans dirty rice, would improve the presentation. Otherwise, grilled tuna and salmon are delicious. The tuna is meaty, the salmon more delicate but not without flavor. Other fish might include grouper, snapper, and swordfish.

The Old Carolina Crab House menu also lists grilled or fried shore dinners, plus a truly delicious mixed seafood grill with linguine. The marinara sauce is lightly spiced with red peppers, or you can get a garlic crab sauce if you prefer. Service is helpful and courteous.

# THE OLD CHURCH INN

KR 17.5/20

Decor 4/4   Hospitality 3.5/5   Food 8/9   Value 2/2

- **American**
- **St. Charles**
- **$$**

18 N. 4th St.
St. Charles
(708) 584-7341
**Troubleshooter:** Brent
Guynn (chef/owner)

**Hours:** Sun brunch noon-3 pm, lunch Tues-Sat 11 am-3 pm, dinner Tues-Sat 5:30-10 pm, Sun 3-7 pm
**Cards:** AE, MC, VISA, CB, DISCOVER
**Reservations:** Accepted
**Bar:** Service bar
**Parking:** Street
**Party Facilities:** For up to 120

The Old Church Inn, as its name suggests, is housed in a de-sanctified church. That strikes me as appropriate, considering the close relationship between religious ritual and food. The restaurant is handsomely appointed, with settings of stained glass, ornate wood-work, and carved angels.

The cooking style is contemporary, though not cutting-edge. The menu lists shrimp de jonghe, rumaki, and snails in garlic butter among its collection of appetizers, though that somewhat passé list is supplemented by something as contemporary as pasta and gorgonzola cheese with walnuts.

A tried-and-true standard, caesar salad, is prepared to perfection. Crisp shards of romaine lettuce are well seasoned with garlic, oil, and all the other components that make up this classic. Though caesar salad is hardly unique, the excellence of this particular rendition is clear.

The excellence is also seen in entrees such as walleyed pike. This is a wonderful freshwater fish; as prepared at the Old Church Inn, it loses none of its freshness. The menu offers the fish either in a creamy lemon butter sauce with almonds, or, for calorie counters, more simply baked.

Several other seafood selections are offered regularly, along with a wide choice of meats and poultry. In a tribute to classic cookery, the menu even features beef Wellington among its best selections, a dish no longer common.

Among a listing of recent evening specials was rolled chicken breast with fresh spinach, served with a coarse chop of tomato for sauce, and sauteed mushrooms. Not only is this a handsome platter to look at, but the preparation is about as good as chicken breast can get. The meat is moist, the spinach not overcooked, the tomato-and-mushroom saucing in proper balance.

A selection of pastas, some in rather trendy exposition, are among other choices on a menu that also makes a bow toward family dining with inclusion of special children's meals. Service, while well-meaning and cheerful, is not nearly as advanced as the food.

# Oo-La-La!
KR 17.5/20
Decor 3/4   Hospitality 5/5   Food 7.5/9   Value 2/2

- **Continental/Eclectic**
- **Chicago/Mid-North**
- **$$**

3335 N. Halsted St.
Chicago
(312) 935-7708
**Troubleshooter:** Callin Fortis,
Nunzio Fresta (owners)

**Hours:** Daily 5:30-11 pm, Sun brunch 10 am-3 pm
**Cards:** MC, VISA
**Reservations:** Suggested
**Bar:** Full
**Parking:** Valet Thursday through Saturday, and street

Oo-la-la! is to decor as vintage clothing stores are to fashion. There is a faux sense of richness, quickly dispelled when one realizes that it is all paint and glitter, swagged curtains, and gaudy chandeliers.

But oh, that food, an engaging mix of French and Italian cuisines, though not limited to either. The cooking is stylish but not particularly cutting-edge. The goal seems to be something akin to bistro food, but with a little more finesse.

That intent is largely achieved. Try something fairly simple, such as marinated chilled vegetables. The platter contains some delicious smoked leek, artichoke hearts, thin slices of roasted zucchini and red peppers, all in a light olive oil and sun-dried tomato vinaigrette. Calamari, so popular in Southern Italian dining, can be ordered deep-fried with an unusual lemon-and-brandy sauce or grilled and served with black olives and an onion/tomato chutney. Simple crostini, toasted bread usually with a brush of tomato sauce, is more original at Oo-la-la! with a topping of artichokes and creamy rich mascarpone cheese.

Pastas play an important part in the Oo-la-la! menu, with more than half a dozen selections offered. Simple tomato sauce is freshened with basil and garlic on your choice of pasta. Penne, the short tubular noodle that lends itself well to al dente cooking, comes with broccoli florettes, roasted red peppers, plus a light garlic-and-tomato saucing. One of the better selections consists of plumped mussels, sweet scented by the sea, with garlic, capers, and small red peppers called pepperoncini, with either a cream or tomato sauce. Among other selections, the twisted corkscrews called fusilli come with small strips of grilled chicken, plus spinach in a tomato cream sauce touched with brandy.

Second-course selections include a tasty version of chicken Vesuvio with plenty of garlic, a daily veal preparation, grilled half chicken with roasted peppers, sun-dried tomatoes, and olive oil in a rather conventional bistro-style recipe. But stuffed breast of chicken filled with spinach and ricotta cheese is an engaging variation, evidently a house specialty.

À la carte salads and desserts conclude an evening of better dining at extremely reasonable cost.

# OPEN SESAME
KR 17.5/20
Decor 2.5/4   Hospitality 5/5   Food 8/9   Value 2/2

- **Middle Eastern**
- **Niles**
- **$**

8743 N. Milwaukee Ave.
Niles
(708) 967-0030
**Troubleshooter:** Nabil Samkari (owner)

**Hours:** Daily 11 am-10:30 pm
**Cards:** AE, MC, VISA
**Reservations:** Accepted
**Handicapped:** Accessible
**Bar:** No alcohol but diners may bring their own
**Parking:** Free lot
**Party Facilities:** Semi-private for up to 55

Only the name has changed in the restaurant that used to be called Old Jerusalem. The dining is as good as ever. Portions are generous, and the cooking is done with a sure and knowledgeable hand.

Start with a selection of appetizers. Go with enough people to order several for more varied sampling. Baba ghanoush, a puree of smoked, roasted eggplant, has an enchanting, dusky flavor. Tabbouli, a salad of cracked wheat, parsley, lemon juice, garlic, and other seasonings, is fresh on the palate. Hummus, a Middle Eastern staple, is a puree of chickpeas and sesame paste called tahini. It is a thick sauce, almost like peanut butter, but with its own distinctive style. Take warm wedges of pita bread and dip into the hummus. Among other appetizer selections, stuffed grape leaves, also available in dinner portion, come warm, with a filling of ground beef and rice and a light, unobtrusive seasoning.

Less-hungry diners might be satisfied with one of the small sandwiches on pita. Kefta kebabs are ground lamb and beef patties that have been char-grilled for the best flavor. Beef or lamb kebabs, all available in dinner portions, can also be ordered as sandwich filling. Felafel is a perfect snack food, a deep-fried patty of ground chickpeas and vegetables, served with tahini sauce, shreds of lettuce, and a bit of tomato for color.

For a full-fledged entree, a combination platter will provide a taste of shish kebab, kefta kebab, and shawrima. The latter, often confused with Greek gyros, is really a much better product. Where gyros uses pressed or ground meat, shawrima is made with slices of lamb taken from a rôtisserie. The seasoning is light, and like other entrees, the dish comes with a side of rice pilaf.

# THE ORIGINAL A-1

KR 16.5/20
Decor 4/4  Hospitality 3.5/5  Food 7.5/9  Value 1.5/2

- **American/Tex-Mex**
- **Chicago/Near North**
- **$$**

401 E. Illinois St. (North Pier Terminal)
Chicago
(312) 644-0300
**Troubleshooter:** John Buchanan (managing partner)

**Hours:** Mon-Thurs 11:30 am-10 pm, Fri-Sat until midnight, Sun until 9 pm
**Cards:** All majors
**Handicapped:** Accessible
**Bar:** Full
**Parking:** Valet, validated lot parking
**Party Facilities:** For 80 sit-down, 150 cocktails
**Heart-Healthy Menu:** Selections on request

The Original A-1 takes restaurant as theater to the max. The large dining room looks as if it were there before Marty Robbins ever found Rosa's Cantina.

The menu is Tex-Mex in large portion. You could begin with an appetizer of guacamole with taco chips, spiced more than most other guacamoles, or a nacho platter with loads of melted cheese, refried beans, mounds of sour cream, even some of that spicy guacamole, and a fiery salsa picante. If you want a bit more elaborate or rib-sticking nacho platter, get it with the house version of Texas chili or shredded chicken.

Any border beanery worth its salsa better have beans. You can get a standard-issue bean soup, with bits of red onion and a fistful of sour cream piled on top. Considering that the caesar salad was invented in Tijuana, I would have expected better of The Original A-1 version. The olive oil dressing is too pronounced, but the salad is still rather bland.

Getting down to the main business of eating, Texas-style barbecue grilled over coals is the big attraction. The chicken and steak both have that smoked flavor, enhanced with a spiced, but somewhat sweet, barbecue sauce. Grilled onions and peppery french fries fill out the platters. Seafood choices vary from day to day. Fajitas come in a variety of ways, loaded with peppers and onions.

# THE PALM
KR 18.5/20
Decor 4/4   Hospitality 4/5   Food 9/9   Value 1.5/2

- **American**
- **Chicago/Near North**
- **$$$**

181 E. Lake Shore Dr. (Mayfair
Regent Hotel)
Chicago
(312) 944-0135
**Troubleshooter:** John
Blandino (general manager)

**Hours:** Mon-Fri 11:30
am-10:30 pm, Sat 5-10:30 pm,
Sundays 5-10 pm
**Cards:** AE, CB, DINERS, MC,
VISA
**Reservations:** Suggested
**Handicapped:** Accessible
**Bar:** Full
**Party Facilities:** For up to 65

**P**atterned after its namesake restaurant, the original Palm in New York, the Chicago Palm has caricatures of celebrities and VIPs on the walls. The sawdust-covered floors and ceiling fans are reminiscent of Chicago's speakeasy days.

The restaurant is famous for its gargantuan portions, from baked potatoes to whole Nova Scotia lobsters, plus huge prime New York cut steaks, tender lamb, and milk-fed veal. All dishes are cooked to order in portions definitely not for bird-like appetites.

For dessert the specialty of the house is cheesecake, rich, heavy, and everything New York-style cheesecake should be. Even though prices are high, the food is uniformly excellent!

# PAPAGUS
KR 18.5/20
Decor 4/4   Hospitality 5/5   Food 7.5/9   Value 2/2

- **Greek/Contemporary**
- **Chicago/Near North**
- **$$**

Embassy Suites Hotel, 620 N.
   State St.
Chicago
(312) 642-8450
**Troubleshooters:** Dave
Wolfgram, Jimmy Banakis
(managing partners)

**Hours:** Mon-Thurs 11:30
am-10 pm, Fri until midnight,
Sat noon-midnight, Sun until
10 pm
**Cards:** All majors
**Reservations:** None
**Handicapped:** Accessible
**Bar:** Full
**Parking:** Validated parking in
nearby lot, and valet
**Party Facilities:** For 12-350

There is no question that the food served at Papagus is excep-
tionally delicious. But typical Greek home cooking? I doubt it. The
presentations and cookery bespeak a very talented chef.

Papagus is handsomely appointed, with cobblestone floors, field-
stone wall accents, an open delicatessen and oven, and some genu-
inely delicious food, at fairly moderate cost. Soon after you are
seated, a waiter takes drink orders, then brings over a large wooden
tray with seven or eight appetizers, called mezzes. You can take right
from the tray or go to the menu and make other selections. There
are some wonderful ideas here, many of them spinoffs of traditional
Greek cooking but with more panache.

Close to the traditional might be dolmades, chilled grape leaves
stuffed with a seasoned, sweetened rice filling. Or taste chicken with
bulghur wheat, a savory experience. Asparagus salad dresses spears
in a balanced blend of oil and herbed vinegar. The choices go on
and on, including potato spreads, with or without garlic; a blend of
peppers, lamb, nuts, and raisins; and roasted eggplant purée. From
the collection of warm appetizers are Papagus versions of moussaka,
saganaki, Greek sausage, and the like.

One could make a meal from the appetizers alone. But should
you move on to entrees, consider skewered fresh fish. Recently,
large cubes of tuna and salmon were served in a slightly sweet herbal
sauce that brought together oil, sun-dried tomatoes, and other fla-
vorings to achieve a well-balanced whole. Lamb, the staple of Gre-
cian dining, is served in several fashions. Slices from a roasted leg
are about as tasty as you can get. The meat comes out with a hint of

pink in the center; this is not the kind of stringy lamb that is over-cooked to disguise its faults. Roasted fresh vegetables accompany the meat, still crisp and textured. One of the more original selections is chicken gyros, in which the chicken is roasted on the vertical gyros spit, flaked into bite-size strips, and served with wedges of pita, dilled yogurt, and thinly sliced red onions. Though not authentic, the dish does demonstrate the imagination always at work at Papagus.

Among desserts, baklava stuffed with walnuts is not to be believed, or you might want to try chocolate pita just as a curiosity.

# PARRINELLO
KR 18.5/20
Decor 4/4   Hospitality 4/5   Food 8.5/9   Value 2/2

| | |
|---|---|
| • **Italian** | **Hours:** Lunch Mon-Fri starts at 11:30 am, dinner Mon-Thurs 5-10 pm, Fri-Sat until 11 pm |
| • **Chicago/Near North** | |
| • **$$** | **Cards:** AE, MC, VISA |
| 535 N. Wells St. | **Reservations:** Suggested |
| Chicago | **Handicapped:** Accessible |
| (312) 527-2782 | **Bar:** Full |
| **Troubleshooter:** Salvatore | **Parking:** Valet |
| Parrinello (owner) | **Party Facilities:** For 40-100 |

Parrinello has the look of a trattoria that could be equally at home in Rome or Brooklyn. That it is in Chicago is our good fortune. The copper ceiling has the patina of age, even to streaks of green running down sections of the plastered walls. Tables are fairly close together, the room made more compact and alive by a small bar to one side. The menu is fairly concise, though it is supplemented by fresh seafood. Among appetizers are such standards as carpaccio, grilled oysters, and grilled mushrooms. In the front window, passersby can see the antipasto platter, its components handsomely presented in a mouth-watering display of asparagus, peppers, a huge cheese wheel, plus other components.

Pasta offers its own rewards. Tortellini are as good as they can possibly be in a light sauce of prosciutto, a smattering of peas, pine nuts, and herbs. Rigatoni is served with an abundant sweet sausage and pepper sauce. A la carte salads can range from simple greens to fresh plum tomatoes, to a mix with gorgonzola cheese and roasted walnuts.

Among a handful of second-course listings, a Northern Italian style of cookery predominates. Scallops of veal in generous portion come with roasted chopped hazelnuts in a butter-and-balsamic vinegar sauce, reminiscent of, but more sharply flavored than, some adaptations of veal picatta.

Tiramisu, cannoli, and gelati define the dessert choices.

# PARTHENON
KR 16.5/20
Decor 2.5/4   Hospitality 4/5   Food 8/9   Value 2/2

| | |
|---|---|
| • **Greek** | **Hours:** Sun-Fri 11-1 am, Sat until 2 am |
| • **Chicago/Near West** | **Cards:** All majors, house accounts |
| • **$** | **Reservations:** For 6 or more |
| 314 S. Halsted St. | **Handicapped:** Accessible |
| Chicago | **Bar:** Full |
| (312) 726-2407 | **Parking:** Free valet, free lot |
| **Troubleshooters:** Chris Liakouras, Peter Liakouras (owners) | **Party Facilities:** For 50-200 |

Parthenon may not be as old as its namesake on the Acropolis, but this restaurant seems to have been a fixture of Chicago's Greek Town just about forever. Now that the restaurant has had a good facelift, it's more enjoyable than ever.

Seafood is a natural specialty for Greek restaurants, and Parthenon is no exception. The red snapper is lovely at market price. Sea bass has a milder flavor and when available should please most any seafood fancier. Each comes broiled, brushed with olive oil, freshly squeezed lemon juice and oregano.

When it comes to portion sizes, more is more. Appetizers are large enough to serve two people. Try the traditional rice-stuffed grape leaves called dolmades with a creamy lemon sauce or little cheese pies in phyllo dough stuffed to bursting.

While the menu presents the tried-and-true Greek specialties found up and down Halsted, there are also some rather unusual choices, such as barbecued whole roast suckling pig for groups of 12 (this requires advance notice). Perhaps most exotic is lamb's head, baked and served with oven-roasted potatoes. For more conventional lamb, try roast loin or leg, or even barbecued on the spit. Most entrees are served with rice or potatoes; some include a side of vegetables.

Combination platters include appetizer mezze priced per person as well as full dinner combinations rounding up the usual suspects: moussaka, pastitsio, roast lamb, potatoes, and vegetables. Desserts are typically sweet, though a homemade yogurt offers a somewhat different alternative to a meal's conclusion.

# PASTEUR
KR 18.5/20
Decor 3/4   Hospitality 5/5   Food 8.5/9   Value 2/2

- **Vietnamese**
- **Chicago/Far North**
- **$$**

4759 N. Sheridan Rd.
Chicago
(312) 271-6673
**Troubleshooter:** Tuan
Nguyen (owner)

**Hours:** Lunch daily noon-2:30 pm, dinner daily 5-10 pm, Sat-Sun to 11 pm
**Cards:** AE, MC, VISA
**Reservations:** Suggested
**Handicapped:** Accessible
**Bar:** Service bar
**Parking:** Street
**Party Facilities:** For up to 70

There is a sense of nostalgia at Pasteur for what never can be again, namely, colonial Vietnam. But that is countered by the enthusiasm and pleasure with which customers are greeted.

The restaurant is named for Pasteur Street in Saigon, and it appears as if everything possible has been done to re-create the way foods might have been cooked and served there. The menu highlights several house specialties, but even when you go with the regular list, there are no mistakes to be made. The traditional Vietnamese spring roll is a delicate, almost translucent, rice paper wrapped around a filling of rice noodles, bean sprouts, and small pieces of shrimp. The spring roll is taken in hand and dipped into a sweet plum sauce, enhanced by the slight bite of peppers, and topped with ground peanuts. Even better among appetizers is an omelette called Banh Xeo. Folded almost like a crêpe, it is filled with shrimp, mushrooms, pork, and bean sprouts, among other ingredients. The idea is to cut off a piece to wrap in a large lettuce leaf, all of which is dipped into a somewhat thin but sweet sauce.

The choices are many and varied, but one other we tasted was deep-fried shrimp with tapioca root. This is listed as a house specialty, and for good reason. The flavors are absolutely marvelous, as the shrimp and sticks of yam are held together in a light binding, all of which, like the crêpe, is meant to be wrapped in a lettuce leaf for handy snacking.

Still more courses lie ahead. Some of the cooking is reminiscent of Thailand. While peppers are used, there is not necessarily that fiery heat characteristic of Thai cooking. For example, stir-fried chicken can be ordered with a seasoning of lemon grass and peppers. But the jalapeño-style peppers have been carefully seeded and washed, which removes most of the heat, leaving a lovely sweet aftertaste. It balances perfectly with the mild chicken and other flavors.

# PEGASUS
KR 17.5/20
Decor 4/4   Hospitality 4/5   Food 7.5/9   Value 2/2

- **Greek**
- **Chicago/Near West**
- **$**

130 S. Halsted St.
Chicago
(312) 226-3377
**Troubleshooters:** John Melidis, James Alexander (owners)

**Hours:** Daily 11 am-midnight
**Cards:** All majors, house accounts
**Handicapped:** Accessible
**Bar:** Full
**Parking:** Free valet parking
**Party Facilities:** For up to 100

**P**egasus is fairly large, but not cavernous. Its handsome white-washed walls create the sense of a Mediterranean villa. The restaurant is fronted by French doors, which are opened in warm weather for a café or taverna ambiance.

The menu is typical of Chicago Greek restaurants, the cooking not really any better or worse than others. I do like the fact that Pegasus uses kaeseri cheese for saganaki and some other dishes, rather than the saltier kefilatori. Pegasus also serves a delicious version of lokaneko, a spicy sausage appetizer. Other appetizers include traditional Greek phyllo-wrapped morsels, one style filled with feta cheese, another with spinach and cheese. The appetizer/salad selection lists about two dozen other choices, hot or cold.

Some appetizers can also be ordered in dinner-sized portions, such as spinach pie or gyros. A combination platter contains several slices of gyros, milder sliced leg of lamb, pastitsio, and dolmades, plus rice, roasted potatoes, and green beans. Meats are not cooked rare in Greek kitchens; thus the leg of lamb is a little too dry, though free of fat. The dolmades, ground meat-stuffed grape leaves, are fairly simple and direct; the light flavor of the filling contrasts with the vegetal flavor contributed by its wrapping. Pastitsio, a macaroni-and-cheese casserole bound in a cream sauce, is lightly seasoned with cinnamon and other aromatics. I noted this moderation in other preparations, too.

I have often said that most of the Greek restaurants up and down Halsted Street serve similar food and thus must be distinguished by other factors. An experience at Pegasus confirms this observation. Soon after we were seated, a group of 20 or more people arrived. After the group had gathered and everyone had found a seat, they all stood, bowed their heads in prayer, and began their meal.

A manager explained they all came from, or had parents who came from, the same village in Greece; this was one of their periodic gatherings. The warmth and intimacy of that group pervaded the dining area, if only for a few moments. Such scenes add a unique touch to Pegasus that underscores the restaurant's warmth and hospitality.

# PIEROGI INN
KR 17.5/20
Decor 3/4   Hospitality 5/5   Food 7.5/9   Value 2/2

- **Polish**
- **Chicago/Northwest**
- **$**

5318 W. Lawrence Ave.
Chicago
(312) 725-2818
**Troubleshooter:** Richard
Zawadzki (chef/owner)

**Hours:** Daily 10 am-8 pm
**Cards:** None
**Reservations:** None
**Handicapped:** Accessible
**Parking:** Free in nearby
Copernicus Foundation lot

There is a certain home-cooked style about Polish foods that you do not find with some other cuisines. The ingredients are filling, soups are hot and hearty, portions tend to be large. With a Polish population in Chicago that's second in size only to Warsaw's, the

Polish restaurants here run the gamut from simple to elaborate. One of the newest, and easily the least presumptuous, is Pierogi Inn.

Just half a block from the Copernicus Foundation, with its imposing tower and onion-bulbed dome, Pierogi Inn is a working-class restaurant where service and foods are simple. The menu is posted on a wall, listing several different kinds of pierogis, plus the soups and entrees of the day.

Begin with a cup or bowl of soup, though be forewarned that the bowl is enormous. But considering how tasty soups at Pierogi Inn are, you'll probably lap up every drop. Naturally, there is mushroom soup, a creamy stock in which float a bounty of sliced and flavorful mushrooms. Chicken soup Pierogi Inn-style is a light golden broth with mild flavor. Polish dumplings called uszka, filled with ground lamb, float in the soup, adding another flavor dimension. Beet borsht is a common find, as is a vegetable soup redolent with fresh-snipped dill.

Pierogis are to Poland what ravioli are to Italy. The dough is cut into rounds and filled with stuffings that range from meats to cheese or mushrooms, or for dessert, various fruits of the season. Chef/ Owner Richard Zawadzki even fills pierogis with oysters Rockefeller or, more commonly, ground whitefish. Containers of thick sour cream are set at the table along with the pierogis. You can order the dumplings with your favorite stuffing or as a combination platter.

Half a dozen pierogis may be accompanied by a sweet cheese blintz and stuffed cabbage. The cabbage is mild; the filling of ground meat and potatoes picks up flavorings during the baking process. In addition to the pierogis, entrees such as veal paprikash, roast chicken, or beef stroganoff are ladled out buffet-style from a steam table. That's in keeping with the direct approach of Pierogi Inn, where portions are large and prices small.

# POMODORO
KR 18.5/20
Decor 4/4   Hospitality 4.5/5   Food 8/9   Value 2/2

- **Italian**
- **Wheeling**
- **$$**

102 S. Milwaukee Ave.
Wheeling
(708) 459-4199
**Troubleshooter:** Lee Keating
(owner)

**Hours:** Lunch Mon-Fri 11:30 am-2 pm, dinner Sun-Thurs 5-9 pm, Fri-Sat until 10 pm
**Cards:** All majors, house accounts
**Reservations:** Suggested
**Handicapped:** Accessible
**Bar:** Full
**Parking:** Free lot
**Party Facilities:** Saturday and Sunday mornings through early afternoons
**Heart-Healthy Menu:** Selections

The cooking at Pomodoro (Italian for "tomato") is fresh and inventive, perhaps a tad richer than usual in Northern Italian cookery, but uniformly good. The restaurant is modern and fresh looking, with a glassed-in café addition that allows diners to enjoy the weather without being adversely affected by it.

To get things started, something as simple and elegant as bruschetti with eggplant can be marvelous. Bruschetti is nothing more than toasted slices of Italian bread brushed with olive oil and garlic, then topped with slices of fresh tomatoes. One can imagine the Italian farmer going off to the field for a day's work in the hot sun with a packet of bruschetti tucked in his sack for lunch. Other appetizers range from fried calamari, to scampi, angel-hair pasta, and goat's cheese, as well as several other selections.

Though salad accompanies entrees, more elaborate à la carte salads can be ordered, as can a traditional pasta course preceding the entree. Among pasta choices, linguine à la marinara comes in a generous portion, with shrimp, scallops, mussels, and calamari topping the pasta, bound with a flavorful tomato sauce spiked with just the right balance of garlic and herbs.

From a selection of meats, veal piccata is characterized by the sheer buttery richness of the sauteed veal.

Desserts include a magnificent fudge-rich flourless chocolate cake and other dolci.

# PRINTER'S ROW
KR 18.5/20
Decor 4/4   Hospitality 4/5   Food 8.5/9   Value 2/2

- **American**
- **Chicago/Loop Area**
- **$$$**

550 S. Dearborn
Chicago
(312) 461-0780
**Troubleshooters:** Michael
Foley (owner), Andrew Bowling
(general manager)

**Hours:** Lunch Mon-Fri 11:30
am-2:30 pm, dinner Mon-Thurs
5:30-10 pm, Fri-Sat until
10:30 pm
**Cards:** All majors
**Handicapped:** Accessible
**Bar:** Full, wine list features 120
vintages
**Parking:** Street or nearby lots
**Party Facilities:** For 10-90
**Heart-Healthy Menu:**
Selections as arranged with
waiter

**W**hen Chef Michael Foley opened Printer's Row, he was pi-
oneering an imaginative, primarily American-based cuisine. Over the
years, Foley has stayed true to that dedication.

His restaurant is somewhat clamorous when busy. Service is
rather formal and impersonal, though not without style and
precision.

The fairly short menu is augmented by evening specials. The en-
tire menu changes every few months. Recent choices have included
some rather imaginative creations. One of the more unusual is the
Printer's Row version of caesar salad, with the menu hardly describ-
ing what Foley has produced. A rather small portion of shredded ro-
maine lettuce leaves lies cupped in a woven potato basket, dressed
as a caesar salad conventionally would be. But the visual impression
is so startling, the surprise so complete, that it becomes evident im-
mediately that Foley is couragous as well as creative.

Other selections, though less shocking perhaps, are no less inno-
vative. Consider a portobello mushroom appetizer. The meaty
fungus is sliced crosswise, much like a beefsteak, and marinated in a
variety of flavors. Vinegar provides an acidic foundation for other
ingredients.

The entree selections incline toward poultry and seafood, in keep-
ing with contemporary tastes, though lovers of beef will find a ten-
derloin roasted with fresh rosemary in natural juices flavored with
shallots. Grilled capon is surprisingly seductive. The bird is silky ten-

der, with a light vinaigrette of vermouth and a touch of sage. Duck gets a roasted treatment, leaving the skin charred black but the meat rosy; influences of honey and orange are found in the sauce. A portion of goose comes embellished with a small mound of couscous. The goose has very little fat, its broad slices from the breast still purple with an underdone quality more fashionable than appetizing.

Other entree choices include monkfish in a cream curry with basmati rice; red snapper wrapped in a brioche dough enhanced with tarragon; or, for vegetarians, eggplant, grilled, then sauced with cumin and lemon-flavored crème fraiche.

# THE PUMP ROOM
KR 17/20
Decor 4/4   Hospitality 5/5   Food 7/9   Value 1/2

- **American**
- **Chicago/Near North**
- **$$$**

1301 N. State Pkwy. (Omni Ambassador East)
Chicago
(312) 266-0360
**Troubleshooters:** Mark Tormey, David Wolfgram (managing partners)

**Hours:** Mon-Thurs 7 am-10 pm, Fri-Sat until midnight, Sun brunch 11 am-2:30 pm, dinner 5-10 pm
**Cards:** All majors
**Reservations:** Required
**Handicapped:** Accessible
**Bar:** Full, band and dancing
**Dress:** Jackets required after 4:30 pm
**Parking:** Valet
**Party Facilities:** Four private suites in hotel
**Heart-Healthy Menu:** Selections

That the Pump Room has a virtually all-American menu says as much about shifting dining tastes and trends as it does about the ability of this most famous of Chicago's restaurants to follow them. Gone are the days when stars traveling coast to coast on the Twentieth Century Limited would stop in Chicago and dine at the Pump Room. Now most of the stars on view in Booth One are of the TV and rock-stage variety.

As for the food, it continues to be handsomely served, with as much attention to detail as is possible in a kitchen geared to serving as many as 200 dinners at one crack. Desserts are top notch, as is the wine list. All in all, the Pump Room has matured considerably since Milton Berle quipped, "Everything comes served on a flaming sword, except the check!"

# RAVINIA BBQ & GRILL
KR 18/20
Decor 3/4   Hospitality 5/5   Food 8/9   Value 2/2

| | |
|---|---|
| • **American** | **Hours:** Lunch Tues-Sat 11:30 am-2 pm, dinner Tues-Fri 5-9:30 pm, Sat until 10:30 pm, Sun 5-9 pm |
| • **Highland Park** | |
| • **$$** | |
| 592 Roger Williams Ave. | **Cards:** MC, VISA |
| Highland Park | **Reservations:** Recommended |
| (708) 433-1111 | **Handicapped:** Accessible |
| **Troubleshooter:** Lou Tannenbaum (owner) | **Bar:** Service bar |
| | **Parking:** Street |
| | **Party Facilities:** For up to 50 |

**I**magine a restaurant where a waitress cuddles a customer's baby and walks around showing the infant to people at various tables. How about a waitress serving food and suggesting that you offer a taste to someone at a nearby table? It may sound odd, but it is friendly, which is the operative word for Ravinia BBQ & Grill. It's almost like going to a party, especially the way owner Lou Tannenbaum visits with guests. Even perfect strangers leave with the sense that they have made a new friend.

Tables are fairly close together, but the portions are as large as the restaurant is small. All dinners include a delicious mixed salad or dill-flavored cole slaw, a choice of cottage-fried, baked, or broasted potatoes, plus a sourdough loaf so good you'll probably want to take any leftovers home with you for toast the next morning. The menu, as the name suggests, leads off with ribs, chicken, skirt steak, and similar barbecue favorites. In addition to the barbecues, salads, and sandwiches that stud the Ravinia BBQ & Grill menu, there are California-style pizzas. One thing that draws many customers is the off-menu specialties, such as fresh fish, generous lamb chops, and an immense veal chop. The chops are almost hidden beneath a mound of crispy browned onion slivers, plus potatoes or rice on the side. Portions of the chops and other entrees are generous enough to serve two people and maybe have some leftovers. Desserts are about as lavish as everything else; fruit pies are featured when in season and are recommended à la mode! A single serving is enough for four or five people. Have fun, come hungry, and leave happy!

# RED LION PUB
KR 16.5/20
Decor 3.5/4  Hospitality 4/5  Food 7/9  Value 2/2

- **British**
- **Chicago/Mid-North**
- **$**

2446 N. Lincoln Ave.
Chicago
(312) 348-2695
**Troubleshooter:** John
Cordwell (owner)

**Hours:** Mon 4 pm-midnight,
Tues-Sat noon-2 am
**Cards:** AE, CB, MC, VISA
**Bar:** Full
**Parking:** Street

There are two common aphorisms about the gastronomy of Great Britain. As one saying has it, "The British know how to eat well, they just don't know how to cook well!" Another epigram maintains, "In Britain the beer is too warm and the bath water too cold!"

The publican at the Red Lion Pub is from England and has done a good job of re-creating the ambiance of his homeland. There is a certain coziness to the Red Lion Pub.

The rather concise menu can offer such dishes as steak and kidney pie, deep-fried fish chips in beer batter, sausage rolls (called "bangers" in the old country), and shepherd's pie. The British like to wrap their meats in pastries of some sort or another. Excluding beef Wellington, you'll find several samples of the genre at the Red Lion Pub.

The bangers are served with a touch of chutney for saucing. The fish is best when liberally moistened with malt vinegar, though you might have to ask for a bottle. The shepherd's pie comes in a baking crock, topped with mounds of browned mashed potatoes covering a larder of meat and a liberal supply of flavorful cooked vegetables. It puts to rest the notion that British foods are as bland as the moors on a dark winter's afternoon. In addition to the short printed menu card, a blackboard lists a few daily items.

The British have a talent for making a wide variety of sausages and an interest in eating same. A shire platter includes a slice or two of coarse-ground terrine blended with slivers of hazelnuts, accompanied by a bland brick cheese and chutney. There are a few sandwiches, including the un-British American hamburger with your choice of toppings, and a newer addition, Buffalo wings. Oh, well! Just chalk it all up to cultural cross-pollination.

Like any decent establishment of its type, the Red Lion Pub has a wide selection of lagers and ales. Desserts can be exceptional: the delicious trifle mounded in a round-bottomed schooner and the open-faced blueberry tart are cases in point.

# RELISH

KR 18.5/20

Decor 3.5/4   Hospitality 5/5   Food 8/9   Value 2/2

| | |
|---|---|
| • **American/Eclectic** | **Hours:** Daily 5:15-11 pm |
| • **Chicago/Mid-North** | **Cards:** AE, CB, DINERS, MC, VISA |
| • **$$** | **Reservations:** None |
| 2044 N. Halsted St. | **Handicapped:** Accessible |
| Chicago | **Parking:** Valet or street |
| (312) 868-9034 | **Party Facilities:** Entire |
| **Troubleshooter:** Ron Blazek (owner) | restaurant available |

**A**s the ever-changing menu points out, the word "relish" is both a verb and noun. Both aspects apply at this appropriately named restaurant. Relish is a bright, kicky restaurant with rock music in the background, imaginative, contemporary graphics on the walls and a sheen reflecting from the hardwood floors.

Servers are knowledgeable and as unpretentious as the food. The emphasis is on creativity. Chef/Owner Ron Blazek begins with fairly traditional conceptions, then adds a twist that transforms the ordinary into the exceptional. Blazek takes the flaky dough of a common strudel pastry and fills it with a collection of mushrooms bound with pesto made not from basil but from arugula, which is then enhanced with roasted garlic. A simple grill of mixed vegetables is given the mild nip of balsamic vinaigrette and mozzarella cheese. Instead of stuffing baked oysters with breadcrumbs, Blazek fills the oysters with the makings of crab cake, delicious in their own right and absolutely luxurious when combined with the sensuous oyster.

Other knockout selections include risotto with lobster and shrimp and an absolutely sensational multicolored striped cannelloni wrapped around a filling of lobster, shrimp, and scallop in a coulis of smoked tomato.

Entrees are similarly provocative. Something as elementary as roast chicken is given snap with an accompaniment of mashed potatoes enriched with asiago cheese. Only a wild game kebab, a mix of meats including venison and quail, among others, failed to please.

More exciting is grouper, the fish literally covered in a crust of smoked salmon that had somehow been processed to an almost crumblike texture. The fish is served with a warm, chunky red-potato salad and a portion of fried leeks. The inspiration continues with a selection of roasted, sliced swordfish in a lobster and smoked shrimp sauce, which the menu describes as vinaigrette. The use of vinegar is adventurous in several selections; the acidity is a natural taste-enhancer in knowledgeable hands.

As for dessert, dried cherry strudel with half a pear and semi-sweet caramel ice cream is not to be missed. A seductively named chocolate dessert attracts attention with its mixed bag of delights. Fruit Napoleon brings a fresh compote with berries and the occasional tropical fruit in between crisp sugar wafers.

# Rigoletto
KR 18.5/20
Decor 4/4   Hospitality 4/5   Food 8.5/9   Value 2/2

- **Italian**
- **Lake Forest**
- **$$**

293 E. Illinois
Lake Forest
(708) 234-7675
**Troubleshooters:** Peter
DeCarl, Jay Weiss (owners)

**Hours:** Lunch Tues-Fri 11:30
am-3 pm, dinner Tues-Thurs
5-10 pm, Fri-Sat until 11 pm,
Sun until 9 pm
**Cards:** MC, VISA
**Reservations:** Suggested
**Handicapped:** Accessible
**Bar:** Full
**Parking:** Nearby lot or street

With neo-modern appointments such as beaded cone lamps over most tables, contemporary graphic art, and comfortable seating at tables or banquettes, the restaurant's decor is sophisticated.

The menu is similarly appealing. The cooking is full-bodied, with an emphasis on pronounced flavors. Thus, a pasta with mushrooms and herbs is almost meaty in taste and texture. With an appetizer such as grilled asparagus with radicchio and balsamic vinegar, the grilling imparts a flavor that works wonderfully with the sharp radicchio and contrasts nicely with the mellowness of the dressing.

A great deal of thought has gone into the Rigoletto menu and its execution. Other choices include fettuccine with roasted duck in cashew butter; sun-dried tomatoes mark the platter with a dark, winelike color. Hot peppers are manifest in an order of penne arrabiata, short tubular pasta in a red pepper-and-tomato sauce with garlic and parsley.

When it comes to meat or seafood, there are similar satisfactions. A large veal chop is served with fleshy portobello mushrooms and a reduced sauce. Roast rack of lamb is brushed with mustard and coated with fresh herbs. On a daily menu recently, tiny capellini, or angel-hair pasta, served as bedding for a zuppa de mare ala fra diavolo. Bathed in a peppered, but not overly spiced, sauce were a selection of littleneck clams, oysters, large mussels, and shrimp. Normally, angel-hair pasta is too delicate to stand up to such heavy accompaniment, and in one sense the pasta was overwhelmed. Yet, since the pasta strands tend to cling to each other, their combined bulk worked with the saucing and seafood.

Desserts include a delicious peanut butter and chocolate mousse torte napped in a vanilla cream sauce, as well as tiramisu and a few other Italian standards, lighter ice creams, and custom-blended fruit sorbets.

# Roditys
KR 17.5/20
Decor 2.5/4   Hospitality 5/5   Food 8/9   Value 2/2

- **Greek**
- **Chicago/Near West**
- **$$**

222 S. Halsted St.
Chicago
(312) 454-0800
**Troubleshooter:** Perry
Senopoulous (owner)

**Hours:** Sun-Thurs 11-1 am,
Fri-Sat until 2 am
**Cards:** AE, house accounts
**Reservations:** Not taken on
weekends
**Handicapped:** Accessible
**Bar:** Full
**Parking:** Valet, lot
**Party Facilities:** For up to 80

**R**oditys is the Greek restaurant Chicago's Greek-American community visits. It is not unusual to find large families from infants to grandparents sitting next to another table surrounded by Greek Orthodox priests or businessmen on convention.

Yet the non-Greek who craves good Hellenic food can find a warm welcome at Roditys. Service is without flaw. Foods may take some time to reach your table, but that is a sign of individual preparation, not of indifference.

Enjoy red snapper still steaming hot from the broiler. Lamb raised to the heights of Greek soul food is braised, broiled, roasted, or barbecued. It is mixed with beef for gyros, served on the bone as a chop, or roasted and sliced from leg, loin, or shoulder.

The typical Greek casserole dishes with tongue-twisting names are uniformly delicious. Another tongue twister, but a balm to the palate, is taramosalata, a creamy fish roe spread. It is mixed with tart seasonings, then spread generously on thick, delicious crusted sesame-studded bread.

After enjoying the feast, sit back with a cup of strong and black Greek coffee. (Be sure not to stir it or you will disturb the grounds at the bottom.) As the Greek toast to health has it, "Sion!"

# ROSDED
KR 18/20
Decor 3/4   Hospitality 4/5   Food 9/9   Value 2/2

- **Thai**
- **Chicago/Northwest**
- **$**

2308 W. Leland Ave.
Chicago
(312) 334-9055
**Troubleshooters:** Namyos
and Chooski Sudhichitt (owners)

**Hours:** Tues-Sat 11:30 am-9
pm, Sun noon-8:30 pm
**Cards:** MC, VISA
**Reservations:** Not taken on
weekends
**Bar:** No alcohol, diners may
bring their own
**Parking:** City lots

This is one of Chicago's first Thai restaurants, and it remains much the same as it has always been. Rosded is the epitome of the tiny storefront restaurant, not overly decorated, housing just a few tables.

The menu lists the 50 or so dishes regularly prepared in the small kitchen behind a service counter. There are certain Thai dishes that serve as benchmarks for my taste. Many Thai soups fall into that category, and those at Rosded are exceptional. Tom kha kai is a good example. This is a peppery hot clear chicken stock loaded with shrimp, scallions, slivers of fresh lemon grass, and burning hot green peppers, among its other ingredients.

Another benchmark for Thai cookery is pad Thai, a noodle dish loaded with bits of egg, ground peanuts, onions, and bean sprouts in a slightly sweet sauce or gravy. The Rosded version has always been among the best served in the city. In fact, no matter what choices you make – mild or hot curries, meat, or vegetarian – you will be well rewarded. Be sure to go with enough people so that you can order a variety of dishes and come away with a rich sampling of what this charming budget restaurant has to offer.

# SAI CAFE
KR 18/20
Decor 4/4   Hospitality 4/5   Food 8/9   Value 2/2

- **Japanese**
- **Chicago/Mid-North**
- **$$**

2010 N. Sheffield Ave.
Chicago
(312) 472-8080
**Troubleshooters:** Jim or Bob
(owners)

**Hours:** Mon-Thurs 4:30-11 pm, Fri-Sat until midnight, Sun 3:30-10 pm
**Cards:** AE, MC, VISA
**Reservations:** Accepted
**Parking:** Street
**Party Facilities:** For 25-30 except Fridays and Saturdays

The term "grazing" was a hot dining buzzword in the '80s. The idea was to sample a little of this and a little of that instead of a single entree. Well, the term may be old hat today, but the concept certainly applies to Japanese sushi.

At Sai Cafe the sushi and sashimi are picture perfect. Though this restaurant may not offer the tranquility found at other Japanese restaurants, tranquility really is not the function of a sushi bar.

Nonetheless, take a moment to enjoy the visual beauty of the hand-wrapped and molded creations set in front of you – either at the sushi counter itself, where you can watch the preparation, or at a table or booth, where there is a bit more privacy.

If you should be confused by the various choices presented on the menu, a very competent staff will explain everything. Sushi can be enjoyed as an appetizer or as a complete dining experience. Should you choose to move on to something more substantial, be sure to try some of the specialty appetizers. Goma-ae is Japan's approach to spinach, and like so much in Japanese cuisine, the spinach is slightly sweet, thanks to its saucing; sesame seeds add some crunch. Be sure to order deep-fried soft-shell crabs when they are in season. The vinegar sauce makes this quite a different experience from the traditional American treatment with butter sauce and almonds. No matter what the season, the pan-fried scallops are always a good selection.

Dumplings show up in almost every culture. In Japan, they are called gyoza. Pan-fried, they come six to the order along with a light soy-based sauce for dipping.

Sai Cafe's version of sukiyaki is not as soupy as other versions of this staple. Instead, a mound of thin-sliced beef on a bed of translucent noodles seems more sauced than bathed in broth. The Japanese make a ritual of the preparation and consumption of buckwheat noodles, which they call soba. Though not considered especially elegant, at Sai Cafe the pan-fried soba noodles come in a mix of colorful julienne vegetables or slices of meat.

Don't look for much in the way of dessert. There isn't any.

# THE SALOON
KR 18.5/20
Decor 4/4   Hospitality 5/5   Food 7.5/9   Value 2/2

- **American**
- **Chicago/Near North**
- **$$**

200 E. Chestnut St.
Chicago
(312) 280-5454
**Troubleshooters:** Roger Greenfield, Ted Kasemir (owners)

**Hours:** Mon-Sat 11 am-midnight, Sun brunch 11 am-3 pm, dinner 3-11 pm
**Cards:** AE, MC, VISA, DISCOVER
**Reservations:** Recommended
**Bar:** Full, extensive wine list
**Parking:** Valet

The Saloon gives diners a hearty taste of straight-on American cooking. Decor is underscored by earth tones and the warmth that style brings to a dining room. Certain American accents are brought together, among them cove ceilings bearing the Southwestern accent of Indian geometric art.

Though not exclusively a steak house, there is no question that beef, and lots of it, sits as a cornerstone of the menu. The steaks range from large cuts of porterhouse to a small 8-ounce filet, as well as New York- or Kansas City-style strip steaks. Veal, lamb, and pork round out the chops selection. But the meat choices do not end there.

In what must be a tribute of sorts to the roadside diner or truck stop, the Saloon offers a stuffed chopped sirloin with mashed potatoes. The waiter even brags that the potatoes are lumpy. The chopped sirloin, meantime, has a center of melted cheddar cheese and is topped with grilled onions. As tasty as this sounds, it really does not come together all that well.

If it is flavor you want, try filet hash, which is a bit more involved than its name implies. Cubes of beef are at the center of this recipe, as are chunked roasted potatoes and large mushrooms, cooked down in a natural gravy. If the filet hash is not to your liking, the Saloon also offers a smoked chicken hash and even a seafood hash, which is held together in a cream sauce.

Blackened salmon, lobster at market price, and grilled tuna are among seafood selections. For a taste of something more unusual, try an appetizer portion of tuna tartare with capers and lemon juice. Among other appetizer selections, a pan-fried crab cake is a bit strong tasting, though blackened scallops are absolutely delicious. Among soups, the spicy gumbo with slices of tasso sausage adds a bit of flavor zip.

Desserts are the kind of decadent delights one would expect at a restaurant where self-indulgence is encouraged. The Key lime pie and chocolate brownie are good, but a variation on bananas Foster should be one for the record books.

# SANTORINI
KR 18/20
Decor 4/4    Hospitality 4.5/5    Food 7.5/9    Value 2/2

---

- **Greek**
- **Chicago/Near West**
- **$$**

138 S. Halsted St.
Chicago
(312) 829-8820
**Troubleshooter:** Demetrios Kontos (owner)

**Hours:** Sun-Thurs 11 am-midnight, Fri-Sat until 1 am
**Cards:** All majors, house accounts
**Reservations:** Accepted
**Handicapped:** Accessible
**Bar:** Full
**Parking:** Free
**Party Facilities:** For up to 100

---

I think I have said before there are many more similarities than differences among Chicago's Greek restaurants. But now and then, one comes along that's seemingly above the crowd. Santorini is such a Greek restaurant. Like elsewhere in Greek Town, it is noisy and festive. Although prices are in line with the others, the restaurant is more upscale in decor, though not necessarily a dressy sort of place.

The large bi-level dining room is Mediterranean bright, with whitewashed walls, wood accents, and a fireplace to one side. There's even a cactus plant, which seems to suggest the American Southwest or Mexico. But never mind all that; the food is decidedly Grecian.

The food at Santorini is on a par with other Greek restaurants, perhaps in some respects a notch or two above. For instance, an occasional special is lamb exohiko. In this preparation, chunks of lamb are braised, topped with cubes of feta cheese, sauced with a dark gravy studded with green peas, and wrapped in a phyllo dough for final baking. The portion is enormous, easily enough for two people. The flavors are in perfect balance as the gravy tends to absorb some of the stronger essence of the feta. The crust remains delicately flaked without becoming soggy.

The printed menu offers a number of other lamb, beef, and chicken dishes. Almost half the menu, though, is given over to seafood. Whole black bass and whole red snapper are market priced. Other fish run the gamut, including Norwegian salmon, orange roughy, grouper, and lemon sole, as well as various shellfish. Shrimp kebabs, like everything else, come in large portion.

Appetizers include such Greek favorites as saganaki and deep-fried calamari. By some standards the calamari can be a little chewy, but it's still great to nibble at, almost like popcorn. The restaurant serves a delicious sliced eggplant, lightly dredged in flour and given a quick dip in hot oil; the slices are topped with grated cheese and a coarse tomato sauce. It makes for delicious snacking.

# SCOOZI!
KR 18/20
Decor 3/4   Hospitality 4.5/5   Food 8.5/9   Value 2/2

- **Italian**
- **Chicago/Near North**
- **$$**

410 W. Huron St.
Chicago
(312) 943-5900
**Troubleshooter:** Steve
Ottman (manager)

**Hours:** Lunch Mon-Fri 11:30 am-2 pm, dinner Mon-Thurs 5-10:30 pm, Fri-Sat until 11:30 pm, Sun 5-9 pm
**Cards:** All majors
**Reservations:** Lunch only
**Handicapped:** Accessible (including Braille menus)
**Bar:** Full
**Parking:** Valet
**Party Facilities:** Semi-private
**Heart-Healthy Menu:** Selections

**S**coozi! is a restaurant where people waiting for tables spend that time at the bar watching other people waiting for tables. Scoozi! is also restaurant as theater to the *ne plus ultra*. But as it turns out, Scoozi! serves some uncommonly – and even surprisingly – good food.

The menu is quite detailed without being exhaustive in its exploration of Northern Italian cookery. Specialties from Tuscany, Piedmont, Lombardy, Venice, Naples, and other regions are featured among the antipasti, entrees, pastas, salads, and pizzas on the menu. A wide range of imported ingredients, including vegetables, cheeses, and herbs, gives the restaurant's chefs the flexibility to offer high quality despite the huge volume and different varieties of dishes that are served.

The best way to begin is by ordering a large pizza from the list of about half a dozen specialty styles. When our waiter brought out two large tomato cans, which he said would be a platform for the pizza, I thought this was just an affectation. Then he brought the pizza, and I realized it did need a platform. It came out on a large board, about 18 inches or more long. Instead of the 9- or 10-inch circle I expected, the pizza was gargantuan, a large ellipse of flavor on a thin, crisp crust. Flavors were absolutely sensational. Scoozi! could earn its reputation just on its pizza.

But there was much more to be ordered. Not only are there some unusual pasta choices, but the kitchen also produces fresh risotto every half-hour. Properly made, it is a soft blend of rice with light seasonings, especially saffron, butter, and cheese. Although risotto Milanese may be the most well-known, there are any number of recipes. Each evening at Scoozi! may bring a different style. Ample enough for a main course is linguine del golfo. This is akin to a zuppa de pesce, linguine mixed with clams, mussels, calamari, and shrimp. All of this gets a bouquet seasoning, highlighted by mild fennel.

Among meat choices, ossobuco, classic veal shanks from Milan, may be on a nightly special in a syrupy, rich gravy with roasted potatoes, mushrooms, and pearl onions. The flavor is full and hearty. Among other choices, veal chop, which the menu describes as "veal T-bone," is breaded and sauteed, then served with a rosemary-accented mustard sauce.

# SEVEN TREASURES
KR 17.5/20
Decor 2.5/4   Hospitality 4/5   Food 9/9   Value 2/2

- **Chinese**
- **Chicago/South**
- **$**

2312 S. Wentworth Ave.
Chicago
(312) 225-2668
**Troubleshooter:** Chung L. Au

**Hours:** Daily 11-2 am
**Cards:** None
**Reservations:** Accepted
**Handicapped:** Accessible
**Bar:** No alcohol
**Parking:** Street

Think of Chinese food, and chances are you think of rice. The fact is that there is a whole world of Chinese noodles – pasta, if you will. If you start your Chinese dining with an egg roll or two, then you are eating a noodle. At Seven Treasures, however, there is a whole different world of noodles, and you won't even have to order an egg roll. Take a look at the restaurant's two menus, one with a large list of choices like most conventional Chinese restaurants and the smaller folder, with its selection of soups, dumplings, and noodles.

Begin with appetizers. Dumplings in oyster sauce are made with a nearly transparent dough, as thin as a sheet of paper. Wrapped inside are fillings such as chopped mushrooms, meat, and whole tiny shrimp. The light sauce clings to each delicious dumpling as you grasp it with chopsticks or fork and enjoy the sensual taste and texture.

Take a platter of braised noodles, with a light topping of fresh ginger and snips of scallions. Braising noodles gives them a texture not unlike the chewy quality found in al dente Italian pastas, yet the flavors and seasonings make them unmistakably oriental. For a different flavor and texture, try a small side order of duck, with crisp skin and meat that practically falls from the bones.

Choosing main courses can be difficult because the selections are so tempting. If you want to eat like the local customers, try one of the soups, which range from clear broth to rice soup, to soup and noodles with a wide choice of toppings. While largely Cantonese, the menu does list some spicier Szechuan dishes. Yet Cantonese dining still has its own charms. The large portion of stir-fried beef comes in a thick brown gravy and a topping of Chinese broccoli, leafy spinach, and other green vegetables.

Seven Treasures is distinctive, since a large portion of its kitchen is open to the front window of the restaurant so that you can actually see the preparation of many of the foods. The restaurant is brightly lit, not unlike a cafeteria or coffee shop of the 1950s. But what makes Seven Treasures distinctive is that this is where the locals go.

# SHAW'S BLUE CRAB
KR 18.5/20
Decor 4/4   Hospitality 4/5   Food 9/9   Value 1.5/2

- **Seafood/American**
- **Deerfield**
- **$$**

660 Lake-Cook Rd.
Deerfield
(708) 948-1020
**Troubleshooter:** GaryNewlin
(general manager)

**Hours:** Lunch Mon-Thurs 11:30 am-4 pm, dinner Mon-Thurs 5-10 pm, Fri-Sat until 11 pm, Sun 4:30-9 pm
**Cards:** All majors
**Reservations:** Suggested
**Handicapped:** Accessible
**Bar:** Full, extensive beer and wine list
**Parking:** Free lot
**Party Facilities:** Semi-private
**Heart-Healthy Menu:** Selections

**N**ot quite as lavish in decor as its big brother downtown (see Shaw's Crab House, following), Shaw's Blue Crab still has plenty to offer in the way of atmosphere. The central bar is a great place for pairing off or group conversation. The large dining areas, like the bar, have an old East Coast oyster house look about them.

Seafood, of course, is what Shaw's Blue Crab is all about. Everything is absolutely fresh, prepared in a variety of ways. Fish can be sauteed, steamed, or broiled; grilled fish is a house specialty. Walk over to the raw bar on an early evening and check out the clams and oysters. Except for the occasional expensive seasonal special, such as Florida stone crabs, most everything on the menu is modestly priced.

Dinners include your choice of soup or salad, although à la carte appetizers add to the fixin's. Maryland crab cake is just about the best to be found this side of the Chesapeake. As for dinners, the house namesake is Shaw's blue crab stew. The potent fish stock is seasoned liberally with the kind of peppers and spices that sneak up on you. The broth is chock full of coarse hand-cut vegetables; you can picture the Shaw family around the kitchen table cutting up ingredients as they while away the afternoon in conversation. The heart of the stew, of course, is the fish. In this case, it's a large cut-up king crab in the shell, smaller lobster tail, oodles of clams, mussels, soft fish, and just enough whole shrimp in the shell to make the stew respectable. Eat all of this at one sitting, and they'll have to roll you home!

Other entrees run the gamut from fried or sauteed frog legs, sea scallops, and the like, to a seafood-and-pasta platter. Evening specials might include blackened Mississippi catfish with red beans and rice, pan-fried lake perch with lemon or garlic butter, or perhaps Hawaiian black bass, sauteed and served with Chinese spices and mushroom sauce.

For those who eschew seafood, a sirloin steak is on the menu, as are two baked chicken recipes. Try the garlic chicken, and you'll wonder why they don't include the word "chicken" somewhere in the name of the restaurant. As for desserts, the Key lime pie tastes as sweet/tart as it would in good old Islamorada.

# SHAW'S CRAB HOUSE
KR 16/20
Decor 4/4   Hospitality 3/5   Food 8/9   Value 1/2

- **Seafood/American**
- **Chicago/Near North**
- **$$$**

21 E. Hubbard St.
Chicago
(312) 527-2722
**Troubleshooters:** Brown and Steve La Halie (managing partners), Yves Roubaud (chef/ partner)

**Hours:** Lunch Mon-Fri 11:30 am-2 pm, dinner Mon-Thurs 5:30-10 pm, Fri-Sat 5-11 pm, closed Sun
**Cards:** All majors
**Reservations:** Suggested
**Handicapped:** Accessible
**Bar:** Two, full
**Parking:** Valet
**Party Facilities:** Available
**Heart Healthy Menu:** Selections

The studied decor is that of an old and well-used East Coast seafood restaurant, perhaps located in a somewhat seedy hotel that has seen better days. Care and attention have obviously gone into the preparation of the food. Dinner should begin with an appetizer, and if you are lucky, it may be soft-shell crab season. These delectable little critters are quickly sauteed in butter, finished with toasted almonds or garlic as you choose. They come two to the appetizer or four to the dinner portion and are unbeatable.

Since dining is à la carte, and very pricey at that, you may want to move right on to a main course, although skipping something like a clam chowder or seafood gumbo may be a mistake. You might want one of the namesake crabs. The crab cakes are large, meaty, perfectly seasoned, and served with a spicy mustard and milder tartar-like sauce. Among shrimp dishes, "N'awlins style" is a spicy rice-and-shrimp casserole influenced by today's popular Creole and Cajun styles of cooking. This particular dish offers five medium shrimp on a bed of highly seasoned, very spicy rice. For almost $14, it's not going to win recognition as one of the best values around town. In fact, the major flaw at Shaw's Crab House is that prices are simply too high for what is offered, as good as it may be. Desserts are quite good, and, I think, more fairly priced. The Key lime pie has all the gusto of the real thing; a chocolate, caramel, and nut tart is worth every delicious calorie.

To the restaurant's credit, service is friendly and well-informed. Tables are rather close together, so if it's quiet intimacy you want, Shaw's Crab House is not the place. Otherwise, cash in a share or two of stock and enjoy the authentic decor, and in most cases, unquestionably good food.

# SHILLA
KR 17.5/20
Decor 4/4   Hospitality 4/5   Food 8/9   Value 1.5/2

- **Korean/Japanese**
- **Chicago/Northwest**
- **$$**

5930 N. Lincoln Ave.
Chicago
(312) 275-5930
**Troubleshooter:** Chan Joung (owner)

**Hours:** Daily 11:30 am-10:30 pm
**Cards:** AE, MC, VISA
**Reservations:** Suggested
**Handicapped:** Accessible
**Bar:** Full, extensive list of oriental beers
**Parking:** Street
**Party Facilities:** Available

**S**hilla takes oriental dining upscale in an expansive dining room with cinnabar-lacquered chairs and contrasting upholstery, plush carpeting, even private dining rooms with Japanese-style teppan tables for individual cooking.

Among appetizers, Korean pancakes are handsomely set on a large platter, like all the appetizers, in a portion easily large enough for three or four diners. Dining in the Korean fashion includes a broad selection of vegetable condiments to be eaten along with the central dinner.

Korean food may be the easiest foreign cuisine for someone accustomed to American cooking to enjoy. Meats are generally charcoal grilled and often seasoned with a barbecue-style sauce. San juk is a good way to begin. The strips of meat are skewered with carrots, scallions, and mushrooms, grilled, and served in a semi-sweet marinade sauce. Similarly attractive is chop chae, a dish of shredded beef with transparent vermicelli noodles and vegetables in a somewhat spicier sauce. Bul goki is perhaps the simplest of all, thin slices of the grilled meat without any sauce at all. Shilla devotes a sizable portion of its menu to Japanese foods, including a handsome sushi and sashimi bar.

# THE SILK MANDARIN
KR 18.5/20
Decor 4/4   Hospitality 4.5/5   Food 8/9   Value 2/2

| | |
|---|---|
| • **Chinese** | **Hours:** Mon-Thurs 11:30 am-10 pm, Fri-Sat until 11 pm, Sun until 9 pm |
| • **Vernon Hills** | |
| • **$$** | **Cards:** AE, CB, DINERS, MC, VISA |
| 4 E. Phillips Rd. (on Rte. 60 west of Hawthorne Shopping Center) | **Reservations:** Suggested |
| | **Handicapped:** Accessible |
| (708) 680-1760 | **Bar:** Service bar |
| **Troubleshooter:** Tasu Tsai (owner) | **Parking:** Free lot |
| | **Party Facilities:** For up to 50 |

**S**entinel good-luck lions flank the entrance of a restaurant that is comfortably appointed, handsomely decorated with Chinese silk screens and other art. The effect is one of luxury, though a peek at the menu reveals prices that are moderate. Waiters dressed in tuxedos take orders and provide accommodating, informed service.

At a time when most Chinese restaurants are more alike than different, the Silk Mandarin is a perceptible cut above. The menu offers most of the selections common to Chinese restaurants that aspire to something more than chop suey. But the cooking is noticeably more elegant and complex than most.

For appetizers, this time pass up the egg rolls and try cold noodles in sesame sauce. Your waiter will bring out a large bowl filled with delicious noodles in a sauce that leaves a light, nutty taste on the tongue. To balance the cold appetizer, try something hot, such as won ton in a hot pepper sauce, delicate shrimp toast, or fried dumplings.

The menu lists several dozen entree choices under meat, poultry, vegetables, and seafood. In addition, there is a listing under the heading of chef's gourmet specials. The choices include rarely seen General Tso's chicken, a recipe with roots in China's past. Just as chicken Marengo originated when Napoleon instructed his field kitchen chef to prepare chicken for him after the battle of Marengo, General Tso ordered his camp chef to prepare fixin's from available sources. The chef obviously knew there was a lot more to battlefield cookery than K-rations!

Chicken, shrimp, and scallops, another above-ordinary choice, comes in a woven edible basket. The sauce, with plenty of spicy bite, clings to each chunk. It is a tribute to the skill of the kitchen that each of the three components holds its own flavor and texture. Like so many other presentations, the dish is a visual masterpiece.

Among other entree selections, orange beef is sauteed, not breaded and fried as in other restaurants. As a result, the meat has a smooth, silky texture. The sauce holds plenty of pepper, which contrasts attractively with the citrus zest of the orange peel.

# SIXTY-FIVE
KR 17.5/20
Decor 3.5/4  Hospitality 4.5/5  Food 7.5/9  Value 2/2

- **Chinese**
- **Chicago/South**
- **$$**

2414 S. Wentworth Ave.
  (Chinatown)
Chicago
(312) 842-6500
**Troubleshooter:** Louis Hong
(owner)

## Other Locations

336 N. Michigan Ave.
Chicago
(312) 372-0306; Mon-Sat 1-9
  pm, Sun until 7 pm
401 W. Armitage Ave.
Chicago
(312) 280-7730; Sun-Thurs
  11:30 am-10 pm, Fri-Sat until
  11 pm

**Hours:** Sun-Thurs 11 am-
midnight, Fri-Sat until 1 am
**Cards:** AE, DINERS,
DISCOVER, MC, VISA
**Reservations:** Suggested
**Handicapped:** Accessible
**Bar:** Service bar
**Parking:** Street or nearby lots
**Party Facilities:** For 140

**S**ixty-Five reminds me of a New York-style Jewish delicatessen. The restaurant is crowded, aromatic, and noisy, with a certain boisterous quality to the service that suggests familiarity, though not rudeness. In short, it is a unique Chinese dining experience.

The cooking is unapologetically Cantonese in a time when other regional Chinese cookery has become more fashionable. There are some exquisite high points to Cantonese cooking, especially in the fullness of steamed vegetables and the abundant seafood.

Seafood is the highlight of Sixty-Five, where lobsters and other crustaceans lie unaware in large tanks, awaiting the hand that will pull them from the water and transform them into delectable dining. Most of the fresh shellfish are at market price. The lobster can be either steamed or stir-fried; the latter method infuses more flavor. Still in the shell, the lobster is hacked into large chunks, from which the meat can be picked out and savored. When served in a garlic and scallion sauce, the lobster is particularly delectable.

The Sixty-Five menu is fairly expansive, though not expensive.

The fat egg rolls are wrapped in a broad noodle crust that is made cracker crisp by deep frying; the stuffing virtually spills out when you bite or cut into one. Other appetizers range from a few different preparations of shrimp or cuttlefish to barbecued spare ribs. There is a more extensive listing of soups than other comparable Chinese restaurants might offer, including winter melon soup, not often seen.

Sixty-Five stumbles occasionally. An order of ginger beef with green onion was on the salty side, though the fresh gingerroot was appropriately flavorful. From among poultry choices listed on a special menu supplement, lemon chicken was actually a blend of lemon and lime in a sweet cornstarch sauce that coated battered and deep-fried strips of white meat. It is a dish whose intensity virtually demands an accompaniment of hot, bitter tea.

Sixty-Five is singular in its approach to inexpensive Chinese dining. The restaurant's large support from the Chinatown neighborhood confirms that fact. By the way, if you are curious about the restaurant's name, your waiter will happily explain.

# SKADARLIJA SERBIAN RESTAURANT
KR 17/20
Decor 3/4  Hospitality 4.5/5  Food 8/9  Value 1.5/2

- **Serbian**
- **Chicago/Northwest**
- **$$**

4024 N. Kedzie Ave.
Chicago
(312) 463-5600
**Troubleshooters:** Mr. & Mrs. Zvonko Klancnik (owners)

**Hours:** Wed-Fri, Sun 6 pm-2 am, Sat until 3 am
**Cards:** AE
**Reservations:** Suggested
**Handicapped:** Accessible
**Bar:** Service bar
**Parking:** Street
**Party Facilities:** For up to 100

Chicago has a long and happy tradition of Middle European night clubs. Fairly new to this scene is Skadarlija, where people come for the food, of course, but also for the music and the conviviality.

The menu is fairly standard for a Serbian restaurant. There are only two appetizers, plus a cold plate that brings together sausages, smoked meats, cheese, and vegetable garnishes. Though it isn't listed on the menu, you should ask for the eggplant purée, called ajvar, and the cheese spread, called kajmak. The former is akin to Middle Eastern roasted eggplant, but milder. The latter is a rich spread, not as tart as American cream cheese, but perfect when lavished on warm bread.

Aside from the à la carte appetizers of plump cheese strudel and cubes of Bulgarian cheese, akin to feta, dinners at Skadarlija are complete from soup to dessert. The soup is a veal and vegetable stock that's almost like stew. Entrees come with an appropriate garnish, usually a sticky, nearly gummy rice with marvelous texture. Most meats in Serbian cookery are grilled. Cevapcici are tubes of ground veal and beef, lightly spiced and served with raw chopped onions. Raznici is Serbian shish kebab made of cubed pork tenderloin rather than lamb. A quartet of veal entrees highlights the menu. They range from a rather simple version of wiener schnitzel to what the menu calls the national specialty, karadorjeva. In this dish, a veal cutlet is rolled with cheese and a meat filling.

For dessert, apple strudel has that homemade flavor. Palacinke are a bit more unusual, akin to crêpes Suzette, with a filling of crushed nuts and preserves.

# SOLE MIO

KR 18.5/20
Decor 3/4   Hospitality 5/5   Food 8.5/9   Value 2/2

- **Italian**
- **Chicago/Mid-North**
- **$$**

917 W. Armitage Ave.
Chicago
(312) 477-5858
**Troubleshooter:** Dennis Terczak (chef/owner)

**Hours:** Mon-Thurs 5:30-10:30 pm, Fri-Sat until 11 pm, Sun until 10 pm
**Cards:** AE, DINERS, MC, VISA
**Reservations:** For 6 or more (waits can be substantial without reservations)
**Bar:** Full, extensive all-Italian wine list
**Parking:** Valet
**Party Facilities:** For up to 30

**T**rattoria dining on trendy Armitage Avenue might suggest contrivance, but Sole Mio is anything but artificial. The restaurant houses several small dining rooms behind the entryway bar room, all crowded with tables. The noise level is usually high because of the restaurant's popularity.

When it comes to pastas, Sole Mio shines. Consider ravioli stuffed with a forcemeat of ground mushrooms. The ravioli are finished on a grill and napped with gorgonzola cheese cream sauce, which is actually much lighter than its description would imply. This is in marked contrast to the intensity of the ravioli stuffing; it fills the mouth with the flavor of woodsy mushrooms. That flavor intensity also comes across in an order of linguine in pesto and shrimp. The emphasis is clearly on the fresh basil, which is at the heart of the pesto. Other pastas from a large selection include such temptations as fettuccine carbonara in Parmesan cream and rigatoni with veal meatballs, escarole, and a fresh tomato basil sauce.

Pastas might serve as an opening course, or even an entree, but a more leisurely way to dine is to select a first course. This might be a conventional carpaccio or something more challenging, such as small spinach crêpe rollups filled with a mix of cheese, resting in a tomato cream sauce. Polenta, which is nothing more than corn meal mush, is only the starting point for a dish centered around a duck confit, the meat dark, chewy, and flavored with prunes marinated in grappa and a syrupy Marsala sauce.

You could do well simply grazing on these or other appetizers, but then you would miss out on entrees. A lightly breaded veal scallop with escarole and pancetta is brought to the table in a mild tomato sauce, not forceful enough to mask other flavors on the platter. Grilled duck breast is sliced and centered on a platter that includes blanched spinach and orzo with a red wine-based porcini mushroom sauce.

Desserts are just as splendid. Among them, lemon tart is intensely flavored and a clear choice over tiramisu, which can be soggy, without definition.

# SPASSO
KR 18/20

Decor 3/4   Hospitality 4.5/5   Food 8.5/9   Value 2/2

- **Italian**
- **Wauconda**
- **$$**

614 W. Liberty (Illinois Rte. 176)

Wauconda

(708) 526-4215

**Troubleshooters:** Carlotta and William Pritt (owners), Andrew Webber (chef/owner)

**Hours:** Lunch Tues-Fri 11:30 am-2:30 pm, dinner Mon-Thurs 5-9:30 pm, Fri-Sat until 10:30 pm, Sun 4-9 pm

**Cards:** AE, CB, DINERS, MC, VISA, house accounts

**Reservations:** Suggested

**Bar:** Full

**Parking:** Free lot

**Party Facilities:** For 20-75

Imagine a shopping center with an indoor archery range. Now imagine a sophisticated Italian trattoria right next to the archery range. That pretty well sums up Spasso.

The restaurant is rather large at first glance, though individual dining rooms are small enough to afford a certain coziness. The setting is faux trattoria, but the interior easily shuts out the shopping mall.

Dining at Spasso can be as simple or as extravagant as you might want. There is a simplicity, even a directness, about the cooking that suggests a no-nonsense approach motivated purely by a desire to please the taste buds. Consider a delicious antipasto of smoked trout, prepared in the restaurant's own kitchen smoker, then embellished with white cannellini beans, a little red onion for color, and olive oil for smoothness. It is a marvelous fusion of texture and flavor.

More elegant is the Spasso version of grilled portobello mushrooms in a garlicky reduction of the mushrooms' essence in a demiglacé. Other choices range from traditional bruschetti with a topping of coarse-chopped tomato, or prawns wrapped in prosciutto, to fried mozzarella and fried calamari. The restaurant also offers a quartet of appetizer pizzas that run the gamut from simple tomato, fresh basil, and mozzarella to one with slices of duck sausage, smoked cheese, peppers, onion, and Parmesan cheese.

Nearly a dozen pastas are on the menu, from a simple spaghetti with marinara, basil, and artichoke hearts to sophisticated black squid ink tagliatelle with shrimp in a saffron cream sauce. The marinara is a pleasant balance of acidity and sweetness.

Entrees range from roast pork tenderloin wrapped in pancetta, seasoned with herbs and garlic in a white wine sauce, to a simple grilled chicken breast in a roasted red-pepper puree. The emphasis is clearly on Northern Italian cooking. As with the rest of the menu, the entrees avoid flashiness and focus more on rustic or intuitive flavors.

# SPIAGGIA
KR 19.5/20
Decor 4/4   Hospitality 5/5   Food 9/9   Value 1.5/2

- **Italian/Northern**
- **Chicago/Near North**
- **$$$**

980 N. Michigan Ave. (One Magnificent Mile)
Chicago
(312) 280-2750
**Troubleshooter:** Manager on duty

**Hours:** Lunch Mon-Sat 11:30 am-2 pm, dinner Mon-Thurs 5:30-9:30 pm, Fri-Sat until 10:30 pm, Sun until 9 pm
**Cards:** All majors
**Reservations:** Required
**Handicapped:** Accessible
**Bar:** Extensive wine selection
**Dress:** Jackets required, neckties optional
**Parking:** In building
**Party Facilities:** For 15-500

**"S**piaggia" means "beach" in Italian, and that's part of the view diners get when they look out the floor-to-ceiling windows. This is the most exciting vista in the city for people-watching. You can look out onto Michigan Avenue, Oak Street, and Lake Shore Drive, with a prime stretch of Oak Street Beach a little farther off. Not only is the view outstanding, so is the interior decor. The restaurant is all marble and brass, with accents of greenery to soften the effect. Chef Paul Bartolotta presents an extensive range of pastas and antipasti, plus a variety of meat, seafood, and poultry choices for entrees.

The restaurant was among the first in Chicago to offer "gourmet pizzas" baked in a wood-burning oven. They, along with all courses, share a certain elegance of preparation and style. Flavors are in balance. Expensive, yes, but certainly a worthwhile experience if sybaritic dining is your pleasure.

# STAR OF SIAM
KR 18/20
Decor 3.5/4   Hospitality 4.5/5   Food 8/9   Value 2/2

| | |
|---|---|
| • **Thai** | **Hours:** Sun-Thurs 11 am-10 pm, Fri-Sat until 11 pm |
| • **Chicago/Near North** | **Cards:** All majors, house accounts |
| •**$$** | |
| 11 E. Illinois St. | **Reservations:** Accepted |
| Chicago | **Bar:** Full |
| (312) 670-0100 | **Parking:** Street or lots |
| **Troubleshooter:** Adirek | **Party Facilities:** For up to |
| "Eddie" Dulyapaibul (owner) | 140 |

Star of Siam is kind of "yuppie-Thai," with an appeal as much urban as ethnic. Located on the first floor of a renovated loft building, the restaurant features a modish decor of bare brick walls and spacious, bench-type seating.

Its food is among the best. Appetizer choices include spring rolls, with honey-like plum sauce glaze and a cool filling of vegetables, tofu, and minced scrambled eggs. In either chicken or beef satay, the meat is lightly grilled and marinated in a bath of sweet coconut milk, its flavors set off with a spiced peanut sauce. Fried tofu, another appetizer, comes in deep-fried thick wedges, best when dipped into a tangy plum sauce.

Thai dining is not complete without a soup course. A large bowl provides enough for at least four people. Thai soups are highlighted by a clear chicken broth accented with a complexity of peppers and seasonings, especially lemon grass and coriander. The tom yom, which has been my benchmark for testing Thai foods over the years, is first-rate at Star of Siam.

For a main-course selection, the menu includes several choices designated as Star's specialties. But even from the regular list of entrees, we found nothing but delightful dining. For example, roast duck consists of slices from the breast in a sauce of honey and soy. The meat is tender and rich, as good duckling can be, but without excessive fattiness. If you like food hot, try the fried spicy basil leaves with shrimp, chicken, or beef.

Star of Siam features several curries, reflecting the Indian influence on Thai food, which is balanced by the Chinese-inspired affinity for rice and noodles. From among noodle choices, pad Thai is a classic in my book. Cool, almost soothing, thin vermicelli noodles are served with crushed peanuts, cooked threads of egg, and oriental ingredients such as bean sprouts and tofu. Entirely different is larb nar, broad, flat wheat noodles in a thickened gravy with collard greens and shrimp. This is a dish in which the texture of the noodles is all important, and when done right, as at Star of Siam, it is completely satisfying.

Although oriental restaurants are not particularly known for desserts, Star of Siam does have some genuine treats. One favorite is Thai star custard, a cake-like preparation rich with the sweet flavor of coconut.

# STAR TOP CAFE
KR 17.5/20
Decor 3.5/4  Hospitality 4.5/5  Food 7.5/9  Value 2/2

- **American/Eclectic**
- **Chicago/Mid-North**
- **$$**

2748 N. Lincoln Ave.
Chicago
(312) 281-0997
**Troubleshooter:** Bill Ammons
(chef/owner)

**Hours:** Tues-Thurs 6-10 pm, Fri-Sat until 11 pm, Sun 6-9:30 pm
**Cards:** AE, MC, VISA
**Reservations:** Suggested
**Handicapped:** Accessible
**Bar:** Service bar
**Parking:** Street
**Party Facilities:** For up to 50 except Fridays and Saturdays

They just do not come any funkier than the Star Top Cafe. This restaurant has even been known to hold a fire sale: "Family style dinner; one big table; sit with strangers and drink a lot!" proclaims the handbill distributed up and down Lincoln Avenue.

Decor in this fairly small storefront is largely understated. Tables are all cloth covered, and yes, there is a cafe style at the Star Top Cafe. The menu changes daily; cooking reflects a lighter, nouvelle-American approach to cuisine. One evening might find a cold pumpkin soup with ginger-flavored cream on the menu, or Cuban black bean soup with a dash of sherry and a dollop of sour cream. While some restaurants serve baked clams with a bread-crumb filling, at Star Top Cafe, the clams are topped with melted brie, accented with shiitake mushrooms and leeks, and flavored with fresh rosemary.

A bit of oriental influence appears in duck confit with snow peas, chilies, shiitake mushrooms, and ground Szechuan peppercorns for bite. For something milder, you might find montrachet goat's cheese with Belgian endive, cut-up apples, and a bacon-honey dressing.

The entree selections are similarly enchanting, most rather complex in the creative use of ingredients. For example, there could be cold fried chicken with guacamole, stuffed poblano peppers, and honey-jalapeño sauce. Other entrees might include sausage and fettuccine with broccoli and garlic for seasoning or an artichoke stuffed with ground beef, seasoned with dill and peppers. Desserts can be similarly elaborate, all kitchen fresh. A lemon chess pie with roots in the American South is a good example.

# SU CASA

KR 17.5/20
Decor 4/4   Hospitality 4/5   Food 7.5/9   Value 2/2

- **Mexican**
- **Chicago/Near North**
- **$**

49 E. Ontario St.
Chicago
(312) 943-4041
**Troubleshooters:** Charles
Tatson (general manager)

**Hours:** Mon-Thurs 11:30 am-11 pm, Fri until midnight, Sat noon-midnight
**Cards:** All majors
**Reservations:** Suggested
**Bar:** Full
**Parking:** Valet

It amazes me that Su Casa remains as consistent as ever, from decor to cuisine to service. Here is an antique-filled, white brick-walled restaurant, with the style of a Spanish colonial hacienda. There are ornate wood statues, heavy carved doors, and large metal ornaments everywhere. Su Casa proves that Mexican food need not be unbearably spicy, and if any criticism can be leveled, it is that the restaurant is a tourist mecca.

The combination dinners offer varied tastes, including Mexican grilled steak, stuffed peppers, delicious chicken enchiladas, cheese tacos, and creamy, cool guacamole. Chicken mole is a special treat, while seafood lovers should enjoy the trout with coriander. Desserts include excellent flan, the classic Spanish custard.

# Szechwan House
KR 18.5/20
Decor 4/4   Hospitality 4.5/5   Food 8/9   Value 2/2

- **Chinese**
- **Chicago/Near North**
- **$$**

600 N. Michigan Ave.
Chicago
(312) 642-3900
**Troubleshooters:** Austin Koo
(owner), Alfred Hsu (maitre d')

**Hours:** Sun-Thurs 11:30
am-10:30 pm, Fri until 11 pm,
Sat noon-11 pm, Sun brunch
11:30-2:30 pm
**Cards:** All majors
**Bar:** Full
**Parking:** Valet
**Party Facilities:** For 60-100

Though the restaurant's name suggests the hot, peppery foods of the Chinese province of Szechwan, Szechwan House offers more sophistication. Certainly, hot and spicy dishes can be found; the restaurant's version of orange beef has always been a favorite. But when it comes to the finer nuances and elusive flavors, hardly anything can match the restaurant's whole steamed fish.

Walleyed pike is delivered to the table under lacy shavings of scallion, with ever-so-fragile flavorings of ginger. The whole fish is displayed, then boned by a server. One still must be careful to watch out for tiny little bones, but the pike's unblemished flavor is a testament to careful preparation.

The Szechwan House menu is so vast that diners should not be hurried in making selections. While servers may offer specific pointers, following your own natural impulse should prove rewarding. The idea is to look for balance in flavors, textures, and ingredients. Try something simple like steamed dumplings, six to an order, best eaten with a touch of sweet ginger soy sauce, though delicious on their own.

Vegetarian chicken is not a contradiction in terms. The "poultry" is actually bean curd, fashioned to look like slices of dark meat, resting on a bed of pickled crisp vegetables akin to turnips or jicama. Even the Szechwan House egg roll is unique, wrapped in a flaky crust rather than the thick, starchy noodle so common at other Chinese restaurants.

Among other selections is coral chicken. Bite-sized pieces are served in a gently flavored dark sauce that gives something akin to a smoky flavor. Try a noodle dish for texture contrast; the chow fun noodles with vegetables may be a simple peasant food to the Chinese, but the dish is nonetheless gratifying. Chinese moo shu is a standout. The crepe wrappings are smooth textured, the fillings a contrast in flavors.

# TAMALES
KR 18.5/20
Decor 4/4   Hospitality 4/5   Food 9/9   Value 1.5/2

- **Mexican/Eclectic**
- **Chicago/Mid-North**
- **$**

3651 N. Southport Ave.
Chicago
(312) 549-TACO
**Troubleshooters:** John and Linda Terczak (owners)

## Other Location

493 Central Ave.
Highland Park
(708) 433-4070; Sun-Thurs
    5-10 pm, Fri-Sat until 11 pm;
    Handicapped accessible

**Hours:** (Summer) Mon-Thurs 4 pm-midnight, Fri 1 pm-midnight, Sat-Sun noon-midnight; (winter) Mon-Thurs 5 pm-midnight, Fri-Sat until 1 am, Sun 5-10 pm
**Cards:** None
**Reservations:** No
**Bar:** Full
**Parking:** Street

**M**ore than a sense of whimsy is at play at Tamales, a stylized Mexican restaurant. Chef John Terczak and his wife, Linda, have given a former bistro a major facelift and created an unusual menu that takes its inspiration from south of the border.

The namesake tamales can be ordered filled with chicken and raisins, chorizo sausage, or seafood. When's the last time you had a tamale with seafood, or for that matter, pumpkin? Yes, pumpkin is offered from time to time. When pumpkin tamales are garnished with a hot salsa verde, sour cream, and mole, and piled atop a corn husk, it is evident that this is not basic taqueria cooking.

The imaginative menu makes wonderful use of fresh vegetables. Roast corn chowder is made with a chicken stock finished with cream and endowed with kernels of corn, pieces of smoky ham, and slivers of hot peppers just to remind you that this is not basic Massachusetts corn chowder.

The menu lists, among a dozen other appetizers, red snapper hash with sour cream. The operative principle at Tamales is to expect the unexpected. Thus, the snapper hash is bound together with potatoes and other ingredients, formed into a large patty, and sauteed. What comes out may look like a crab cake, but it is something unique.

Diners could make a meal from a handful of the smaller appetizer dishes, ranging from spinach and cheese chimichanga to a fried-egg tostada. Other items found on conventional Mexican menus get unconventional treatment. That is certainly true of the larger entree portions. Tacos can be ordered vegetarian-style, while a roast leg of pork comes with five separate garnishes.

A recent fish of the day, tuna, came grilled with chayote, a Mexican squash with the pale color and crisp feel of jicama or turnip, but a flavor that hints of lemon. A garnish of freshly grilled vegetables completes the platter. Among other selections, grilled cornish hen is surrounded by grilled vegetables and completed with a reddish orange achiote sauce, its flavor delicate and mild.

Though Tamales is casual in atmosphere and tone of service, the food is assuredly not assembly-line fare. You will pay for taco chips and salsa that are complimentary at most Mexican restaurants, but then Tamales is not just any Mexican restaurant.

# T'ANG DYNASTY
KR 16.5/20
Decor 4/4  Hospitality 3.5/5  Food 7.5/9  Value 1.5/2

- **Chinese**
- **Chicago/Near North**
- **$$**

100 E. Walton Pl.
Chicago
(312) 664-8688
**Troubleshooter:** Charles Lin
(manager)

**Hours:** Sun-Thurs 11:30 am-10:30 pm, Fri-Sat until 11 pm
**Cards:** AE, DINERS, MC, VISA
**Reservations:** Accepted
**Handicapped:** Accessible
**Bar:** Full
**Parking:** Valet
**Party Facilities:** For 10-200

The trend in Chinese restaurants recently has been toward elaborate design and handsome, upscale surroundings. That certainly would describe T'ang Dynasty, where oriental art framed with imported mahogany and brass fittings adorns the walls. The restaurant is part of a chain of local restaurant enterprises, so diners may recognize certain selections and ways of preparation.

T'ang Dynasty is a restaurant that scores in some areas, but hardly impresses in others. Strong points include the handsome plating and presentation, especially in a house specialty called T'ang Dynasty scallops. Pouches made of rice noodles contain a mix of scallop pieces, minced vegetables, and mushrooms in a pearlescent sauce. The promise is of exquisite taste wrapped inside such packaging. In fact, the flavors are rather bland except for the limited flavor released by the mushrooms.

On the other hand, General Tso's chicken, a recipe found on better Chinese restaurant menus, is exceptional. Chicken chunks are stir-fried in a mélange of flavors that includes a bouquet of peppers and just enough ginger to add bite. The elaborate menu leads logically from one course to another, though one group of appetizers is separated from another and dubbed "dim sum" in an apparent effort to capitalize on that fad.

Vegetable dumplings are wrapped spinach noodles steamed with a forcemeat of minced vegetables. Taiwan escargots are exceptionally delicious. Forget about the garlic butter with which French snails are sauced and enjoy these morsels with their sharp pepper spicing. Scallion pancake is perhaps a bit more flavorful than those served at other Chinese restaurants. Back in the entree domain, or-

ange beef is tender and well glazed but could use more citrus bite.
Lamb in Peking sauce is a treat, with an amalgam of flavors that borders on the sweet and just enough complexity to make it work.

The lavish menu goes on for more than a dozen pages, climaxing
with elaborate desserts.

# TANIA'S
KR 19/20
Decor 4/4   Hospitality 5/5   Food 8/9   Value 2/2

- **Cuban/Mexican**
- **Chicago/Northwest**
- **$$**

2659 N. Milwaukee Ave.
Chicago
(312) 235-7120
**Troubleshooters:** Elias and
Martha Sanchez (owners)

**Hours:** Daily 11-4 am
**Cards:** All majors
**Handicapped:** Accessible
**Bar:** Full
**Parking:** Valet in evening
**Party Facilities:** Available

Tania's is festive, with a cathedral ceiling and terraced dining a
level above the main dining room. It is as if you were on vacation in
Latin America, dining in the best restaurant your hotel has to offer.
Service is on a par with some of the best French restaurants. The
waiters are knowledgeable and eager to assist, with close attention to
detail.

Though the menu is divided between Cuban and Mexican
choices, the influence is more Spanish than Latin American. Taste a
tapa or two from the hot or cold listings. The tortilla Española is akin
to a frittata, an egg pie as tall as a cake, with mild onion and potato
flavors. Abalone gets delicious handling in a peppery fresh tomato
sauce, flush with garlic. Delicious little pastries, empanadillas, are
stuffed with creamy ricotta cheese and leafy spinach in a perfectly
golden crust. Other tapas range from chickpea salad and mussels or
baked clams to grilled chorizo, squid salad, or stewed tripe with
chickpeas.

There are four Mexican entrees. Tania's also serves a perfect steak
Milanese in a mildly seasoned flour dredging. Other selections in-
clude grilled shrimp, whole deep-fried snapper in garlic sauce with
potatoes, as well as other seafood and steak. Cuban entrees include
typical pork and beef recipes.

The purely Spanish influence is represented by Tania's paella. While the paella is tasty and ample, the lobster is consistently overcooked. Lobster cannot tolerate long cooking times as well as some other shellfish. Lumping all ingredients in the same pot simultaneously is a mistake. Aside from the overcooked lobster, however, the paella is wonderfully flavorful, with ample additions of scallops, large prawns, clams, mussels, and even a meaty chicken leg.

Dinners can be finished with elaborate desserts or after-dinner coffees, flamed and presented with a flourish. Tania's is one of the more festive restaurants in the city; when the weather gets you down and a vacation south of the border is beyond reach, Tania's is not a bad substitute, if only for an evening.

# TAVERN IN THE TOWN
KR 19/20
Decor 4/4   Hospitality 4.5/5   Food 9/9   Value 1.5/2

- **American**
- **Libertyville**
- **$$$**

519 N. Milwaukee Ave.
Libertyville
(708) 367-5755
**Troubleshooter:** Rick Jansen (owner)

**Hours:** Lunch Tues-Fri 11:30 am-2 pm, dinner Tues-Sat 6-11 pm
**Cards:** All majors
**Reservations:** Suggested
**Handicapped:** Accessible
**Bar:** Full, excellent wine and beer lists
**Parking:** Street
**Party Facilities:** On request

Tavern in the Town is lots more than a tavern. The setting is turn-of-the-century, with lots of wood polished to a sheen, handsome use of stained-glass skylights, brass, and top-of-the-line table appointments. Lace tablecloths soften what might otherwise be too hard an effect. Lighting is low, even romantic.

Though the ambiance speaks of another time, when women wore full-length skirts and high-buttoned shoes and men wore sleeve garters and spats, the cooking is as contemporary and stylish as it comes. The menu looks deceptively sparse, and if there is any failing it may be that choices are a bit limited. For instance, only three appetizers and a soup of the day are on the printed menu, though the choice is usually expanded by a daily special or two. Recently, sauteed snails came around a center of julienne vegetables and bits of smoky flavored bacon. Though the snails were presented in a brown sauce, their flavor clearly came through, leaving that woodsy, unmistakeable footprint that is often lost when snails are overpowered in a traditional garlic butter sauce.

Among other choices was an order of mussels, so perfectly prepared that there was not a trace of grit. The mussels had been steamed in white wine with a bit of garlic butter enrichment. They were served in a large bowl, bathed in a chive-accented beurre blanc.

There is attention to detail in virtually everything presented to diners. Platters are handsomely composed, as if each entree or appetizer were being prepared for a photographer to capture on film.

Meat choices include a combination of grilled and roasted meats that can change daily. Roasted breast of chicken comes stuffed with leeks and wild mushrooms, while black angus beef comes in a Bordelaise sauce with shallots.

Seafood changes daily, with a choice of either poached or grilled fish. Recently, diners were served grilled salmon and red snapper together on the same platter. Two sauces complemented the fish in both color and flavors.

Desserts, each more lucious than the next, can be chosen from a platter presented at the end of the meal.

# TAYLOR STREET BISTRO

KR 17.5/20

Decor 3/4   Hospitality 5/5   Food 7.5/9   Value 2/2

---

- **French/Bistro**
- **Chicago/Near West**
- **$$**

1400 W. Taylor St.
Chicago
(312) 829-2828
**Troubleshooters:** Chef
Joseph and Ann Doppes
(owners)

**Hours:** Lunch Mon-Fri 11:30 am-2 pm, dinner Mon-Sat 5:30-10:30 pm
**Cards:** MC, VISA
**Reservations:** Suggested
**Handicapped:** Accessible
**Bar:** Full
**Parking:** Valet weekends, street otherwise
**Heart-Healthy Menu:** Selections

---

**H**ere is French bistro dining right in the heart of Little Italy. Café curtains and a Belle Époque poster or two frame waiters and waitresses bustling about in full-length aprons, their order pads tucked in back. There is a sense of conviviality at the Taylor Street Bistro from first greeting to goodbye.

The menu presents some typical bistro fare and more. Among appetizers, diners will find something as simple as a platter of steamed mussels or snails in garlic butter to something well beyond the basics, such as veal sausage with arugula and warm Alsatian-style potato salad. A recent daily menu presented delicious lamb sausages, spiced with a mild curry and served with couscous spiked with bits of red pepper.

The menu also features bistro pizza, more Californian than either French or Italian. Though our waitress said the crust was brioche dough, it had a crispness that worked fine with toppings of shrimp, broccoli, and goat's cheese. Goat's cheese also appears in at least one salad, plated with spinach and a light warm bacon dressing. As for specific Italian overtones, there are two pastas, angel hair with shrimp and sun-dried tomatoes in a light cream sauce or a more traditional linguine with clams in a white wine, butter, and garlic sauce. The latter is truly delicious and, like its companion pasta, can be ordered in appetizer or entree portion.

From other entree choices, the mix is traditional bistro fare plus choices a bit more contemporary. Duck is made deliciously rich, glazed with ginger and honey. There are also simple pepper steak and grilled salmon brushed with Pommery mustard.

# TEHRAN
KR 17/20
Decor 3.5/4   Hospitality 4/5   Food 7.5/9   Value 2/2

- **Middle Eastern**
- **Chicago/Far North**
- **$**

6619 N. Clark St.
Chicago
(312) 338-0677
**Troubleshooters:**
Mohammad Hossiniyan, Hassan
Maadelat (owners)

**Hours:** Daily 11 am-11 pm
**Cards:** All majors
**Reservations:** Accepted
**Bar:** No alcohol, but diners may bring their own
**Parking:** Street
**Party Facilities:** Catering only

In the Orient, the emphasis is on a balance of flavors and textures. In Middle Europe, foods are hearty and robust. In Italy and France, sauces make the difference.

For the Middle East, where the influences stretch from Gibraltar east into northern India, cookery can be as varied as the famed carpets that come from this vast region. But one characteristic stands out. This is food noted for distinct and subtle seasonings, particular spices, and an aromatic approach to food preparation. Here in Chicago, Tehran is popular among members of the Iranian community, as well as budget diners and seekers of good, even exotic dining.

Tehran is housed in a standard Chicago storefront. But lights from graceful chandeliers, the whitewash of the walls, and crisp tablecloths give the restaurant an appearance of refinement.

First, taste some of the appetizers, several of which may also be ordered in full dinner portion. Dolmeh, grape leaves wrapped around a filling of rice and spiced beef, has many incarnations in the Middle East. At Tehran the flavors remain distinct, yet subtle; the light tomato sauce served with the dolmeh does not obscure other flavors. Eggplant is a favorite vegetable of the region. Smoked and pureed, seasoned with garlic and a few spices, it makes a delicious spread on warm pieces of pita bread. Among other choices, charbroiled chicken kebabs are simply flavored with fresh lemon juice and grilled over hot coals.

All dinners include soup, dessert, and your choice of an American-style or Persian salad. Choose the latter and enjoy a wedge of lightly salted farmer's cheese, radishes, parsley, and sliced raw onions. Grilled meats get excellent treatment at Tehran. The Iranian version of Middle Eastern kufteh, in this case called koubideh, is a mix of ground lamb and beef skewered and roasted over the coals, certainly more exotic than the traditional American way of backyard grilling. Many meats come in sauces, like stews. In one dish, beef meatballs are served in a sweet, thick dark pomegranate sauce with walnuts. Another entree features meat with yellow split peas and lime in a light tomato-based sauce. There are several lamb entrees ranging from stews to the whole grilled shank. Fluffy steamed rice topped with threads of saffron is served along with all the entrees.

Finally, for dessert try creamy rice pudding, or order a sweet pastry à la carte.

# THAI BORRAHN
KR 18.5/20
Decor 4/4   Hospitality 5/5   Food 8/9   Value 1.5/2

- **Thai**
- **Chicago/Near North**
- **$$**

247 E. Ontario St. (second floor)
Chicago
(312) 642-1385

**Troubleshooters:** Vallop and Chan Pen Rattana (owners)

**Hours:** Mon-Thurs 11:30 am-10 pm, Fri until 11 pm, Sat 4-11 pm, Sun 4-10 pm
**Cards:** AE, MC, VISA
**Reservations:** Accepted
**Bar:** Full
**Parking:** Street, public lots
**Party Facilities:** For up to 30

The name Thai Borrahn refers to antiques. It seems appropriate for a restaurant that is so pretty. Tucked out of the way on the second floor, the restaurant houses a small collection of Thai and Buddhist art in a dining room where patrons may sit at Western-style tables or on floor mats at low tables.

No matter where you choose to sit, you will find the food and presentations impressive. Be sure to order the truly exceptional steamed red snapper casserole. The fish is pureed to a consistency much like a French quenelle and may even be bound with egg whites to smooth out its texture. Small mounds are placed in a dimpled ceramic platter. The flavor is a complexity of mild peppers, the snapper, and basil resting on a bed of napa cabbage. Another approach to seafood is found in deep-fried fish cakes, eaten with ground peanuts in a vinegary cucumber sauce. Shrimp and squid tempura are among other appetizer choices at Thai Borrahn. Golden baskets, as another selection is called, are small pastry cups filled with a mix of husked corn, shrimp, and chicken that yields a slightly sweet flavor.

Curries play an important part in Thai dining. They can be either red and mild or green and hot. Even the spicier choices are not so blazing as to discourage tastings. Curries are made of beef, chicken, pork, or fish, as well as in vegetarian varieties. Much like stews, they come in portions that can be generously divided among four people. You might want to try more than one curry to get an idea of the diversity available. For example, beef curry offers one approach, while fried catfish curry is more exotic.

Be certain to order a noodle dish along with your curries. The pad Thai is a classic at Thai Borrahn. Translucent noodles are at the heart of this creation, a mix that also includes shredded cooked egg, bits of pork and shrimp, chunks of turnip and tofu for texture, and a lightly sweetened sauce that unifies the varied ingredients.

# THAI CLASSIC
KR 18.5/20
Decor 4/4   Hospitality 4.5/5   Food 8/9   Value 2/2

- **Thai**
- **Chicago/Mid-North**
- **$**

3332 N. Clark St.
Chicago
(312) 404-2000
**Troubleshooter:** Ms. Sammy
Lertpanichpon (owner)

**Hours:** Mon 5-11 pm, Tues-Sat noon-11 pm, Sun (buffet) noon-10 pm
**Cards:** AE, MC, VISA
**Reservations:** Weekends
**Handicapped:** Accessible
**Bar:** No alcohol, diners may bring their own
**Parking:** Free lot
**Party Facilities:** For up to 60
**Heart-Healthy Menu:** Vegetarian menu

Imagery reminiscent of *The King and I* is found in the decor of Thai Classic, with suggestions of Victorian architecture in the posts and rails that define the dining areas. At the same time, there are examples of more traditional Thai art, including a large Buddhist altar that stands to one side of the handsome restaurant.

Diners may sit at conventional tables or on floor cushions with foot wells to make such an accommodation more comfortable. The Thai

Classic menu is modestly priced and compares favorably with those of many other storefront Thai restaurants where the ambiance is less luxurious.

Thai food, like so much of Asian dining, lends itself to grazing. Order several appetizers, such as deep-fried triangles of tofu, which can be dipped into a semi-tart fruit sauce. Skewered chicken satay features the grilled meat in ample portion, eaten with a peanut pepper sauce that is somewhat milder than similar sauces found at other Thai restaurants. Sticky sweet rice, called mee grob, is suggestive of candy, but the complexity of flavors makes it something more substantial.

Something sweet is appropriate as prelude for subsequent courses, in which peppers bring a moderated heat to the dining experience. Many of the Thai soups offer a bouquet of seasonings and spices. Thai Classic soup brings in the influence of coconut milk, an ingredient common in Thai cookery and a welcome counterpoint to the concentration of peppers and spices. This is not to suggest that seasonings are too heavy at Thai Classic. Curries have balanced flavors, and noodle dishes are pleasantly mild in most cases.

# THAI LITTLE HOME CAFE
KR 18/20
Decor 3.5/4   Hospitality 3.5/5   Food 9/9   Value 2/2

- **Thai**
- **Chicago/Northwest**
- **$**

4747 N. Kedzie Ave.
Chicago
(312) 478-3944
**Troubleshooter:** Oscar Esche (owner)

**Hours:** Lunch Mon-Fri 11:30 am-2:30 pm, dinner Mon-Fri 5-9:30 pm, Sat-Sun noon-9:30 pm (closed Wednesdays)
**Cards:** AE, MC, VISA
**Reservations:** Suggested
**Handicapped:** Accessible
**Bar:** Service bar
**Parking:** Street
**Heart-Healthy Menu:** Nutritional information available about menu selections

A pioneer among Chicago's coterie of Thai restaurants, Thai Little Home Cafe remains as good as ever, maybe even more refined. Once marred by lackluster service, even that aspect has improved.

Starting with appetizers, try the egg rolls, spring rolls, and an order of satay. The last is grilled cubes of meat, like a shish kebab, made even more delicious with a peppered peanut sauce. The egg rolls have a crisply fried crust and are studded with coarse chopped vegetables and meat. The spring rolls are shredded cabbage and sausage wrapped chilled in a thin crêpe. It's an interesting alternative to the egg roll, now ubiquitous in Asian restaurants.

Thai Little Home Cafe has more than a dozen soups. For some real flavor, try one of the tom yum lemon grass soups with beef, chicken, or shrimp. Among entree choices, although the menu describes beef with basil leaf as hot, there is balance to this dish, so the flavor of the basil is clearly detectable. For fish, order whole deep-fried red snapper with hot peppers, which are an exotic influence without overpowering the mild flavor of the fish. For poultry, one of the better selections is chicken with garlic.

# THAI TOUCH
KR 18/20
Decor 4/4   Hospitality 4.5/5   Food 7.5/9   Value 2/2

| | |
|---|---|
| • **Thai** | **Hours:** Sun, Tues-Thurs noon-9 pm, Fri-Sat until 10 pm (closed Mondays) |
| • **Chicago/Northwest** | |
| • **$$** | |
| 3200 W. Lawrence Ave. | **Cards:** CB, DINERS, MC, VISA |
| Chicago | **Reservations:** Accepted |
| (312) 539-5700 | **Handicapped:** Accessible |
| **Troubleshooter:** Art Lee (owner) | **Bar:** Full |
| | **Parking:** Street |
| | **Party Facilities:** For up to 80 |

Thai Touch is more than just another ethnic storefront restaurant. Diners are seated in a stylish atmosphere accented with trappings that suggest Thai royalty and culture. The menu showcases foods recognizable to diners familiar with Thai restaurants, but the cooking has a refinement not found in all of them. And there are sparks of originality that make dinner a unique experience.

For starters among appetizers, try gold cups. Small baked dough cups hold a blended mixture of chopped peanuts, minced chicken, corn, and carrots topped with an edible piece of gold leaf. The taste is mild but satisfying.

Thai cuisine draws upon the crosscurrents of culture that influence Southeast Asia. Chicken satay is prepared in a curry sauce and served with a Thai peanut sauce whose sharpness is balanced by a salad of thin slices of cucumber and scallions in a sweet brine. Other appetizers range from egg, shrimp, or spring rolls to grilled skewered shrimp, deep-fried crab in a noodle pocket, and deep-fried fish cakes.

A trio of soups is highlighted by delicious lemon grass broth with chicken or shrimp, a complexity of seasonings perfumed by lime juice and cilantro to counter the peppery heat of the broth. Thai dining need not be exclusively hot, but at least one fiery course is in order for a balanced meal. Red curry with chicken is spicy hot, but too much anise flavor is slightly jarring. On the other hand, roasted five-spice duck is a complete success, the Chinese-influenced spicing perfectly in balance with the crisp roasted duck, whose fatty skin easily peels away from the dark flesh.

A dish so rich calls for contrast. Pad Thai serves as a perfect counterpoint. The noodles have a slightly chewy texture and are mixed with ground peanuts plus julienne carrot strips and raw red cabbage for crunch and color. Among meat entrees, choices include pork flavored with garlic or cinnamon, along with vegetables. Basil beef features the meat stir-fried with peppers in a spiced sauce with the unmistakable flavor of basil leaf.

Desserts include coconut ice cream, rice pudding, and delicious Thai coconut custard. Service is warm, though it can also be slow. But Thai Touch is such a comfortable place to visit that, unless time is of the essence, it hardly matters.

# THAI VALLEY
KR 18.5/20
Decor 3/4   Hospitality 4.5/5   Food 9/9   Value 2/2

- **Thai**
- **Chicago/Northwest**
- **$**

4600 N. Kedzie Ave.
Chicago
(312) 588-2020
**Troubleshooter:** Manager on duty

**Hours:** Tues-Sat 11 am-10 pm, Sun until 9 pm
**Cards:** AE, MC, VISA
**Reservations:** Accepted
**Handicapped:** Accessible
**Bar:** No alcohol, diners may bring their own
**Parking:** Street

This neat-as-a-pin storefront is family run; the food is as delicious as any I have found. Aside from minimal wall decor, there is little to distinguish Thai Valley visually. Orders come bustling out of the tiny kitchen, where senior family members steam, stir-fry, and perform any of the other minor miracles that produce the exotic platters set before hungry customers.

Service can sometimes be a little on the sluggish side, but as small as this restaurant is, no one will shoo a customer out merely to turn a table. That speaks well for the restaurant's hospitality. The menu lists several dozen items readily recognizable to anyone familiar with Thai cuisine. Newcomers to this food will find short English-language descriptions, though words can hardly do justice to the intricate flavors of Thai cookery.

From among appetizers, spring rolls and pork satay are probably most familiar. Fried tofu with Thai peanut sauce can serve as a meatless alternative. Mee krob, deep-fried Thai noodles, are held together candy-like in a sweet sauce, garnished with fried tofu, bits of scrambled egg, and fresh, crunchy bean sprouts to balance textures. Deep-fried fish cakes, called tawd mun, are another delicious appetizer, eaten with vinegary cucumber and crushed peanut sauce.

The classic tom yum soups at Thai Valley are almost meals in themselves; if you ask for highly spiced soup, the hot peppers will make your eyes water and your throat roast. But the delicious flavor of lemon grass balances the heat. Be sure to order at least one of the noodle entrees. Try pad Thai, in which rice noodles are almost gummy, served with crushed peanuts, tofu, bean sprouts, and a garnish of scallions and lime wedges.

Then order one of the curries, perhaps with chicken in a coconut milk gravy, spiced with a complexity of peppers and seasonings. Whole deep-fried red snapper at market price is a house specialty.

# THAT STEAK JOYNT
KR 17/20
Decor 4/4   Hospitality 4/5   Food 7/9   Value 2/2

- **American**
- **Chicago/Mid-North**
- **$$$**

1610 N. Wells St.
Chicago
(312) 943-5091
**Troubleshooter:** Billy Siegel
(owner)

**Hours:** Mon-Sat from 5 pm,
Sun from 4 pm
**Cards:** All majors
**Reservations:** Suggested
**Handicapped:** Accessible
**Bar:** Full, extensive wine list,
Wed-Sat live music
**Parking:** Valet, or reduced
rates at nearby garage
**Party Facilities:** For 20-300
**Heart-Healthy Menu:**
Selections

That Steak Joynt has been an Old Town fixture for more than 30 years, and the customers keep coming. The restaurant serves up about as good a piece of beef as you'll find. And it continues to do so with variety: broiled, char-broiled, peppercorned, sauteed, with or without onions, garlic . . . you name it, and That Steak Joynt can do it. While beef is the prime attraction, and justly so, the restaurant has made a major impact with its barbecued pork ribs. The ribs are good enough that the name of the restaurant could be changed to That Rib Joynt.

Other aspects of the menu are in keeping with tastes in the '90s. Seafood is highlighted; try salmon cartoccio, in which the fish is baked in a paper bag, then served with a light lemon and sun-dried tomato sauce with a bouquet of fresh vegetables on the side. In keeping with contemporary tastes, several Italian choices have been added. Cappellini in a sweet marinara is served with half a dozen large broiled shrimp and is delicious.

Each dinner includes Italian-style marinated vegetables, soup, salad, and potatoes. Dessert can be as simple as a steaming cup of espresso or cappuccino or delicious apple strudel baked in the restaurant's kitchen, sauced with applejack brandy. Located next to

Second City, That Steak Joynt has a variety of dinner/theater packages.

The atmosphere remains 1880s San Francisco bawdy house; the ornate antique bar may be the only one in town with a piano built in. Service, while friendly, sometimes does not live up to the elegance of the decor.

# TIMBERS
KR 18.5/20
Decor 4/4   Hospitality 5/5   Food 7.5/9   Value 2/2

* **American**
* **Highland Park**
* **$$**

295 Skokie Hwy.
Highland Park
(708) 831-1400
**Troubleshooter:** Jim Errant
(owner)

**Hours:** Lunch Mon-Fri 11:30 am-4:30 pm, Sat noon-4 pm, dinner Mon-Thurs 5-10 pm, Fri-Sat until 11 pm, Sun 4:40-8:30 pm
**Cards:** AE, MC, VISA
**Reservations:** Accepted
**Handicapped:** Accessible
**Bar:** Full
**Parking:** Free lot
**Party Facilities:** For up to 60
**Heart-Healthy Menu:** Selections

Timbers is a Western-style American eatery, with the emphasis on meat and fish. The dining room is huge, but thanks to the good service, diners never feel lost or forgotten. There's no fancy saucing, except for the ribs, and no pretensions to "cuisine." They do food here! The mesquite grilling isn't yuppie affectation but rather a natural way to enhance those heartier fish and meats. This is basic good eating, without frills. The soups are hearty, not insipid little broths with French-kitchen pedigree. Even the salads are substantial. The house salad is a good mix of greens and tomatoes with your choice of excellent dressings. The Caesar chicken is mesquite-grilled skinned breast meat sliced on a bed of romaine lettuce, with pungent Caesar dressing. A half-dozen other dinner-size salads are offered for lighter or specialized appetites. Desserts can be lavish including the great American favorite, hot fudge sundae. Other choices are similarly mainstream American.

# TOKYO MARINA
KR 16/20
Decor 3/4   Hospitality 3.5/5   Food 7.5/9   Value 2/2

- **Japanese**
- **Chicago/Mid-North**
- **$$**

5058 N. Clark St.
Chicago
(312) 878-2900
**Troubleshooter:** Noboru
"Jim" Asato (owner)
**Note:** Restaurant is undergoing
remodeling and is scheduled for
reopening in summer, 1993.

**Hours:** Sun-Thurs 11:30
am-10 pm, Fri-Sat until 11 pm
(closed Thanksgiving and
Christmas)
**Cards:** MC, VISA
**Reservations:**
Recommended, especially
weekends
**Handicapped:** Accessible
**Bar:** Service bar
**Parking:** Street
**Party Facilities:** For up to 50

**F**reshness is the heart and soul of sushi and sashimi. At a time
when the eating of raw seafood is coming into question, Tokyo Ma-
rina is especially reassuring.

Tokyo Marina offers just about anything you can find at any of
Chicago's better Japanese restaurants, but at lower cost. Before or-
dering, you will want to check the handwritten listing of special fish
and other seafood, as well as the different kinds of maki, the sea-
weed-wrapped sushi that can contain any number of other ingre-
dients ranging from avocado to omelette. If you choose to order à la
carte, you will have more fun when you sit at the sushi bar and tell
the chef what you want. More economical, and with nearly as much
variety at hand, are combination platters that include sushi made
from mackerel, yellowtail, octopus, tuna, or other seafoods, depend-
ing upon what is fresh and available.

The restaurant is perfect for grazing. Try several appetizers.
Chicken yakitori features two large skewered sticks of grilled poultry
and vegetables in shish kebab fashion, but with distinctly Japanese
seasonings. Tempura can be too oily, but otherwise the vegetables
and shrimp are cooked perfectly. One of the best choices is scallops
butteryaki. Large sea scallops are stir-fried in butter with sliced button
mushrooms. Something like this would be perfectly at home in a
more elaborate French or continental setting.

Tokyo Marina serves a number of noodle dishes and soups, as
well as casseroles such as sukiyaki and a quartet of nabes, which are
vegetable and meat one-pot meals, often cooked at tableside. Unless

you sit at the sushi bar, service can be sluggish. But considering the value at hand, Tokyo Marina should be on your list of regular haunts for Japanese food.

# TOPOLOBAMPO
KR 18.5/20
Decor 4/4   Hospitality 4/5   Food 9/9   Value 1.5/2

- **Mexican**
- **Chicago/Near North**
- **$$**

445 N. Clark St.
Chicago
(312) 661-1434
**Troubleshooters:** Rick and Deanne Bayless (chef/owners)

**Hours:** Lunch Tues-Fri 11:30 am-2 pm, dinner Tues-Thurs 5:20-9:30 pm, Fri-Sat until 10:30 pm
**Cards:** All majors
**Reservations:** For 6 or fewer (the largest table seats 6)
**Handicapped:** Accessible
**Bar:** Full
**Parking:** Street, valet parking for dinner
**Party Facilities:** Sundays and Mondays
**Heart-Healthy Menu:** Suggestions on request

Topolobampo is literally a restaurant within a restaurant, tucked inside Frontera Grill. But while Frontera Grill is noisy and crowded, Topolobampo is shut off by doors and glass. The mood is placid, though the foods can be as exotically seasoned as at the restaurant's larger sibling. At Topolobampo the menu changes every two to three weeks. It is studded with recognizable terms in Mexican cookery but also features some preparations and ideas that are not so commonly seen in Chicago-area restaurants, Mexican or not.

You might choose an appetizer called pibipollo, a terrine or pâté that is a Yucatan version of chicken tamale. Chicken flavored with mild but distinctive achiote peppers and a tomato sauce enhanced with chilies and orange juice is wrapped in banana leaves and baked. When unwrapped, it holds its wedge shape, resting on a bed of banana leaves, napped with the tomato-chili sauce.

Something as common as sopa Azteca, the Mexican version of chicken soup, gets unusual treatment. The dark broth is accompanied by a platter of white Mexican cheese, chunked avocado, tortilla strips, sour cream, and dried pasilla chilies. You add these to the soup according to taste.

Another treat that pops up on the changing menu might be roasted poblano pepper. The large green pepper is split to form a basket, which holds a mixture of chunked roasted potatoes, tomatoes, avocado, chilies, and the heart of the dish, smoked marlin. The surprise is the heat generated by the poblano, which in most recipes, such as chilies rellenos, is almost bland.

Entrees, like appetizers, are handsomely plated on Mexican chinaware with a blue floral pattern. Pork tenderloin may come in half a dozen chunks, arrayed around a center of Mexican pumpkin and bathed in an unconventional mole made of chili peppers plus a bouquet of crushed nuts. Beef eaters can order a tenderloin crosshatched from a wood-fired grill. The beef is framed by rajas, strips of garlicky marinated cooked peppers. A small tostada chip holds some black bean sauce.

From the oceans, tuna is grilled with red onions, served with peppers, and garlic-enhanced rice and peas. Other entrees include rabbit or pheasant as well as seafood. Topolobampo's desserts go well beyond basic flan or sopapillas and include fruit tarts, ice creams, and exquisite crêpes, lavishly cooked in butter and served with a tangy caramel sauce made from condensed goat's milk. If all that were not enough, Topolobampo also serves Chicago's best coffee.

# TOULOUSE
KR 17.5/20
Decor 4/4   Hospitality 3.5/5   Food 8/9   Value 2/2

- **French**
- **Chicago/Near North**
- **$$$**

49 W. Division St.
Chicago
(312) 944-2606
**Troubleshooter:** Bob
Djahanguiri (owner)

**Hours:** Tues-Sat 6:00-10:30 pm, Fri-Sat until 11:30 pm, late menu 10:30-1 am
**Cards:** AE, CB, DINERS, MC, VISA
**Reservations:** Suggested
**Bar:** Full, cabaret entertainment at piano bar
**Parking:** Valet
**Party Facilities:** For 25-75 Sundays or luncheon daily
**Heart-Healthy Menu:** Selections

Open since March 1979, Toulouse remains one of the better spots in town for dining and lingering, thanks to its intimate atmosphere and the piano bar, not to mention a menu that is short but satisfying.

Diners are seated fairly close together at tables capped with white cloths, fresh flowers, and cut-glass candle holders. As the evening progresses, overhead and accent lighting is dimmed. The setting remains perfect for a romantic dinner.

Entrees could include as a daily special roast strip sirloin with Bordelaise sauce. Large twin slices of meat rest in a Bordelaise reduction, a thin but flavorful sauce. Roasted boned lamb with couscous, duck with green peppercorn sauce, roasted red snapper with oriental vegetables and ginger sauce, and veal sauteed in butter with lemon and capers are the core of the printed menu. Fish and pasta of the day are also featured, as is the chef's selection. One recent chef's selection has been roasted whitefish with a mushroom, herb, and pepper sauce. The idea of roasting fish may seem unusual, but it worked beautifully, transforming common Lake Superior whitefish into something, if not elegant, at least challenging. The peppery sauce was not so strong as to mask the flavor of the fish.

Pepper also shows up among the appetizer selections in an order of escargots forestier with mushroom sauce. Here, as with the fish, there is an abundance of sliced mushrooms, as well as bits of translucent onion, a complexity of herbs, and a liberal accent of pepper. It all works well, especially when coupled with a glass of the house red wine, a California cabernet.

Other appetizers might include a house duck pâté, onion soup, a seafood platter, and chilled asparagus spears in a vinaigrette. Toulouse serves two salads, the basic house array of greens and a tasty leek salad with a roquefort terrine. A generous slice of the terrine studded with slivered almonds sits atop a bed of sliced leek, in a mild bacon dressing. Fingers of Belgian endive form a crescent at the top of the platter, each endive piece holding a dab of relish. This is a salad not to be missed, if only for the delicious terrine.

Desserts include fruit tarts, flourless chocolate cake, and cheesecake. Our service was somewhat impersonal, a quality that is out of sync with the romantic mood otherwise created at Toulouse.

# TRATTORIA BELLAVIA
KR 18/20
Decor 3/4   Hospitality 5/5   Food 8/9   Value 2/2

- **Italian**
- **Chicago/Northwest**
- **$$**

3811 N. Harlem Ave.
Chicago
(312) 286-5568
**Troubleshooter:** Lisa Vaccaro (owner)

**Hours:** Daily 4-11 pm
**Cards:** AE, MC, VISA
**Reservations:** Suggested
**Handicapped:** Accessible
**Bar:** Full
**Parking:** Street
**Party Facilities:** For up to 60

Though Chicago's South Side and west suburban Italian communities are perhaps more widely known, Harlem Avenue on the Northwest Side of the city has its own Italian character, too. The San Francisco café, adjoining Trattoria Bellavia, seems to cater to neighborhood regulars, who look curiously at newcomers. But at the Bellavia the welcome mat is evident.

The cooking at Trattoria Bellavia is direct, homestyle, and often innovative. For example, the house namesake, vitello alla Trattoria, seems to be a variation on standard Italian themes. Sauteed veal and eggplant are combined with melted cheese and a fresh tomato sauce. In essence, the recipe marries the best of veal Parmigiana and eggplant Parmigiana into a single creation that works perfectly. The sauteed veal is first-rate and tender; the eggplant has been sliced ever so thin and layered over the meat, then topped with cheese for final baking. The sauce is somewhat sweeter than many. Like all dinners, the veal comes with a side of freshly cooked pasta, soup, and salad.

The soups are homemade. Minestrone is a garden of vegetables in a slightly thickened broth. In straciatelli, small starbursts of pasta are served in another stock rich with bits of chicken.

As for pasta, there are several different kinds; many, such as cavatelli, manicotti, ravioli, and tortellini, are homemade. The linguine with clam sauce is excellent. Here, whole small clams still in the shell top pasta that is abundant with garlic. Several seafood entrees, a number of veal dishes, and chicken round out the menu at Trattoria Bellavia.

À la carte appetizers include a couple of real gems. Arancini, deep-fried rice balls, are classic. Panzerotti, like a pizza that has been folded into a half-moon shape, is highlighted by a pastry-like crust.

Service is effortlessly hospitable to match the cooking. Trattoria Bellavia is a step or two above the ordinary in Italian dining.

# TRATTORIA NO. 10
KR 19/20
Decor 4/4   Hospitality 5/5   Food 8.5/9   Value 1.5/2

- **Italian**
- **Chicago/Loop**
- **$$**

10 N. Dearborn

Chicago
(312) 984-1718
**Troubleshooter:** Peggy McAtamney (manager)

**Hours:** Lunch Mon-Fri 11:30 am-2 pm, dinner Mon-Thurs 5:30-9 pm, Fri-Sat until 10 pm
**Cards:** All majors, house accounts
**Reservations:** Suggested at least 3 days in advance
**Handicapped:** Accessible
**Bar:** Full, extensive list of Italian wines
**Parking:** Valet at night
**Party Facilities:** For up to 50

Trattoria No. 10 lies underneath the heart of the Loop. Its narrow entryway leads to the unexpected . . . a series of dining rooms and a large bar that have authentic Old Country charm.

The best way to partake of Italian cooking is to order a course or two, enjoy them, then order another, and so on through the meal.

This method ensures a leisurely pace and aids digestion. Happily, the staff at Trattoria No. 10 understands and makes no effort to rush people through an evening.

Even before ordering, enjoy the house bread, warm, thick crusted as if it were fresh from a wood-fired oven, with a stuffing of sun-dried tomatoes. For antipasti, taste excellent sea scallops, grilled and served with a relish made of cooked fennel leaves flavored with the zest and pulp of fresh oranges. It is an unusual combination, but one that works to perfection and an excellent example of the imagination that characterizes contemporary Italian dining.

For something a bit more traditional, consider the Trattoria No. 10 version of roasted peppers, served cold with a dusting of oregano. Other appetizers include steamed mussels, traditionally prepared with garlic and a sauce made with fresh tomatoes.

In addition to a handful of pastas, Trattoria No. 10 serves a daily version of risotto, the extravagant Milanese rice. Risotto cannot be allowed to stand; it must be made and served fresh. Depending upon ingredients, seasonings can be intense, leaving something akin to a burn at the back of the throat and a lingering reminder of how rich the best risotto can be.

Among better entrees is farfalle con anatra, a sizable bowl of bow-tie noodles with chunks of roasted duck breast. All of this is enhanced with tomatoes, asparagus, and heavily caramelized onion cooked down into an intense veal sauce. Roast rack of lamb is another demonstration of the ordinary made imaginative, with a serving of Tuscan beans and a mix of vegetables alongside a chop grilled with garlic and a bouquet of fresh herbs.

# TRATTORIA ROMA TERZA
KR 16.5/20
Decor 3.5/4  Hospitality 4.5/5  Food 7.5/9  Value 1/2

- **Italian**
- **Chicago/Near West**
- **$$**

1119 W. Taylor St.
Chicago
(312) 226-6800
**Troubleshooter:** Franco
Zalloni (owner)

**Hours:** Lunch Mon-Fri 11:30
am-3 pm, dinner Sun-Thurs
4-10 pm, Fri until 11 pm, Sat
5-11 pm
**Cards:** All majors
**Reservations:** Suggested
**Bar:** Full wine list
**Parking:** Valet or street

**A**t Trattoria Roma Terza the walls are painted to give a look of rustic age, though the restaurant is one of the newest on the Taylor Street Italian restaurant scene. The idea is to create a kind of Old World ambiance. To one side of the dining room stands a low table with platters of antipasti waiting to be taken to tables by quick-moving waiters. In warm weather, a patio is open for people who prefer dining outside.

Trattoria food is meant to be casual, yet robust enough to satisfy. That certainly describes what is happening at Trattoria Roma Terza, though prices tend to be high. From a lengthy list of antipasti, hungry diners will find small pizzas, unconventional by most standards. Try the quattro formagi, or four cheeses – mozzarella, mascarpone, blue, and Swiss – melted more or less together on a fairly crisp crust. Fried calamari are virtually greaseless; bruschetti ala Romana is classic toasted bread brushed with olive oil and topped with tomato. The rather short pasta and entree menu lists only a half dozen or so choices from each of those categories. Trattoria Roma Terza serves a pasta akin to gnocchi, called gnocchetti, that falls short of the chewiness that should make it so satisfying as a pasta course.

But an order of gnocchetti segreto is tasty enough, with a cream sauce plus broccoli, pieces of Italian sausage and grated Parmesan cheese. Somewhat lighter is gnocchetti mozzarella, made fresh with a splurge of basil leaves. Another choice is spaghetti in a Northern-style tomato-and-cream sauce with fresh green peas, diced small pieces of prosciutto, mushrooms, and Parmesan cheese.

From among entrees, scampi griglia features eight large grilled shrimp in the shell, flavored with a squeeze or two of lemon juice, olive oil, and a dash of paprika. Even better is pollo con pepperoni, chicken sauteed in tomato sauce and served with a generous bounty of sliced sauteed green and red peppers, with plenty of onions for accent.

# TUCCI MILAN
KR 19/20
Decor 4/4   Hospitality 5/5   Food 8/9   Value 2/2

* **Italian**
* **Chicago/Near North**
* **$$**

6 W. Hubbard St.
Chicago
(312) 222-0044
**Troubleshooters:** Steve Ottman, Howard Katz (managing partners)

**Hours:** Mon-Thurs 11:30 am-10 pm, Fri-Sat noon-11 pm, Sun 5-9 pm
**Cards:** All majors
**Reservations:** Limited
**Handicapped:** Accessible
**Parking:** Valet, street, or lot
**Heart-Healthy Menu:** Selections

The neo-modernist lighting accents, open kitchen, and guests who are often dressed as stylishly casual as is the food set the stage for sophisticated cooking. Many travelers agree that for all the appeal of Rome, Milan is increasingly becoming an Italian destination of choice. Certainly, the city is heir to a fabulous gustatory tradition, notably that delicate rice casserole known as risotto.

At Tucci Milan, the risotto is prepared fresh, the arborio rice slow-cooked in a flavored broth, finished with whatever ingredients the chef's whim and market availability may dictate. Risotto is traditionally eaten after one has tasted the antipasti. The selection at Tucci Milan can be as urbane as carpaccio and designer pizzas or as simple as prosciutto, peppers, and goat's cheese or eggplant baked with a topping of chopped tomatoes and melted cheese. The carpaccio is sprinkled with a coarse grind of Parmesan cheese and accompanied by artichokes and arugula greens, the thin slices of raw beef lightly brushed with olive oil.

Among the single-portion pizzas is one with a puree of eggplant seasoned with basil to emulate pesto, brushed over a thin crust and baked to a crisp, with a topping of chopped fresh vegetables. Dinner-sized salads can be rewarding selections, especially in warm weather. A recent order consisted of lettuce frisée with tiny slivers of beet, cracked walnuts, and a generous round of goat's cheese with a light olive oil dressing.

The menu is somewhat shy of meat, offering two styles of chicken, a grilled veal chop, and poached salmon, choices supplemented by four or five daily specials, often featuring additional pastas. The pastas are generally imaginative but not contrived. Rigatoni with a selection of shrimp, scallops, and finned fish has been among delicious offerings. Tucci Milan also offers what it calls the sandwich of the day. One recent sandwich was made with focaccia, a round bread loaf baked with tomatoes and brushed with oil. To make the sandwich, the bread was sliced, then layered with generous chunks of grilled boned chicken, lettuce, tomato slices, even mayonnaise. The clincher was melted smoked mozzarella cheese, which really defined the flavor. For desserts, Italian ices and ice creams are supplemented by a selection of pastries.

# TUFANO'S VERNON PARK TAP
KR 15.5/20
Decor 2/4   Hospitality 4/5   Food 7.5/9   Value 2/2

| | |
|---|---|
| • **Italian** | **Hours:** Tues-Fri 11 am-10 pm, |
| • **Chicago/Near West** | Sat 4-11 pm, Sun 3-9 pm |
| • **$** | **Cards:** None, house accounts |
| | **Reservations:** No |
| 1073 W. Vernon Park | **Handicapped:** Accessible |
| Chicago | **Parking:** Valet |
| (312) 733-3393 | **Party Facilities:** Sundays, |
| **Troubleshooter:** Joseph | Mondays, and Saturday |
| DiBuono (owner) | afternoons |

Though its official name is Tufano's, most people know it as the Vernon Park Tap. Whatever you want to call it, this restaurant is a part of Chicago history.

The restaurant is a holdout against urban expansion; it stands on the line separating what once was a much larger Italian community from the sprawling University of Illinois at Chicago campus. In all the years the restaurant has been around, it has changed little. The interior is as simple as its exterior, not much different from the row of houses on either side.

The Tufano family opened the restaurant almost 60 years ago, and it remains a small, family-style gathering place for locals, students from the nearby campus, and area politicians who find it a hospitable respite.

At first blush the menu seems to be prosaic, featuring everyday Italian fare: spaghetti, stuffed shells, lasagna, chicken, and chops. Many of the courses are served family-style. Order a special Tufano's salad and get a large platter overflowing with tomatoes, cucumbers, Italian salami, mozzarella cheese, onions, artichoke hearts, lettuce, peppers, the list seems endless. On Fridays the restaurant serves its special seafood salad, cold chunks of squid, shrimp, snow-white codfish, tuna, and Italian scungilli, which is a type of mollusk.

Weekends are the time to come for homestyle cooking. Large, handmade ravioli in the house tomato sauce are served only on Saturday and Sunday, as are the delicious dumpling-like cavatelli. Friday is fish day, when orange roughy, available every day, is enhanced with calamari, pasta, and clam sauce, baked codfish, called baccala, and steamed littleneck clams by the dozen or half dozen.

If you have difficulty finding the restaurant, just ask someone in the neighborhood. Everybody knows where it is.

# TUSCANY
KR 19/20
Decor 4/4   Hospitality 5/5   Food 8/9   Value 2/2

- **Italian**
- **Chicago/Near West**
- **$$**

1014 W. Taylor St.
Chicago
(312) 829-1990
**Troubleshooter:** Phil Stefani
(owner)

**Hours:** Mon-Thurs 11 am-11 pm, Fri until midnight, Sat 5 pm-12:30 am, Sun 2-9:30 pm
**Cards:** AE, DINERS, MC, VISA
**Reservations:** Suggested
**Handicapped:** Accessible
**Bar:** Full
**Parking:** Valet
**Party Facilities:** Two private rooms

**A**t Tuscany, the fashionable crowds are as much a part of the decor as is the open kitchen, the French café doors that open up the front of the restaurant in warm weather, and the bare brick and hardwood. Tuscany is not the typical mom-and-pop restaurant that made Taylor Street's Little Italy a dining mecca for so many years.

It is, however, typical of what is happening today in Italian dining. The restaurant is crowded and noisy. It eschews overcooked spaghetti, spicy meatballs, and red-checkered tablecloths. Instead, diners are finding herbed olive oil, designer pizzas, and unusual pastas with non-traditional saucing.

From the list of designer pizzas, all on thin crusts, taste one piled high with fresh chopped tomato, basil, slices of grilled eggplant and onion, and a liberal amount of melted goat's cheese. The crust is crisp without being burned, the toppings flavorful. A simple bruschetta topped with chopped tomatoes and basil is another choice, short of a full antipasto spread. Tuscany offers a house version of carpaccio as well as typical appetizers such as fried calamari and baked clams.

Each evening features some house specials. Recently, risotto with rabbit was being served, as were grilled salmon and several other entree selections. If you choose the risotto, let your waiter know right away because its preparation takes 35 minutes.

Back on the printed menu, several pastas, ranging from mezzaluna stuffed with chicken and vegetables in a prosciutto-laced cream sauce to gnocchi with a quartet of cheeses, are regularly served. Though pasta is a separate course in true Italian dining, an order of linguine with shrimp in a spicy diavolo sauce is a meal in itself. A variation might be to forgo the marinara and have a lighter oil-and-garlic combination with a bite of hot peppers. The shrimp are firm and fresh, the pasta al dente.

On the back wall of the main dining room at Tuscany is a large wood-fired rotisserie in which whole chickens are slowly roasted. One version presents the chicken split with an accompaniment of deliciously seasoned roasted potatoes. Even with the skin of the chicken stripped away in the interest of healthy dining, the meat has a woodsy, fresh flavor. Other meats on the menu include several grilled steaks and chops, as well as some traditional sauteed veal preparations. Desserts are typical – tiramisu, cannoli, and the like – but we think it more fun after dinner to walk a couple of blocks west on Taylor Street and get an Italian ice at Mario's.

# Tuttaposto

KR 19/20

Decor 4/4   Hospitality 4.5/5   Food 8.5/9   Value 2/2

---

- **Italian/Mediterranean**
- **Chicago/Near North**
- **$$**

646 N. Franklin St.
Chicago
(312) 943-6262
**Troubleshooter:** Tony
Mantuano (chef/owner)

**Hours:** Lunch Mon-Fri 11:30
am-2 pm, dinner Mon-Thurs
5-10 pm, Fri-Sat until 11 pm,
Sun until 9 pm
**Cards:** All majors
**Reservations:** Suggested
**Handicapped:** Accessible
**Bar:** Full
**Parking:** Valet or street
**Party Facilities:** For up to
50; semi-private space for larger
groups

---

Tuttaposto is probably the most original new Chicago restaurant in years. The decor is alive and contemporary, with bare brick walls, open kitchen, wood-burning oven, and hand-hewn beams. But what really sets off Tuttaposto is its imaginative menu. Chef/Owner Tony Mantuano draws not only on his native Italian heritage but also from the entire Mediterranean region.

Thus a seafood stew, named for the cataplana copper cooking pot in which it is brought to the table, is meant to be a re-creation of what might typically be found in a small Portuguese fishing village. It is somewhat akin to bouillabaisse in the sense that it is a gathering of various seafood in a clear, garlic-accented stock. The cataplana also includes couscous, the millet grain common to North African cooking.

Chef Mantuano draws on Italy for inspiration with a spaghetti, but his tomato sauce is considerably more peppery than that usually considered Italian. His pizza, with a thin, cracker-style crust, melted cheese, fresh herbs, and tomatoes, is right out of Naples. Another pizza, however, is more ad libbed, displaying caramelized garlic with goat's cheese.

The menu conveniently spells out particulars of each presentation, with descriptions augmented by service people who seem to practice their profession with more than a touch of pride.

Gnocchi is served in an intense mushroom sauce, so good by itself that the added grated cheese only introduces an unwelcome saltiness. But Tunisian chicken wings, heartily spiced with peppery harrisa, are enhanced by the addition of cheese.

Tuttaposto happens to be fine for traditional multicourse dining, but ordering two or three tapas provides more variety. Seafood sausage comes from the wood-stoked ovens with a side of chopped arugula. A black bean salad is enhanced with octopus in basil olive oil. Empanadas, pastry turnovers with edges crimped around a plumped center, are filled with ground salt cod and coupled with a red-pepper puree. Even more unusual is the restaurant's version of Sardinian focaccia. This is not the round flat bread of Italy, but rather a crisp cracker baked in large sheets. In this case it is served with hummus, salmon roe caviar, and smoked eggplant puree for dipping.

# Un Grand Café
KR 17/20
Decor 3.5/4   Hospitality 4/5   Food 7.5/9   Value 2/2

- **French/Bistro**
- **Chicago/Mid-North**
- **$$**

2300 Lincoln Park West (Belden Stratford Hotel)
Chicago
(312) 348-8886
**Troubleshooters:** Gabino Sotelino (managing partner), Chris Randall (general manager)

**Hours:** Dinner Mon-Thurs 6-10:30 pm, Fri-Sat to 11:30, Sun 5-10 pm
**Cards:** All majors
**Reservations:** Accepted
**Bar:** Full
**Party Facilities:** For up to 125, Sundays only
**Heart-Healthy Menu:** Selections

**P**robably not old enough to be called "venerable," Un Grand Café has nonetheless been a Lincoln Park fixture for about a decade or so. It was one of the restaurants that introduced bistro-style cooking to Chicago diners, and it continues to do so with a newly revised menu.

The most popular dinners are still there. Café regulars can still expect to find steak with pomme frites, roasted chicken, traditional onion soup baked in a crock, and a selection of choice pâtés.

But now there are some additions to tempt diners. Among appetizers is escargot farcie, new potatoes filled with snails in garlic butter.

Mussels are served in a cream sauce with leek and fennel, while duck sausage sits atop a fresh salad frisée.

From a selection of new entrees, the menu lists pork loin stuffed with prunes; mashed potatoes are the accompaniment. Somewhat more elaborate is baby pheasant over grilled vegetables splashed with mustard vinaigrette, while lamb shanks are braised and served with couscous, ratatouille, and French flageolet beans. Seafood lovers will find an exciting new version of bouillabaisse. The bistro menu is fleshed out with other, more classic choices, including several elegant fish and game entrees.

# UNCLE TANNOUS
KR 19/20
Decor 4/4   Hospitality 5/5   Food 8/9   Value 2/2

| | |
|---|---|
| • **Middle Eastern/ Lebanese** | **Hours:** Mon 5-10:30 pm, Tues-Thurs noon-10:30 pm, Fri until 11 pm, Sun until 10 pm |
| • **Chicago/Mid-North** | **Cards:** AE, DINERS, DISCOVER, MC, VISA |
| • **$$** | **Reservations:** Suggested |
| 2626 N. Halsted St. | **Handicapped:** Accessible |
| Chicago | **Bar:** Service bar |
| (312) 929-1333 | **Parking:** Valet |
| **Troubleshooter:** Joseph Skaff (owner) | **Party Facilities:** For 10-100 |

Lebanese cuisine, like others from the Middle East, is designed to be not only nourishing but the heart of an elaborate and often ritualized social encounter. It is the role of the host to offer his guests the best of what he has. This seems to be at the heart of dining at Uncle Tannous.

A waiter welcomes diners with the printed menu, but quickly adds that there is an evening special or two. When fish is served, he may even invite you back into the kitchen to inspect the freshness of the seafood before it is cooked.

The menu is enticing, to say the least, with its various grilled meats, fried or broiled seafood, and softly seasoned vegetables characteristic of the Levant.

Should you choose to be a bit adventurous and your appetite is up to the demands, order the Lebanese maza, an offering of smaller portions of several foods spread across your table to pick and choose as you might in a Lebanese home. The maza features at least 20 different selections, ranging from simple vegetables and sliced tomatoes to grilled liver, kidneys, and other Lebanese choices. There are felafel, hummus, baba ghanoush, spinach, and meat pies. There are stuffed grape leaves, green beans in olive oil with herbs, spices, and light tomato sauce, fava beans and okra, tabbouli salad, slices of cucumbers, seasoned onions in oil – a veritable cornucopia.

Should you choose to order à la carte, various kebabs and broiled cuts of lamb should please. Sometimes served as a special is kafta in the pan. Kafta is grilled ground beef patties, sauteed with a coating of cracked wheat for texture, served with slices of potato in a tomato sauce. Desserts include traditional baklava, rice pudding, and crème caramel. The baklava is made without honey, bound together instead by finely ground nuts sandwiched between layers of phyllo dough.

# VA PENSIERO
KR 18.5/20
Decor 4/4  Hospitality 4.5/5  Food 8.5/9  Value 1.5/2

- **Italian**
- **Evanston**
- **$$**

1566 Oak St.
Evanston
(708) 475-7779
**Troubleshooters:** Tim and Barbara Gorham (owners)

**Hours:** Lunch Mon-Fri 11:30 am-2 pm, dinner Mon-Thurs 5:30-9 pm, Fri-Sat until 10 pm
**Cards:** AE, DISCOVER, VISA, MC
**Reservations:** Suggested
**Handicapped:** Accessible
**Bar:** Wine list includes 50 Italian regionals
**Parking:** Valet Fri-Sat
**Party Facilities:** For up to 100, 125 cocktails

Va Pensiero has an ambiance much like an older Italian resort of half a century or more ago. Peach-colored walls enclose a setting rich with terra-cotta accents and comfortable, upholstered seating.

The menu changes seasonally. Among antipasti, roasted artichoke hearts are filled with a creamy blend of peppered mozzarella cheese, liberally laced with fresh lemon juice. Roasting the artichoke hearts leaves them plump and tender, though a certain oiliness may be apparent. Polenta makes a studied contrast to something as rich as the artichoke, baked with a sauce of gorgonzola cheese and slices of apples. If ever two flavors were meant for each other, they are this fine blue-veined cheese and apples.

Soup changes daily at the discretion of the chef. From a selection of pastas, risotto, that uniquely simmered rice from the Milan area, might be cooked with mussels. This is a dish to savor for the texture of the individual grains, which absorb the flavor of the stock. Sometimes, risotto can be too salty; this risotto has a gentler flavoring. Another pasta, ravioli, may come in a very light marinara, with a creamy goat's cheese filling. The texture of the pasta is all important, just resistant enough to the bite so that it does not fall apart.

The rest of the printed menu, which leans toward the Italian north, is fairly short but not without interest. Even a simple veal chop gets support from a cooked salad of arugula, tomatoes, and onions dressed with balsamic vinegar. In another version of the veal chop, oven-roasted tomato has been peeled but retains some texture. For hearty diners, Va Pensiero sometimes serves bollito misto, a collection of meats in their own juices. The platter comes with a fan of sliced beef tenderloin, lamb, and slices of spiced duck sausage in a broth reduced to emphasize seasonings.

Desserts include a lovely flourless Italian torte, freshly made gelati, and other sweets.

# VILLA MARCONI
KR 18/20
Decor 3/4   Hospitality 5/5   Food 8/9   Value 2/2

- **Italian**
- **Chicago/South**
- **$$**

2358 S. Oakley Ave.
Chicago
(312) 847-3168
**Troubleshooter:** Lillian
Marconi (owner)

**Hours:** Mon-Fri 11 am-10 pm,
Sat 5-11 pm (closed Sundays)
**Cards:** AE, CB, DINERS, MC,
VISA
**Reservations:** Accepted
**Bar:** Full
**Parking:** Street

If I were to describe the perfect casual restaurant, I would want it to be a family-owned and -operated neighborhood place, with pleasant decor, friendly service, really good food, and excellent value. If it happened to be Italian, that wouldn't be so bad. This, in a nutshell, is Villa Marconi. The restaurant is rather large, brightly lit, and festive, although a critical eye might describe it as garish.

Fried appetizers such as calamari or zucchini sticks are virtually greaseless. Baked clams are steaming hot, succulent, and flavorful with a seasoned breadcrumb blanket. Minestrone soup tastes like the kind simmered all day with fresh vegetables and homemade stock.

From among a selection of pastas, our waitress was kind enough to suggest something not on the menu, or on the chalkboard – linguine with mussels. A large oval platter, the kind used for family-style dining, was brought out from the kitchen with more than two dozen mussels arrayed on the edges. In the center was a mound of pasta, lightly oiled and garlicky, but not so highly seasoned as to overwhelm the fresh taste of steamed mussels.

From a selection of entrees, chicken Vesuvio is classic in its simplicity. Veal Parmigiana is a large cutlet, like a golden pillow all puffed up with its light flour-and-egg crust. Beef braciole is a bit different from the usual, wrapped with mortadella for a sausage spiciness instead of milder prosciutto.

Desserts include cheesecakes and Italian ice creams.

# VIVERE
KR 18.5/20
Decor 4/4   Hospitality 4.5/5   Food 8/9   Value 2/2

| | |
|---|---|
| • **Italian** | **Hours:** Lunch Mon-Fri 11:15 am-2:15 pm, dinner Mon-Thurs 5-10 pm, Fri-Sat until 11 pm |
| • **Chicago/Loop** | |
| • **$$$** | **Cards:** All majors |
| 71 W. Monroe St. | **Reservations:** Accepted |
| Chicago | **Handicapped:** Accessible |
| (312) 332-4040 | **Bar:** Full, award-winning wine list |
| **Troubleshooters:** The Capitanini family (owners) | **Parking:** Valet |
| | **Party Facilities:** For up to 50 |

**V**ivere features a surreal wash of earth tones and molded coppers, paint-splashed glass ornamentation, swagged curtains, curving woodwork, furnishings, and trim. Wherever the eye turns, there is something of interest. But, like other restaurants, Vivere must succeed or fail on its food. Executive Chef Peter Schonman has put together a menu that displays some excellent selections from the realm of contemporary Italian dining.

Among appetizers, consider such choices as a wild mushroom soufflé, a small timbale resting in a pooled cream-and-onion sauce. Try delicious smoked salmon and trout, with understated accents of fennel and lesser statements of coriander and parsley. More substantial are crêpes layered with a duckling forcemeat, garnished with a sweet tomato marmalade.

Things get even better with the selection of second-course pastas. Most interesting is pappardelle di spinaci con scamorza. Here, a broad noodle is presented in a cream-based sauce flavored with house-cured pancetta and pungent, hard Italian grated cheeses. Another excellent choice is small tortelli stuffed with sharp cheeses in a sauce of crushed cherry tomatoes and fresh basil. Tastes and textures are exquisite.

Vivere features a daily risotto, using a short-grained rice rather than arborio. Nonetheless, the grains plump up, bound together into chewy bundles of flavor.

Among entrees, rabbit with garlic, tomato, and rosemary is sweet flavored, with no trace of gaminess. Chicken breasts are distinctly flavored with garlic, sage, and red pepper. Entrees are served with an assortment of fresh vegetables.

Desserts are sensational, whether a simple fruited sorbetto or a rich chocolate cake with cappuccino sauce. There is even sweetened eggplant with a chocolate sauce and layered ricotta cheese, not as contrived as it sounds and somewhat cake-like in texture. The wine list is extensive – simply put, one of the finest in the Midwest if not the entire nation.

# VIVO
KR 19/20
Decor 4/4   Hospitality 5/5   Food 8/9   Value 2/2

---

- **Italian**
- **Chicago/Near West**
- **$$$**

838 W. Randolph St.
Chicago
(312) 733-3379
**Troubleshooters:** Jerry Kleiner, Dan Krasny, Howard Davis (owners)

**Hours:** Lunch Mon-Fri 11:30 am-2:30 pm, dinner Mon-Thurs 5 pm-midnight, Fri-Sat until 1 am, Sun 4:30-11 pm
**Cards:** AE, CB, DINERS, MC, VISA
**Reservations:** Mandatory
**Handicapped:** Accessible
**Bar:** Full
**Parking:** Valet
**Party Facilities:** Large lounge upstairs

---

It's almost a toss-up as to whether the food or the people-watching is the stronger attraction at Vivo. Both are fascinating. Vivo, in the heart of Chicago's Near West Side produce market, is on the cutting edge of fashion and dining.

The restaurant is post-modern, with high ceilings, pinpoint spot lighting, dark woods, and handsome granite accents. The food is Italian, but with "neo" embellishments. While many dishes are firmly rooted in tradition, the style of service and presentation, not to mention the overall ambiance, make Vivo different.

While a combination of bruschettas with four separate toppings of chopped mushrooms, chopped tomatoes, grilled peppers, and olivida is ordinary, the mixed antipasto brought from the sideboard near the restaurant's entrance is without fault. The platter is loaded with grilled and roasted fresh vegetables, including slices of eggplant, zucchini, and whatever else is seasonally fresh, plus delicious sauteed peppers, snatches of olives, and mushrooms. Speaking of mushrooms, grilled portobello on a bed of greens is as meaty as a cut of steak, only much more healthful. Other antipasti include a couple of salads, classic prosciutto with melon, and grilled shrimp with zucchini.

Vivo features several pasta selections, ranging from simple spaghetti with garlic, basil, and fresh tomatoes to fettuccine with an imaginative lamb ragout. The restaurant also features a daily risotto. Spaghetti with a mix of seafood is substantial enough to serve as either a pasta course or entree. Fresh mussels and clams still in their shells ring a platter that includes shrimp and scallops, in a marinara sauce with enough bite to be interesting. For something a bit more earthy, rigatoni with spicy Italian sausage would also satisfy as a main course.

Elsewhere on the menu are whole grilled red snapper and sauteed salmon, among other seafood choices. Grilled chicken with endive is well flavored, certainly more interesting than many styles of roasted chicken, which is often bland. A breaded veal chop, sliced sirloin in Barolo wine sauce, and medallions of veal with artichokes are among other dinner selections.

# THE WATERFRONT
KR 18/20
Decor 4/4   Hospitality 4/5   Food 8/9   Value 2/2

| | |
|---|---|
| • **Seafood/American** | **Hours:** Sun-Thurs 11:30 am-midnight, Fri-Sat until 1 am |
| • **Chicago/Near North** | **Cards:** AE, DINERS, DISCOVER, MC, VISA |
| • **$$** | |
| 16 W. Maple St. | **Reservations:** Accepted |
| Chicago | **Bar:** Full |
| (312) 943-7494 | **Parking:** Nearby lots or street |
| **Troubleshooter:** Basil Georgeson (owner) | **Party Facilities:** For 12-50 |
| | **Heart-Healthy Menu:** Selections |

Though not the trendsetter for seafood that it once was, the Waterfront more than stays afloat by offering delicious, imaginatively prepared seafood dinners at reasonable cost. This was the first Chicago restaurant I know of that served cioppino, the delicious seafood stew that traces its roots to Portugal by way of San Francisco.

The menu is somewhat behind the times by contemporary standards. I cannot imagine ever finding salmon in raspberry sauce here.

But if you want good, old-fashioned seafood prepared in a hearty manner with plenty of side dishes, this is the place to visit.

Diners sit in captain's chairs or church-pew benches at copper-topped tables, surrounded by weathered wood, bare brick, and fixtures that would be at home on a brigantine set for rough seas and ports unknown.

Carpetbagger steak stuffed with a motley crew of broiled oysters is still a menu fixture, as are old favorites like cioppino and various styles of shrimp, lobster, and fish. The restaurant has recently added a section devoted to spa cooking. And to keep up with the Joneses, if not the Mendozas, diners can also enjoy a selection of Spanish-inspired tapas; ask what's available each evening. There's nothing stuffy about the Waterfront, where good seafood and good fun have prevailed for many years.

# WAYSIDE MANOR
KR 17/20
Decor 3/4   Hospitality 5/5   Food 7/9   Value 2/2

---

- **American**
- **Crete**
- **$$$**

1216 Main St.
Crete
(708) 672-8080
**Troubleshooters:** Jim Howard (chef/owner)

**Hours:** Tues-Sat 5:30-10 pm
**Cards:** MC, VISA
**Handicapped:** Accessible
**Bar:** Small wine list
**Parking:** Free lot
**Party Facilities:** For up to 40

---

Scan any local restaurant guide and it quickly becomes evident that there is a dearth of fine dining in the south suburbs. When South Side and south suburban diners look for something special, more often than not they must journey north. But there are a handful of good south suburban restaurants, some even worth the trip for North Siders. One to know about is Wayside Manor.

The drive, which takes you past scattered barns and pleasant farmland, leads to the small downtown section of Crete. A short ride up Main Street takes you to the Victorian home that houses this restaurant. Inside are a trio of cozy dining rooms, each somewhat different, though all charming with nineteenth-century ambiance.

Chef/Owner Jim Howard works the stoves and ovens to create what he calls cuisine à la minute. That does not mean fast food; rather, everything, including sauces, is prepared at the last minute, on request. More often than not, the dining at Wayside Manor proves to be worth the time and effort.

Recent appetizers have included delicious smoked duck breast served cold with a traditional English cumberland sauce, made from a base of currant jelly, port wine, and citrus zest. The home smoking of the duck adds a fine-flavored finish.

Entrees are preceded by a rather lavishly arranged house salad whose mixed lettuce leaves are piled high on a large platter in an artistic arrangement. As for entrees, we found some hits and some near hits. Ravioli stuffed with lobster is absolutely superb, thanks in large part to the deliciously fresh basil cream sauce in which it is napped. Pale pork tenderloin comes in a pastry crust, looking for all the world like beef Wellington. In fact it is served in a sauce that would do justice to beef, as well as pork. Among a handful of seafood selections at Wayside Manor have been grilled Norwegian salmon and tilapia. Large Gulf shrimp are served as a quartet in a brandy-based butter sauce highlighted by a hint of ginger and a garnish of pasta.

Among dessert choices, chocolate mousse is the dark, deep-flavored kind, served on a semi-sweet chocolate round and bathed in a pool of chocolate sauce.

# THE WEBER GRILL
KR 18.5/20
Decor 3.5/4   Hospitality 5/5   Food 8/9   Value 2/2

- **American**
- **Wheeling**
- **$$**

920 N. Milwaukee Ave.
Wheeling
(708) 215-0996
**Troubleshooter:** Robert Fox
(general manager)

**Hours:** Lunch Mon-Fri 11:30
am-2:30 pm, Sat noon-2:30
pm, dinner Mon-Thurs 4:30-10
pm, Fri-Sat until 11 pm, Sun
3-9 pm
**Cards:** All majors
**Reservations:** Suggested
**Handicapped:** Accessible
**Bar:** Full, extensive wine list
**Parking:** Free lot
**Party Facilities:** For up to 40

The Weber Grill seems to be an idea whose time has come. Almost everybody loves the flavor of foods grilled over charcoal in the backyard. But except for weekends, you might not feel like lugging out the charcoal after a hard day's labor, firing up the grill, then standing out in the yard to do all the work yourself. That's where the Weber Grill comes in.

The idea is simple. The kitchen has a bank of huge, professional-sized Weber cauldrons, all manned by professionals. The menu features most of those meats and fish you would associate with grilling: steaks, ribs, chicken, and chops.

There are views into the kitchen from two windows, so you can watch how things are done. Dinners include a soup of the day or salad. Salad dressings are excellent. Among à la carte appetizers, a platter of onion curls consists of a huge mound of crisp fried onions that are great for finger snacking. Selections from the grill in appetizer portion include grilled scallops with bacon in a ginger-and-lime marinade, chicken kebabs, and beef kebabs. In the case of the beef, here is grilling by the masters of the craft.

Among dinners, barbecued ribs in full- or half-slab portion will be a rib-picker's delight. The ribs are given a good smoking, which makes the meat look oddly red, and then they are finished over the charcoal. You can have a sweet-and-sour or spicy red sauce. Either way, the meat is tender and almost falls from the bones. Among seafood choices, a mixed grill could include scallops, tuna, and monkfish. Each variety holds its own flavor and texture. Grilled tuna is a particular treat.

Desserts include cheesecakes, ice creams, custards, and other yummies.

# WILD ASPARAGUS
KR 19/20
Decor 3.5/4   Hospitality 4.5/5   Food 9/9   Value 2/2

- **American/Eclectic**
- **Evanston**
- **$$**

1709 Benson Ave.
Evanston
(708) 866-8181
**Troubleshooter:** Greg
Kaminski (owner)

**Hours:** Mon-Thurs 11 am-9 pm, Fri-Sat until 10:30 pm
**Cards:** MC, VISA
**Reservations:** For 4 or more at dinner
**Handicapped:** Accessible
**Bar:** Wine and beer only
**Parking:** Street
**Party Facilities:** Catering only

Though its name suggests some kind of counterculture health-food store or restaurant, Wild Asparagus is one of the more upbeat and interesting, though smaller, dining spots to be found in the northern suburbs. Technically, this is a gourmet carryout food shop. Tables for diners are set around a central core of counters and coolers. You might think that a waiter reaching for the dried cepes on a shelf could drag his sleeve in your soup, but, fortunately, the place is not as crowded as all that.

Appetizer choices run from any of several pasta salads to delicious fresh soups. Smoked cold salmon has a mild tang and is accompanied by an unusual sweetened dill sauce. Among soups, a corn chowder tastes garden fresh, with the zip of some semi-hot peppers and the crunch of tortilla chips for texture balance.

Wild Asparagus is the kind of restaurant where entrees all look so tempting, it is difficult to make a selection. Hunter's stew features chunks of beef and veal in a sauce laden with carrots, zucchini, and pea pods inside a loaf of crusty bread. The bread is the bowl, and when it comes to dunking in the leftover sauce, this presentation is ready-made for such goings-on.

Seafood varies according to availability. Baked flounder was recently served stuffed with crabmeat. Seafood ravioli is a platter of half-moon ravioli, evidently shaped by hand. Each is filled with a coarse grind of scallops, shrimp, and crabmeat, bound with ricotta cheese. The ravioli are lightly masked with a wonderfully flavored lobster sauce that says worlds about the kind of kitchen talent at work here.

Somewhat lighter in the pasta department is pasta primavera. The assorted sauteed fresh vegetables come in a light garlic butter sauce, garnished with intensely flavored sun-dried tomatoes. Among other selections, a roasted duckling comes with a seasonal cranberry orange glaze. A side of wild rice complements the richness of the duck.

Certainly desserts are not to be missed. They include firm pumpkin cheesecake, triple chocolate cake, or an equally towering white chocolate mousse cake, as well as assorted fruit tarts and strudels.

# THE WINNETKA GRILL
KR 18.5/20
Decor 3.5/4   Hospitality 5/5   Food 8/9   Value 2/2

| | |
|---|---|
| • **American** | **Hours:** Mon-Thurs 5:30-9 pm, Fri until 10 pm, Sat 5-10 pm, Sun until 9 pm |
| • **Winnetka** | |
| • **$$$** | |
| 64 Green Bay Rd. | **Cards:** All majors |
| Winnetka | **Handicapped:** Accessible |
| (708) 441-6444 | **Bar:** Service bar |
| **Troubleshooter:** Henry | **Parking:** Free lot |
| Markwood (owner) | **Heart-Healthy Menu:** Selections |

The à la carte menu is as unpretentious as the food is elegant, supplemented by daily selections of seasonal fish, produce, and the like. Presentation matches the handsome neoclassic surroundings of the small, noisy dining room.

That noise and the closeness of tables are my only complaints about a nearly perfect restaurant. True, some selections may not be up to the level of others, but there are plenty of excellent offerings from which to choose. Though Maryland crab cakes with a light mustard mayonnaise dressing were Chesapeake Bay fresh and delicious, New York duckling foie gras was a disappointment in a sauce that had all the grace of a dry onion-soup mix. The foie gras itself lacked the satiny smoothness that is the reason the dish commands the attention of gastronomes. Other appetizers may include tantalizing pasta in a gorgonzola cream and walnut sauce, ceviche-style bay scallops, and domestic caviar.

Dinners come with a light salad of mixed greens and a fresh vegetable or stylized potato. The style of cooking leans toward nouvelle, but richness is there when demanded to underscore taste or texture. Thus breast of duck with cracked peppercorn sauce is charred black on the outside, the slices of meat handsomely pink inside. The cream-based sauce retains a lighter character than one might suspect, nonetheless richly flavored. Another duckling, with crisp skin and a fruity glaze, is closer to the classic recipes that emphasize the rich fattiness of duck. But in this case, the bird is leaner, less ponderous.

Among other entrees, pasta with crayfish, scallions, and sun-dried tomatoes comes in a lightly flavored lobster cream sauce. It's as satisfying a way to enjoy fresh pasta as ever was created. The menu is fleshed out with a good array of seafood (shell and fin) and lighter meats. The Winnetka Grill is, after all, a grill room, so proper attention is paid to steaks and chops.

From the dessert cart, choices include delicious deep-dish apple pie in a lightly burned caramel sauce, homemade carrot cake, sweetly spiced, and a marvelous three-layer chocolate mousse cake with light, dark, and white chocolate. Service is informed and unrushed.

# YOSHI'S CAFÉ
KR 18/20
Decor 4/4   Hospitality 5/5   Food 7/9   Value 2/2

- **French**
- **Chicago/Mid-North**
- **$$$**

3257 N. Halsted St.
Chicago
(312) 248-6160
**Troubleshooter:** Yoshi
Katsamura (chef/owner)

**Hours:** Tues-Thurs 5:30-10 pm, Fri-Sat until 10:30 pm, Sun 5-9 pm
**Cards:** AE, DINERS, MC, VISA
**Reservations:** Mandatory
**Bar:** Full
**Parking:** Valet or street
**Heart-Healthy Menu:** Selections

In past reviews, I awarded a 20/20 rating to Yoshi's Café. But if my most recent visit is typical, Yoshi's Café no longer deserves that accolade.

The chic, upscale, bistro dining room is still handsome. Service is detailed. The menu descriptions are as exciting as they have always been, almost lovingly recited by the staff. But the unwavering excellence of the food seems to have been compromised.

An appetizer of grilled shad roe with a garnish of fresh ginger and an oriental beurre blanc was wonderfully prepared. Just as successful was the pheasant pâté. Among other appetizers, a platter of smoked salmon rolled and stuffed with salmon mousse, a bit of caviar, and a coating of flying fish roe was equally successful. Similarly, taste and texture were balanced in an order of sauteed squid and bay scallops atop soba noodles with a sauce that brought together soy, tomato, and sesame flavors.

Had the rest of the dinner lived up to the appetizers, there would have been no problem. Soup, a jellied consommé combined with a watery vichyssoise, was an unworkable conception that we sent back to the kitchen. A salad selection almost made up for the fault, a large oven-dried tomato serving as bedding for chunks of gorgonzola cheese embellished with radicchio and fingers of endive. All would have gone well had not the balsamic dressing been so harsh. On the other hand, a platter centered on fried goat's cheese was virtually perfect in conception and execution.

From among entree choices, there were too many misses. The herbed lamb sausage on a platter that included two grilled lamb chops was fatty. Grilled mackerel teriyaki was strong and unpleasant.

On the other hand, petrale sole bedded on udon noodles with duglere sauce was perfect.

Slices of medium-rare duck breast on a variety of lettuces in a vinaigrette was too sweet and unbalanced. Finally, among desserts was a kiwi sorbet that smelled and tasted like anchovies. A pecan-and-raisin torte was dry, crème caramel nearly bland, tarte tatin delicious, but its crust almost rubbery.

I could not help but notice that Chef Yoshi spent much of the two and one-half hours we were there in the dining room greeting guests. Perhaps more time spent supervising, and less as celebrity chef, would return his kitchen to its former excellence.

# YU LIN'S CHINESE DUMPLING HOUSE
KR 19/20
Decor 3.5/4   Hospitality 5/5   Food 9/9   Value 1.5/2

- **Chinese**
- **Highland Park**
- **$$**

1636 Old Deerfield Rd.
Highland Park
(708) 831-3155
**Troubleshooters:** Yu Lin and C.P. Hsueh (owners)

**Hours:** Sun-Thurs 4:30-9:30 pm, Fri until 10:30 pm, Sat until 11 pm
**Cards:** None, house accounts
**Reservations:** Suggested
**Handicapped:** Accessible
**Bar:** Service bar
**Parking:** Free lot
**Party Facilities:** For luncheons

**R**egular diners at Yu Lin's Chinese Dumpling House have come to expect more than the ordinary. Many of the dinners are "firepot," which means that meats and vegetables are cooked fondue-style at your table. Some require at least a day's advance notice because of the elaborate ingredients. What tends to set the restaurant apart from most others featuring Chinese cuisine is the special use of sauces. Here they are not just some liquid to be absorbed by rice; sauces make a serious contribution to the flavor balances the kitchen staff is trying to achieve. Yu Lin's Chinese Dumpling House is perfect for special, but not necessarily expensive or dressy, occasions. Children always seem to enjoy Yu Lin herself; if you should be at a loss for what to order, let Yu Lin be your guide.

# YVETTE
KR 18.5/20
Decor 4/4   Hospitality 4.5/5   Food 8/9   Value 2/2

- **French**
- **Chicago/Near North**
- **$$$**

1206 N. State Pkwy.
Chicago
(312) 280-1700
**Troubleshooter:** Bob
Djahanguiri (owner)

**Hours:** Sat-Sun brunch/lunch 11 am-3 pm, dinner Mon-Thurs 5 pm-midnight, Fri-Sat until 1 am, Sun 5-11 pm
**Cards:** AE, DINERS, MC, VISA
**Reservations:** Suggested
**Handicapped:** Accessible
**Bar:** Piano bar
**Parking:** Street
**Party Facilities:** For up to 155

One of the trendier of Chicago's wining and dining spas, Yvette is at the heart of the see-and-be-seen neighborhood. Just north of busy Division and State, the restaurant is classier than the meet markets around the corner, thanks to its panache and style, as well as the good food. In summer months, French doors are opened to create a street-side café for people-watching and al fresco dining. Inside is a *fin de siècle* bistro with a long mahogany bar, behind which is suspended a large blue Parisian mirror. To underscore the international flavor of Yvette, clocks show the time in Paris, Rome, Tokyo, and London.

Unique to the restaurant are its two grand pianos, belly to belly at the core of the entertainment area. Each night, precisely at eight o'clock, glass doors behind the pianos slide apart dramatically to reveal the main dining room, which is on three levels.

While most of the floor space is given over to the bar, the restaurant area to the rear offers some *formidable* dining. The style of cookery leans toward light classical French, with a Mediterranean accent here and there, coupled with a degree of urban finesse in plate arrangements and seasonings. Look for the fresh fish every day, including a seared tuna salad with lime juice and chive-infused olive-oil dressing. House smoked salmon is served with oriental vegetables and ginger sauce, while chicken and shrimp étouffée offers something a bit spicier on a bed of scallion-touched rice. Striped sea bass is roasted and served in a butter-based clam sauce.

Among meatier choices, pork tenderloin comes with a spicy pear sauce and herbed spaetzle. Grilled veal sirloin is enhanced by a complement of roasted peppers and fennel with a piece of polenta flavored with asiago cheese. Somewhat simpler is roast lamb in its own juices with ratatouille and roasted potatoes. Beef eaters will be tempted by twin tournedos sauteed with sweet-and-sour onions in a classic red-wine Bordelaise sauce.

Desserts tend to the elaborate, with lots of feuilletage pastry and cream fillings.

# ZARROSTA GRILL
KR 19/20
Decor 4/4   Hospitality 4.5/5   Food 8.5/9   Value 2/2

- **Italian/Eclectic**
- **Oak Brook**
- **$$**

118 Oakbrook Center
Oak Brook
(708) 990-0177
**Troubleshooter:** Manager on duty

**Hours:** Mon 11:15 am-9:30 pm, Tues-Thurs until 10 pm, Fri-Sat until 11 pm, Sun noon-8 pm
**Cards:** AE, MC, VISA
**Reservations:** Suggested
**Handicapped:** Accessible
**Bar:** Full, extensive wine list
**Parking:** Free lot
**Party Facilities:** For up to 30

**Z**arrosta Grill begins with a stylized concept of Northern Italian fare and then lets imagination and creativity take flight. The restaurant is fun, kicky, in tempo with '90s dining. The dining room has high ceilings and open ductwork; the walls affect the look of crumbling plaster with brick behind; poster art catches the eye anywhere you turn.

Just off the dining area is an open kitchen and adjacent wood-burning pizza oven, alongside a rôtisserie. Dinners come à la carte or for a few dollars more, with pizza appetizer, your choice of soup or salad, and dessert.

California pizza with cloves of roasted garlic and caramelized onions is topped with mild fontina cheese. Or consider duck sausage with slivers of dried tomatoes and a touch of cheese. Pesto pizza is almost like a grilled salad, with its topping of black olives, spinach pesto, sun-dried tomatoes, and small shrimp pieces. Speaking of pizza and salad, there is a pizza salad – not grilled, to be sure. Basically it is a step or two above the typical tossed salad with mushrooms, onions, a little Genoa salami, and other pizza toppings mixed in with the greens and flavored by a pungent herb vinaigrette.

Though pastas can be ordered as entrees, they stand better as a separate course. Gorgonzola tortellini is a good example, the cheese more an understatement than a pronounced flavor, with a mix of scallions, broccoli florets, and other vegetables in a light sauce highlighted by fresh basil.

From among fresh seafood selections, a platter of mussels circles a mélange of vegetables, scallops, and pasta shells flavored with olives, capers, onions, and other ingredients. Norwegian salmon, the best variety of that fish, is coated with five kinds of peppercorns and given oven broiling. Since the fish is thick, its center comes out still moist; the peppercorn crust protects the outside from burning.

Several styles of chicken come from the rôtisserie. Chicken Southwest is rather timid, despite its marinade of cumin, chili powder, peppers, and other spices awash in beer. From among meats, veal with California figs and roasted garlic is as good as its name. The figs add a pervasive sweetness against the sharp garlic flavor. A Marsala wine and cream sauce adds sexiness.

Dessert choices vary from night to night; Key lime pie was tops. The wine list is excellent, and service people seem to have as much fun as customers.

# ZAVEN'S
KR 19/20
Decor 4/4   Hospitality 5/5   Food 8.5/9   Value 1.5/2

* **Continental/Armenian**
* **Chicago/Near North**
* **$$$**

260 E. Chestnut St.
Chicago
(312) 787-8260
**Troubleshooter:** Zaven
Kodjayan (owner)

**Hours:** Lunch Mon-Fri 11:30 am-2:30 pm, dinner Sun-Thurs 5:30-10 pm, Fri-Sat until 11 pm
**Cards:** All majors, house accounts
**Reservations:** Suggested
**Handicapped:** Accessible
**Bar:** Full, extensive wine list
**Parking:** Garage across street
**Party Facilities:** For 10-40

**Z**aven's is one of the more romantic hideaways on the city's dining scene, perfect for that special dinner for two. Handsome appointments add to the overall feeling of warmth and comfort that envelops diners. This is not especially trendy dining; on the contrary, it is a remembrance of more traditional approaches to food and ingredients. The taste combinations and textures remind me of the way chefs used to cook before "nouvelle" became a gastronomic byword. Soups and sauces are abundant with cream or butter. A smooth lobster bisque is copiously rich in flavor. From among entrees, I love the steak armagnac, a must for any lover of pepper steak. The waiter works tableside with his preparation cart, heating a skillet to melt a chunk of butter. Then in goes the large cut of meat, perhaps fourteen ounces, sizzling on both sides, sauced with Worcestershire and Dijon mustard, and, of course, heavily seasoned with fresh cracked pepper. Next comes a sizable splash of armagnac, flaming the meat. To complete the preparation, a thick Bordelaise sauce is poured into the pan and finished with a large dollop of sour cream. It's the kind of cooking that might give cardiologists a fit, but it does make for satisfying dining.

While preparations and atmosphere suggest old-style continental dining, some of the better selections on the menu are Armenian. Thus a tabbouli salad of cracked bulghur wheat with olive oil, lemon juice, and parsley makes an interesting alternative to the traditional leafy greens found in a spinach or caesar salad. The Armenian version of steak tartare is called kibbi, and though it's usually served as an appetizer, Zaven's offers it in a dinner portion. By the way, traditional steak tartare is not neglected, and as the menu points out,

"Champagne is not for all palates and neither is raw beef; for those who fancy it, however, this is a very special treat."

Kufta kebabs, grilled ground lamb seasoned with parsley, tomatoes, onions, and herbs, would be the choice for somewhat less adventurous diners.

# ZUM DEUTSCHEN ECK
KR 19/20
Decor 4/4   Hospitality 4/5   Food 9/9   Value 2/2

- **German**
- **Chicago/Mid-North**
- **$$**

2924 N. Southport Ave.
Chicago
(312) 525-8121
**Troubleshooter:** Al Wirth, Jr. (owner)

**Hours:** Mon-Thurs 11:30 am-10:30 pm,Fri-Sat to midnight,Sun noon-10 pm
**Cards:** All majors
**Reservations:** Suggested
**Bar:** Full
**Parking:** Free lots
**Party Facilities:** For 25-400

In the heart of a Chicago winter, there's little else that can satisfy like German food on a cold night. While Chicago has numerous German restaurants, few are as handsome as Zum Deutschen Eck. A refurbishing in recent years has produced a refectory rich with dark wood trim and moldings, with comfortable seating in any of several dining rooms. Shelves are laden with knickknacks that underscore the Old World charm.

All of this would mean nothing if the food were not so good. Though the menu ostensibly changes nightly, diners can count on several regular choices that draw people back.

Usually you will find such German classics as smoked pork loin, called kassler rippchen, plus several kinds of sausages and schnitzels. Hasenpfeffer, roast duckling, and various other roasted meats are part and parcel of the filled and filling dinner platters.

Though Zum Deutschen Eck is certainly a meat-and-dumplings kind of place, there are a few seafood choices for those who want something lighter. Broiled whitefish comes with boiled potatoes, but our waitress was willing to substitute a potato pancake. Broccoli was served as the green vegetable. The whitefish is about as good as it can get, sweet, flaky, substantial. By the way, don't miss the potato pancakes. Though not listed on the menu as a side dish, they can be ordered that way.

Desserts include a couple of cheesecakes, traditional Black Forest kirsch torte, even an old-fashioned cherries jubilee. But apple strudel always strikes me as the perfect end to a German dinner, and the one at Zum Deutschen Eck is plump, warm, sweet, and tasty. All dinners include home-style soup or other appetizer and your choice of salad. Service is prompt and somewhat distant unless you make the effort to warm up to your waiter or waitress.

Nuevo Leon, 183
Su Casa, 230
Tamales, 232
Topolobampo, 249

## Middle Eastern

Arbela, 8
Cafe Phoenicia, 39
Ha Shalom, 114
Helmand, The, 117
Open Sesame, 189
Tehran, 239
Uncle Tannous, 262
Zaven's, 280

## Polish

Mareva's, 166
Pierogi Inn, 198

## Romanian

Little Bucharest, 155

## Seafood

Bob Chinn's Crab House, 24
Cape Cod Room, 48
Catch 35, 53
J.P.'s Eating Place, 129
Nick's Fishmarket, 182
Oceanique, 184
Old Carolina Crab House, The, 185
Shaw's Blue Crab, 217
Shaw's Crab House, 218
Waterfront, The, 268

## Serbian

Skadarlija, Serbian Restaurant, 223

## Spanish

Arco de Cuchilleros, 9
Cafe Ba-Ba-Reeba!, 37
Emilio's, 90
Geja's Cafe, 100

## Swedish

Ann Sather, 7

## Thai

Dao Thai, 69
Lanna Thai, 142
Rosded, 209
Star of Siam, 228
Thai Borrahn, 240
Thai Classic, 241
Thai Little Home Cafe, 242
Thai Touch, 243
Thai Valley, 245

## Turkish

Konak, 134

## Vegetarian

Blind Faith Cafe, 21
Chicago Diner, The, 63

## Vietnamese

Lac Vien, 138
Le Bistro, 147
Pasteur, 196

## "$$$" Dinner for two over $50, plus tax, tip, and drinks

## Restaurants Recommended if Cost, Time, Location, and Diet Do Not Matter

# Eat Well & Stay Healthy

## with Good Health Books from Surrey

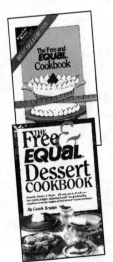

**The Free and Equal® Cookbook**
by Carole Kruppa
From appetizers to desserts, these 150-plus, *sugar-free* recipes will make
your mouth water and your family ask for more! Includes soups, salads,
entrees, desserts, snacks—even breakfast treats. Now you can make great
dishes like cioppino, Caesar salad, shrimp Louisiana, stuffed peppers, and
chicken cacciatore, yet keep control of calories, cholesterol, fat, and
sodium. Calorie counts and diabetic exchanges.

**The Free and Equal® Dessert Cookbook**
by Carole Kruppa
Make cheese cake, black bottom pie, chocolate bon bons, cookies, cakes,
and much more *all sugar-free*. More than 160 delicious recipes that help
you control calories, cholesterol, and fat. Calorie counts and diabetic
exchanges.

### The Microwave Diabetes Cookbook
by Betty Marks
More than 130 delicious, time-saving, *low fat, sugar-free* recipes for everyone concerned with heart- health, and especially those with diabetes. Easy-to-follow directions for everything from appetizers to desserts, vichyssoise to pizza. Complete nutritional data, calorie counts, and diabetic exchanges.

### The Restaurant Companion: A Guide to Healthier Eating Out
by Hope S. Warshaw, M.M.Sc., R.D.
All the practical information you need to order low-fat, high-nutrition meals in 15 popular cuisines! At Chinese, Italian, or Mexican restaurants (plus many others), fast-food chains, salad bars—even on airlines—you'll *learn how to stay in control* of calories, fat, sodium, and cholesterol when eating out.

### The Love Your Heart Low Cholesterol Cookbook, Revised Second Edition
by Carole Kruppa
Give your taste buds a treat and your heart a break with 250 low-cholesterol recipes for everything from appetizers to desserts. Enjoy the great tastes—with *no cholesterol*—of deviled eggs, Italian bean soup, oriental chicken salad, chocolate cake, and many more easy-to-make delights. Nutritional data, diabetic exchanges, and calorie counts.

### The Love Your Heart Mediterranean Low Cholesterol Cookbook
by Carole Kruppa
Hearty, exotic, traditional, delicious—all great words to describe these mouth-watering dishes from the south of France, Italy, Spain, Greece— even Morocco. Yet the 200-plus recipes—from appetizers to desserts—are *streamlined for heart health.* Keeping the tempting, sun-drenched flavors while controlling fat, cholesterol, sodium, and calories is this book's genius! Complete nutritional data and diabetic exchanges.

## ☎ FOR EASIER ORDERING, CALL 1-800-326-4430

*Prices include postage, insurance, and handling. Allow 4–6 weeks for delivery.* Please s

____The Free and Equal® Cookbook  $12.45
____The Free and Equal® Dessert Cookbook  $12.45
____Skinny Beef  $15.45
____Skinny Pizzas  $15.45
____Skinny Potatoes  $15.95
____Skinny Seafood  $15.45
____Skinny Soups  $15.45
____Skinny Spices  $15.45

____Skinny Cookies, Cakes and Sweets  $15.45
____The Microwave Diabetes Cookbook  $13.45
____The Restaurant Companion  $14.45
____The Love Your Heart Low Cholesterol
  Cookbook  $15.45
____The Love Your Heart Mediterranean Low
  Cholesterol Cookbook  $15.45

Name _____

Address _____

City _____ State _____ Zip _____

Enclosed is check or money order for $ _____ Amex/Visa/MasterCard No. _____

Exp. Date _____ Signature (If using credit card) _____

Send order to: **Surrey Books, 230 E. Ohio St., Suite 120, Chicago, IL 60611**

SATISFACTION GUARANTEED OR YOUR MONEY BACK

# "Skinny" Recipes for Great Low-Fat Meals

**Skinny Beef** by Marlys Bielunski, Susan Lamb Parenti and Irene Yeh
Over 100 healthy, *low-fat recipes* for America's favorite entree. Enjoy great
tastes of beef in all its varieties: stir-frys, salads, barbecues, roasts, and easy-to-
make 30-minute meals that combine beef with other ingredients for delicious
entrees. Nutritional data for each recipe.

**Skinny Pizzas** by Barbara Grunes
Our national fun food now qualifies as our *national good-health food, too!*
These 100-plus tempting, easy, economical recipes trim away excess fat,
cholesterol, and calories so you can serve pizza without guilt. Includes:
shrimp, spinach, chicken, teriyaki, stir-fry, vegetarian, Creole, scallop,
Szechwan, cheesecake pizzas and dozens more. Plus 18 pizzas for the
barbecue. *Follows AHA guidelines* of 30% or fewer calories from fat.
Nutritional data for each recipe.

**Skinny Potatoes** by Barbara Grunes
Can the inexpensive, readily available, easy-to-cook potato be reinvented as an
entree? an appetizer? even a dessert? Can this undervalued but heart-healthy
tuber turn up with chicken and peanuts as the star of a stir-fry? Can baked
potatoes—topped with everything from shrimp and tofu to chicken and
chili—win acclaim as delicious one-course meals? Emphatically "YES," as
these 100-plus recipes prove! *All follow AHA low-fat guidelines* and include
nutritional data.

**Skinny Seafood** by Barbara Grunes
The sea's bounty affords happy, healthy eating—especially when it's prepared
to increase natural flavor while controlling fat, cholesterol, and calories. These
101 creative recipes range from steamed lake trout and grilled snapper to
seafood pizza, finnan haddie, scallop burritos, whole Maine lobster, Cajun
catfish, Cantonese fish soup, jambalaya, shrimp salad—even a Wisconsin fish
boil! *Follows AHA guidelines* of 30% or fewer calories from fat. Complete
nutritional data.

**Skinny Soups** by Ruth Glick and Nancy Baggett
More than 100 delicious, hearty yet calorie-wise soups from elegant crab and
mushroom bisque, exotic Malaysian chicken scallion, and unusual Italian
garden to standbys such as French onion, chicken-rice, and New England fish
chowder. *Recipes keep calories from fat under 30%,* and emphasize low
sodium, low cholesterol, and high-fiber ingredients. Complete nutritional data.

**Skinny Spices** by Erica Levy Klein
50 nifty homemade spice blends, from curries and chilis to herbal and ethnic
concoctions that make even diet meals exciting! Spice blends require no cooking and add *zero fat, cholesterol, or calories* to food. Includes 100 spicy recipes.

**Skinny Cookies, Cakes and Sweets** by Sue Spitler
It *is* possible to create over 100 low-fat desserts and sweets, *none exceeding
250 calories per serving*—not even the cheesecakes! Sue Spitler proves it with
carrot cake, baked Alaska, apple pie, caramel flan, oatmeal cookies, plums in
port, chocolate cake, and 100 more marvelous treats slimmed down to AHA
guidelines of 30% or fewer calories from fat. Easy to prepare—delicious.
Nutrition data for each recipe.

A o ɛ y (nig—)

51/2cq